CAMBRIDGE MANUALS IN ARCHAEOLOGY

Series editors

Don Brothwell, *University of London*
Barry Cunliffe, *University of Oxford*
Stuart Fleming, *University of Pennsylvania*
Peter Fowler, *University of Newcastle upon Tyne*

Already published

J. D. Richards and N. S. Ryan, *Data processing in archaeology*
Simon Hillson, *Teeth*
Peter G. Dorrell, *Photography in archaeology and conservation*
Lesley Adkins and Roy Adkins, *Archaeological illustration*
Marie-Agnès Courty, Paul Goldberg and Richard MacPhail, *Soils and
  micromorphology in archaeology*

Cambridge Manuals in Archaeology are reference handbooks designed for an
international audience of professional archaeologists and archaeological scientists in universities, museums, research laboratories, field units, and the public
service. Each book includes a survey of current archaeological practice alongside
essential reference material on contemporary techniques and methodology.
Volumes on excavation and field survey and specific aspects of environmental
archaeology are in preparation.

FISHES

FISHES

Alwyne Wheeler
Formerly of Department of Zoology,
British Museum (Natural History)

and

Andrew K. G. Jones
Department of Biology,
University of York

Illustrations by
Rosalind Wheeler

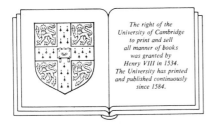

The right of the
University of Cambridge
to print and sell
all manner of books
was granted by
Henry VIII in 1534.
The University has printed
and published continuously
since 1584.

Cambridge University Press

Cambridge
New York   Port Chester   Melbourne   Sydney

Published by the Press Syndicate of the University of Cambridge
The Pitt Building, Trumpington Street, Cambridge CP2 1RP
40 West 20th Street, New York, NY 10011, USA
10 Stamford Road, Oakleigh, Melbourne 3166, Australia

First published 1989

Printed in Great Britain at the University Press, Cambridge

British Library cataloguing in publication data
Wheeler, Alwyne, *1929–*
Fishes. – (Cambridge manuals in archaeology).
1. Archaeological investigation. Sources of evidence:
Fish
I. Title II. Jones, A. K. G.
930.1′028′5

Library of Congress cataloguing in publication data
Wheeler, Alwyne.
Fishes / Alwyne Wheeler and Andrew K. G. Jones: illustrations by
Rosalind Wheeler.
        p.   cm. – (Cambridge manuals in archaeology)
Bibliography.
Includes index.
ISBN 0-521-30407-5
1. Fish remains (Archaeology) I. Jones, Andrew K. G. II. Title.
III. Series.
CC79.5.A5W53   1989
930.1′028 – dc 19 89-544   CIP

ISBN 0 521 30407 5

WD

CONTENTS

vi   *Contents*

FIGURES

TABLES

ACKNOWLEDGEMENTS

No book is the total unaided work of its authors. We both owe a debt to colleagues and friends who have provided advice, criticism, inspiration and learning which together have added to the knowledge which led to the preparation of this book. Both of us owe much to many friends in archaeology and ichthyology who have often (sometimes unwittingly) added to our knowledge of the two disciplines.

We both wish to acknowledge the effort made by our artist Roz Wheeler who has drawn, patiently discussed, and redrawn the illustrations, often in the small gaps of a busy life.

We have both benefited from the advice of Don Brothwell (Series Editor) and Peter Richards of Cambridge University Press, whose experience in archaeology and publishing respectively have always been at our disposal. Both have been remarkably patient in waiting for us to finish the book.

Andrew Jones would like to thank his colleagues at the Environmental Archaeology Unit, University of York, for numerous discussions and for their help in other ways. In particular, he would like to record his indebtedness to Julie Jones for reading the early chapters of the book (and in the past for tolerating so many unpleasant fishy smells).

Alwyne Wheeler wishes to thank Sita Fonseka for typing his share of the text with her usual accuracy and speed. He is also strongly indebted to Cicely Wheeler for providing the milieu in which thought and constructive writing are possible.

Julie Jones created the index; we would both like to thank her for making so important a contribution to the usefulness of the book.

Together we acknowledge the York Archaeological Trust for photographs of the tank in use in fig. 4.3, R. Hunter, Biology Department, University of York for drafting fig. 4.4, and Mads-Peter Heide-Jørgensen of Danbiu ApS, Hellerup, Denmark, for permission to reproduce fig. 9.1 from T. Härkönen's *Guide to the otoliths of the bony fishes of the northeast Atlantic* (1986). We are also grateful to Johannes Lepiksaar and Alfonso Rojo for helpful comments on bone element terminology.

PREFACE

Fishes have been an important source of food for hominids since at least Upper Pleistocene times. Unlike mammals and birds, their exploitation has mainly been by the capture of free-living individuals, the cultivation of fishes (although an ancient art) having been on only a local scale, chiefly in Asia and Europe, until the middle years of the twentieth century. The capture of free-living animals, often indiscriminately as to kind or size, has resulted in a greater diversity of species being used for food than is the case for other vertebrate groups. As there are more species of fishes than all mammals, birds, reptiles and amphibians worldwide (and generally within local faunas also), the problem of identifying fish remains in archaeological sites is complicated both by the wide range in size of fishes represented and by the number of species involved.

The study of fish remains has much to offer environmental archaeologists, especially those concerned with coastal, riverine and lacustrine sites. Properly handled and analysed, fish bones can provide information on the species exploited, and from a knowledge of the habitats of the fishes, the archaeologist can advance hypotheses concerning the methods used to capture the fish and the level of technology required to sustain such methods. Within limits, fish remains can also be used to establish the numbers and sizes of individuals, their body weight and sometimes seasonality of capture.

This book contains chapters concerned with the anatomy of fishes, in particular the hard structures of relevance to the archaeologist, the preparation of comparative skeletons of specimens and their curation, methods of recovery of fish remains, discussions of taphonomy, and aspects of fish ecology. The second chapter includes a world overview of the families of fishes of potential importance for food. Other topics discussed involve the estimation of size from the hard remains of fishes, the calculation of seasonality of capture from both ecological information and the analysis of fish growth, as well as the interpretation of fishing activity based on the analysis of fish remains.

The main thrust of the book is to give practical information as simply as possible. This is not a manual which puts forward theoretical approaches to fish archaeology using techniques culled from fisheries research. Such techniques are certainly valid in their own discipline but are based on the collection of data from thousands of specimens over a short period of time. Their

xiii

relevance to archaeological fish remains, which are often damaged, have a wide temporal distribution, and are rarely available in statistically significant quantity, is dubious. For this reason such techniques and methods are merely outlined here and their potential use to archaeologists is indicated, but the archaeologist is warned not to expect too much of them. While many of the examples used in this book are from European sites and fishes, the application of the information, especially of methods and techniques, is worldwide.

Above all, we hope that this book will prove useful to environmental archaeologists and will encourage and enable others to discover the fascination we have experienced during our dealings with the remains of ancient fishes.

INTRODUCTION

The study of fish remains from archaeological sites is an exciting and important element of environmental archaeology, a subject which is principally a development of the second half of the twentieth century and is concerned with the relationship between mankind and the rest of the natural world. Although pioneering studies of fish bones were carried out more than a century ago, the study of fish remains from archaeological sites could only emerge as a discipline in its own right once ichthyologists and archaeologists had developed their subjects, techniques and expertise, and had become aware of fields of mutual interest.

The earliest studies on archaeological fish remains appear to have been mainly the result of eminent and experienced zoologists being invited to examine remains recovered from excavations without necessarily being involved in their interpretation. As a result the identification of species was unassailable, but their importance was not always appreciated, and sometimes dubious explanations of their significance were advanced.

An early critical study of fish remains was made in the 1840s by the distinguished Dutch zoologist Herman Schlegel of the Rijksmuseum van Naturlijke Historie in Leiden. According to Clason (1986), Schlegel studied the remains of fishes, together with those of other animals, from excavations at the early medieval town of Dorestad in 1842. The fishes he identified included the sturgeon, *Acipenser sturio*, the pike, *Esox lucius*, and the wels catfish, *Silurus glanis*, the last being a particularly significant, but for a long time unrecognized, identification. According to Clason, the Danish zoologist, Japetus Steenstrup was involved in the identification of fish remains from Ertebølle settlements or shell mounds around 1851, although this work has rarely been cited by zoologists. Somewhat later, the French zoologist Henry Emile Sauvage examined material attributed to the Upper Palaeolithic period from caves in the Dordogne region of France and reported his findings in a little-known 'Essai sur la pêche pendant l'époque du renne' (Sauvage, 1870). He also contributed to Lartert and Christy's *Reliquiae Aquitanicae* (1875), which is usually cited as the original publication.

The true significance of these studies was not always realized. Thus, the occurrence of the remains of wels catfish at Dorestad showed that this species was endemic to the Netherlands. *Silurus glanis* is today very rare in the area and it has been frequently alleged that this species was introduced from the Danube. Its status as an endemic species was firmly established by Brinkhuizen (1979b), who found *Silurus* bones at other archaeological sites in the Netherlands, thus confirming Schlegel's earlier record. This is an example of important evidence from archaeological work which was long overlooked by zoologists. The opposite is true of Sauvage's work. Sauvage concerned himself with interpretation of the fish remains from the 'Reindeer Age' sites, relating his findings to human settlement patterns and procurement activities. He noted that head bones of salmon were absent while those of the smaller members of the carp family were present in the assemblages he examined. From this he postulated that the heads of salmon captured at some distance from the sites were removed before the bodies were brought to the cave. This was seized upon by Clark (1948) and apparently supported by analogy with aboriginal fishing practices in British Columbia. Clark suggested that members of the Palaeolithic community cut off the heads of salmon, but retained the vertebrae (eventually to serve as beads), thus facilitating transport of the edible portions of the fishes. As Wheeler (1978a) pointed out, this appealing picture is seriously flawed. During their residence in rivers, mature salmon resorb most of the calcium from their cranial skeletal elements, reducing them to weakly mineralized cartilage, which is unlikely to survive in archaeological sites. Although necklaces formed from salmonid vertebrae have been found with Palaeolithic inhumations in the Grimaldi caves in south-east France, salmonid vertebrae have a relatively large central hole, which carries the notochord from head to tail throughout the animal's life, and not all have been used in the manufacture of necklaces. This example shows that without sound ichthyological knowledge interpretation of fish remains may lead to dubious conclusions.

As wet-sieving samples becomes standard practice, the fish remains recovered from excavations will become more representative of the exploited fauna. The fish bone researcher has therefore to be prepared to identify small elements from a wide range of species and to recognize minute fragments of common food fishes. Knowledge of the habitats and natural history of fishes has expanded enormously in recent years and a great deal of information is now available to archaeologists. Fish bone studies containing statements such as 'fish bones of cod size were recovered' and wrongly identified illustrations of fish remains are not acceptable. (Both may be found in the literature, although it would be invidious to name the authors of these reports in this context.)

Although this book is about fishes and archaeology, it concentrates on fish remains, i.e. the fragments of fishes likely to be recovered from archaeological sites. It does not aspire to be a survey of the interactions between fishes and man. As a result the fascinating topic of the development of methods of capture of fishes is only touched on here, although references are made to detailed sources on this aspect, amongst them Wing and Reitz (1982), Brinkhuizen (1983), Brandt (1984) and Gunda (1984). Much can be learned of mankind's knowledge of fishes from the study of pictorial representations, in cave drawings such as those in Europe and Australia, decorations on pottery, in mosaics as at Pompeii and Carthage, while ancient Egyptian representations of fishes have been much discussed. Absorbing as the study of these pictorial representations is, it can serve as only a rough guide to the knowledge the respective cultures possessed of their fish fauna and is not covered in detail here.

Fish remains are powerful aids to understanding human exploitation of the environment. At a very basic level, identification of the fishes present at archaeological sites allows archaeologists to state whether freshwater or marine environments were exploited, and further to suggest the habitats which were fished. Analyzed with caution, fish remains may reveal seasonal exploitation, the methods by which fishes were captured and hence something of the level of technology of a culture.

The techniques involved in studying fish remains have greatly improved in recent years, and no doubt will continue to evolve and be refined. In the future we can confidently expect zooarchaeologists to study fish remains from a well-established basis, which will make a fundamental contribution to the knowledge we have of fishes and their exploitation in the past.

2

FISHES AND THE ARCHAEOLOGIST

The importance of fishes to human economy
Because fishes live in water and as part of their strategy for survival are generally cryptically coloured, fast-moving and shy, they are not very conspicuous to land-based animals like man. As a result it is difficult for us to appreciate the diversity and abundance of the fishes inhabiting seas, rivers and lakes. Fishes outnumber all other vertebrates in both numbers of individuals and numbers of species. They live in almost all the waters of the earth. They are often astonishingly fecund, releasing enormous numbers of eggs at spawning times. For example, a herring may shed up to 50,000 eggs. As a result of this breeding strategy, immense populations of fish can be sustained despite heavy mortality from predation and adverse environmental factors.

The interaction between man and fish has been considerable in historic times and is known to have been so in prehistoric periods despite the inconspicuous nature of fishes.

The influence of the herring, *Clupea harengus*, on the fortunes of the Hansa merchants (generally known as the Hanseatic League) in northern Europe is well known. The Hanseatic League, which was a dominant economic and eventually a social force in Europe, controlled the herring trade from the Baltic for some two hundred years. The herring, which is represented in the Baltic by a small-sized race or possibly a subspecies, like many of its relatives in the family Clupeidae, is well known for dramatic fluctuations in abundance, which are not necessarily connected with over-fishing (although this may have a bearing on the fluctuations in modern fisheries). Such a decline in abundance during the fourteenth century led to the Hansa losing much of their power. The later rise of Dutch, Scottish and English herring fisheries in the North Sea led to considerable economic and social progress by each country in succession. Herring and wool were the key industries in England from the twelfth to the seventeenth centuries and Samuel (1918) suggests that the herring trade was important not only in supplying food but also in stimulating strong traditions of ship-building and seamanship, which in time helped to secure maritime dominance for that country.

Moreover, in the late nineteenth and early twentieth centuries the migrations of the herring southward in the North Sea during the summer and early autumn were followed by the fishing fleet (then mostly vessels using floating drift nets) from Scotland and northeast England and an associated

4

overland migration by Scottish women who, following the fleet, processed the catch on landing (Hodgson, 1957). As well as securing an income of sorts for the men and women employed in catching and processing the fish, considerable economic benefit accrued to the fishing ports in East Anglia. More recently still, over-fishing of young herring in the North Sea has led to fishing being suspended for periods of several years with subsequent adverse effects on the livelihood of the fishermen and their communities.

Comparable examples can be found elsewhere. The Atlantic cod, *Gadus morhua*, which lives in the western North Atlantic, as well as in European seas, was one of the abundant natural resources which attracted European explorers and later settlers to the coasts of northern North America. The competing fleets of Portuguese, French and British fishermen played a part in the settlement of the northern Atlantic coast, as well as providing financial returns for merchants sending out these ships. Even earlier, the migrations of Vikings to the North American coast may have been related to the abundance of both cod and herring there (Jensen, 1972), and there is evidence of seasonal fishing expeditions for herring along the Norwegian coast, as well as established fishing stations in Iceland in the tenth century (Goodlad, 1971). Grahame Clark has recently suggested that the desire to exploit cod 'may have helped significantly in opening up the sea routes implied by the megalithic tombs of the Atlantic seaboard' (Clark, 1980).

Migratory fishes have been of particular significance in primitive societies. This is particularly true of anadromous species, such as the Pacific salmon, *Oncorhynchus* spp., on the west coast of North America, which formed a major food resource for riverine communities (Schalk, 1977). Other anadromous species (fishes which migrate from the sea into fresh water to spawn) such as the Atlantic salmon, *Salmo salar*, and various shads, *Alosa* spp., in Europe and eastern North America, and menhadens, *Brevoortia* spp., in eastern North America may have proved to be locally as important as the Pacific salmon. On the Pacific North American coast, the eulachon, *Thaleichthys pacificus*, played an important part in the early Indian coastal economy as a source both of food and of fat (Hart, 1973). The importance of anadromous fishes to aboriginal societies lies in their concentration in a confined space, even if only for a short season, thus making them highly accessible.

Similar spawning-related migrations brought herring close inshore and made them vulnerable to even primitive fishing methods, as were schools of shore-spawning capelin, *Mallotus villosus*, in Arctic waters, particularly Greenland (Jangaard, 1974).

Within the tropical Pacific Ocean the colonization of island groups was only possible because of the unfailing protein resources the sea offered. In his excellent analysis of archaeological fishing as an aspect of oceanic economy, Reinman (1967) addressed this topic from the evidence of early fish hooks, archaeological fish remains and some ichthyological data, and concluded that a mastery of the techniques of catching fishes contributed greatly to the invasion by man of the islands. Moreover, it has become increasingly evident that many of the fish hooks produced by the aboriginal inhabitants of Oceania, made from mollusc shell, wood or bone, were often specifically evolved to catch a single desired species of fish, or groups of fishes, and were highly efficient. The wooden, steeply angled hook with a strongly recurved tip, used for catching escolar or castor-oil fish, *Ruvettus pretiosus*, is a particularly well-known example. Similar specialized hooks were evolved to capture the Pacific halibut, *Hippoglossus stenolepis*, by Indians along the coastal regions of the North Pacific and the Gulf of Alaska. According to Thompson and Freeman (1930), the halibut was, next to the salmon, the most important food fish available to the Indians and very large quantities were caught between June and August and consumed or preserved. The highly evolved wooden hooks of the Indians proved to be more efficient than modern European wire, barbed hooks.

However, this book is not concerned with the part played by fish and fishing in the past; it is about the remains of fishes that can be found in archaeological sites. That small fish bones survive in a recognizable form in archaeological deposits for thousands of years may seem surprising in view of their size and fragility. In fact, fish remains are extremely common in certain archaeological deposits but few site reports include adequate accounts of the recovered fish bones. Until the mid-1970s it was common to see archaeological reports referring to all fish remains simply as 'Fish' rather than identifying them accurately (e.g. Harcourt, 1969); such incomplete identifications are still to be found in excavation reports (e.g. Cruse and Harrison, 1983). Although these and other similar unspecific references to fish are for small assemblages of remains, they illustrate the way fishes have been neglected by many archaeologists.

Yet text-books and general accounts of past cultures attempt to assess the importance of fishes and fishing. All too often authors are forced to make sweeping generalizations. For example, 'Mesolithic inhabitants of northern Europe drew upon birds, fish, marine mammals, shell-fish and plants for sustenance, as well as land based mammals' (Clark, 1980, p. 49).

There are several reasons why fish remains have been so neglected in the past. Firstly, there were, and still are, only a few people who can produce competent fish bone studies. The major difficulty for students, be they archaeologists or biologists, is access to adequate reference collections. Few institutions have skeleton collections which contain specimens of all the species likely to occur in archaeological deposits.

Secondly, there is a shortage of practical written accounts of how to carry out the work. Casteel's book, *Fish remains in archaeology and paleo-environmental studies* (Casteel, 1976) gives copious examples of what could be achieved by studying fish remains from archaeological sites, based on what fishery biologists do with contemporary fish, but fails to give much practical advice for those finding fish bones for the first time.

Thirdly, fish remains are often neglected because they are relatively small and fragile. Many important food fish have small bones which are easily overlooked even if sieving to 1 cm is carried out. Because water offers more support to a fish than air does to a terrestrial vertebrate, fish bone is less dense and has different mechanical properties from other kinds of bone. Most fish bone is more easily fragmented than mammal or bird bone.

Finally, widespread ignorance concerning the information that can be gleaned from fish remains has meant that archaeologists have not always insisted that their fish material was accurately identified. It is only in the last few decades that archaeologists have begun to appreciate how abundant and informative fish remains can be. Fish bones can provide invaluable information on three main areas of interest: human diet; the economy of a settlement or culture; and the natural environment of a site.

For a long time it has been accepted that mammal and bird bones (which are often referred to as 'animal bones') should be collected and reported, and in the last 20 years or so many archaeologists have realized that small mammal bones, plant remains, insect fragments, etc. can also provide valuable information about life in the past. In order to recover these kinds of materials sieving techniques have been developed. These have resulted in the recovery of a wide spectrum of fish remains, which once were recovered rather sparsely. As a corollary, modern recovery techniques have produced a much greater range of fish material, which has increased the challenge of identification.

Furthermore, many excavators share the view that, because excavation is a destructive process, there is a duty to record what is present, however small, if it provides information concerning the life of the site's inhabitants.

Two main assumptions are generally accepted in archaeology. The first is that remains of past cultures reflect people's everyday lives and that an accurate understanding of the material culture will provide insights into past societies. The second is that ancient remains are of interest 'in their own right'. It is these two concepts which demand that all archaeologists ensure that fish remains are adequately recovered and studied.

Evidence of diet, economy and trade

While fish remains are intrinsically fascinating and their study can be justified on these grounds alone, they can also yield a wealth of information concerning life in the past. The most obvious is that they are an excellent source of information about human diet. There can be little doubt that most of the fish bones recovered on archaeological sites were deposited either after the flesh had been consumed, or after the flesh had been processed for later consumption. Fish remains are often the waste from kitchens and tables and may even comprise food remains which passed through the gut of the inhabitants of the site. An example of kitchen waste was provided at Barnard Castle, County Durham, England (Donaldson *et al.*, 1980). The contents of a drain running from the kitchen to the curtain wall of the medieval castle were carefully sieved and a large range of fish, mammal and bird remains recovered. Material from pits, floors, yards and other features within medieval tenements at Alms Lane, Norwich, England (Jones and Scott, 1985) showed that a restricted range of fish was consumed by the urban population from the twelfth to the eighteenth centuries. There did not appear to be major differences between the fish assemblages from the various tenements and from different feature types. The bones from this site can best be regarded as a component of domestic waste, discarded in an indiscriminate manner.

Evidence that fish bones were swallowed and passed with faeces comes from several sites where multidisciplinary studies of animal and plant remains have been undertaken. They clearly demonstrate that human excrement can contain large numbers of fish bones. Follett (1967) examined desiccated human coprolites containing fish remains from cave deposits in Nevada, North America. The Coppergate site, at York, England, contained many latrines or cesspits, which were recognized by the enormous numbers of eggs of two kinds of intestinal nematode worm parasites, whipworm, *Trichuris trichiura*, and the large roundworm or maw-worm, *Ascaris lumbricoides*. Plant remains from these same features were dominated by small fragments of the spermoderm (bran) of cereals (either wheat, *Triticum* spp., or rye, *Secale cereale*). In addition, seeds of fruits like raspberry, blackberry, apple, sloe and plum testify that the deposits were faecal in origin. These layers also contained substantial numbers of fish bones, mainly vertebrae of eel and herring. Many of the vertebrae bore signs of having been crushed during mastication.

Not only are fish bones found in unconsolidated layers rich in food debris and parasite ova; they are also occasionally found in 'faecal concretions' in waterlogged urban sites. Faecal concretions are a mixture of bran fragments, parasite ova and other faecal material bound by calcium phosphate into amorphous lumps. They are insoluble in water. Sometimes the lumps contain recognizable food remains e.g. sloe stones or fish vertebrae. Very rarely the vertebrae are crushed in a manner consistent with their having been chewed.

Indirect evidence for human consumption of fish has been revealed by parasitological investigations of ancient faeces. A number of researchers have examined archaeological faecal samples and identified eggs of the fish tapeworm *Diphyllobothrium latum*. This intestinal parasite depends on three kinds of host – the freshwater invertebrate *Cyclops*, a fish and a mammal – for the various stages in its complex life-cycle. Humans (and other mammals) become infected when they eat uncooked fish containing the immature worm (plerocercoid). The first archaeological record of fish tapeworm eggs is the account describing the intestinal contents of 'Karwinden Man', a peat-bog burial from Eastern Prussia, dated to AD 500 (Szidat, 1944). A recent review of records of parasite eggs, including *Diphyllobothrium latum*, from latrine fills has been given by Herrmann (1985).

Coastal sites and those located on rivers occasionally yield such large concentrations of fish remains that they must be interpreted as the remains of fish that have been processed for later consumption (e.g. Batey *et al.*, 1982).

While almost all fish bones found on archaeological sites are the remains of food waste, food offerings, or have been used by man in some way, a small percentage may have been brought onto sites by agents other than man. For example, at coastal sites the wind can deposit bones washed up on the beach; likewise otters, sea birds and other scavengers can bring fish carcasses onto a site or they may pass faeces or pellets rich in fish remains. A good example of animal-deposited fish remains recently came to light when bones from Orkney were studied (Colley, 1984a). A stone floor, thought to be in an abandoned building, was found to be overlain by a concentration of small fish bones, which at first sight resembled finely divided tobacco leaves. Closer examination showed that many of the fish were small species of shore fish which were unlikely to have been eaten by man. Otters were suggested as the depositing agents. It was also thought that otters were responsible for some of the bones reported in the Quanterness tomb, Orkney (Wheeler, 1979a). Similar finds of small mammal bones have been attributed to roosting owls (O'Connor, 1983).

Fish remains can yield valuable and interesting information, given careful and critical recording. The species represented may reflect the social status of the people inhabiting the site. Bones from twelfth-century levels in the Misericorde of Westminster Abbey, then a wealthy monastery in London, clearly demonstrated that the monks enjoyed a varied diet including over 20 kinds of fish. Of particular interest were relatively large numbers of remains of sturgeon, *Acipenser sturio*, John Dory, *Zeus faber*, and turbot, *Scophthalmus maximus*, species that are highly prized for their eating qualities. All are excellent food fish and today command the highest prices in fish markets (Jones, 1976).

Often the size and sometimes the age at death of the fish can be determined. At Great Yarmouth (Wheeler and Jones, 1976), measurements on cod jaw bones were used to estimate the size of the fish present in medieval layers. Noe-Nygaard (1983) presented similar information for pike lower jaws (dentaries) and after careful scrutiny of incremental growth rings on vertebrae of 100 modern pike caught at known dates throughout the year, she estimated the season of capture for Mesolithic pike from Praestelyngen, Denmark.

By considering the habits and ecology of the various species recovered, it is possible to reconstruct the sources likely to have been exploited by ancient fishermen and to learn something of the methods used to catch the different kinds of fish. Another approach to reconstructing fishing techniques is to compare histograms of the frequency of the different sizes of fish recovered from an archaeological assemblage with hypothetical selectivity curves for various kinds of fishing gear. Balme (1983) showed that three sites in the Darling Basin, New South Wales, Australia gave length distributions of golden perch, *Macquaria ambigua*, which indicated that gill nets were used.

Fishing practices develop as a local response to the geography and distribution of fish. For example, the Mesolithic community of Bua Västergård Goteborg, Sweden, engaged in line fishing for large cod (Wigforss *et al.*, 1983). Finds of large cod, *Gadus morhua*, and ling, *Molva molva*, bones have been also reported from Mesolithic material at Morton, Scotland (Coles, 1971). At Varanger Fjord in northern Norway a seasonally occupied Neolithic site yielded an assemblage of fish remains dominated by large cod (Olsen, 1967), indicating that line fishing was practised.

Spears were used by Mesolithic Danish lake fishermen, for a pike with spear tips *in situ* has been excavated (Clark, 1948). Wicker baskets and nets have also been found in Mesolithic deposits in Europe (Clark, 1980). All are essentially simple technologies using locally available renewable resources. It is therefore probable that traditional fishing methods have ancient roots in many places. This has been elegantly demonstrated by Enghoff (1983) for coastal fisheries in Denmark. The bones of many small cod and whiting, *Merlangius merlangus*, were found in Mesolithic middens. The traditional fishing method in the area, still practised in this century, was setting wicker weirs at low tide and collecting trapped fish (mostly small cod and whiting) on subsequent low tides.

All these methods, harpooning, hook and line fishing, and building tidal traps, have been discussed in relation to early fishing in Oceania (Reinman, 1967); likewise, harpooning, line fishing, bow and arrow, and nets are used today by the aboriginal inhabitants of Amazonia (Smith, 1981) even though modern materials are now employed.

Evidence of environmental conditions

An assemblage of bones from a site is likely to reflect contemporaneous local ecological conditions in addition to providing economic information. For example, bones of stickleback, *Gasterosteus aculeatus*, and small dace, *Leuciscus leuciscus*, recovered from Roman drainage ditches in Southwark (Jones, 1978), provide evidence of the contemporaneous fish fauna. The distribution of stickleback remains at Bronze Age Fen-edge West Row, Mildenhall, Suffolk, England, indicated which areas of the site were flooded seasonally. The fish bone data provided complementary evidence to that from investigations of the plant macrofossils at West Row and helped to produce a convincing picture of past flooding (Murphy, 1983).

During the last few thousand years man has modified his environment dramatically. Drainage, urbanization and industrial pollution have had a major impact on the freshwater biota. These changes have been particularly well documented for the river Thames, England, and its fish fauna (Wheeler, 1979b). Many of the rivers of lowland Britain and other industrial areas of the world have been altered: the water has been polluted by sewage and industrial effluent; weirs have been built to control the flow of water and banks erected to narrow the width and increase depth. These changes all influence the fish population. In Europe there are approximately 390 species of fish which, for at least some part of their lives, inhabit freshwaters (Blanc *et al.*, 1971). Some favour fast-flowing well-oxygenated streams, others prefer slow-flowing or even still waters which are poorly oxygenated, while a few live mainly in tidal waters. Given a source of information on the requirements and preferred habitats of fishes identified from an archaeological site, it is possible to postulate the kind of river being exploited.

The past distribution of fishes

Fish remains provide clear evidence for the distribution of fish in the past. There are few other lines of investigation that are capable of providing information about the changing fish fauna of a region in the recent past. Some evidence is available from studies describing bones recovered from natural peat and other deposits laid down during the Pleistocene and Holocene (e.g. Stuart, 1982).

Historical records, while they can be of immense value, give only occasional reference to fishes and it is not always possible to be certain that the name used by the writer refers to the species known by the same name today. Sometimes names in ancient documents defy translation. Occasionally, however, in medieval documents such as Kitchener's Rolls, lists of fish are itemized with their cost and amount purchased. Such records are obviously of considerable interest to historians and archaeologists. Sadly, historical records rarely survive for more than a few centuries.

The information gleaned from historical records and assemblages of ancient fish remains can be very helpful to present-day biologists managing fish stocks, whether marine or freshwater. Today most fish populations are subjected to heavy fishing pressures from commercial and sport fishermen. Evidence of the age and size structure of past fish populations can be inferred from archaeological material and the evidence considered during the development of a management strategy.

A blend of biology and archaeology

To study fish remains from archaeological deposits is to bridge two academic disciplines. It is essential to have a sound knowledge of fish osteology as well as an understanding of the principles of stratigraphy. All too frequently fish bone reports are spoilt by incorrect use of scientific names or mis-spellings. Such errors cast a cloud over the report and cause the reader to question the accuracy of the determinations and the credibility of the conclusions. On the other hand, naive assumptions such as 'all the fish remains from a layer are contemporaneous with the pottery found in that layer' would cause many archaeologists to wince. In brief, there is a need to understand the rules, conventions and assumptions of two areas of study and to combine them sensitively.

At the risk of offending zoologists, some basic guidance on the classification of animals and the use of scientific names is given. Living things are divided into two kingdoms, animals and plants. The animal kingdom is subdivided into large units called phyla (singular phylum) e.g. Arthropoda (animals with jointed legs: crabs, insects, spiders, etc.) and Chordata (animals with backbones: fishes, birds, reptiles and mammals). Each phylum is divided into orders, suborders, families, genera and species. Species may be subdivided into subspecies, varieties and races, though these can rarely be detected by studying bones alone.

For centuries it has been the convention to describe and name animals and plants in Latin. Indeed, many of the common food fish are known by scientific names which are latinized versions of terms used by classical writers like Aristotle, names which have been adopted by later writers. Over the years naming organisms has developed into a discipline of its own – taxonomy. Codes of practice exist which ensure that the names used for animals (and plants) satisfy quite elaborate yet specific sets of rules; an International Commission exists to clarify points of difficulty.

Usually it is possible to identify to species at least some remains in an archaeological assemblage. A generally accepted definition is that a species is a population of organisms which, under natural conditions, produce fertile offspring by sexual reproduction. Species are known by Latin or latinized scientific names consisting of two parts: the first the generic name, which is always spelled with an initial capital letter; and the second, the specific epithet, which begins with a lower-case letter. Scientific names for species are usually printed in italic; where this is impossible the name is underlined. This form reflects the tradition of describing animals in Latin in a single sentence. Sentences always begin with a capital letter. Finally, the full name ends with the name of the person (authority) who first described it by that name and the date on which the description was published. The authority name is sometimes abbreviated. For example, the Atlantic herring is universally known as *Clupea harengus* L., 1758. The generic name is *Clupea*, a name derived from

Pliny (Macleod, 1956) and the specific name *harengus* (which is the latinized form of the Dutch *haring* – Anglo-Saxon *haering*). The 'L.' is an abbreviation for Linnaeus, and the date 1758 represents the year in which Linnaeus used the name in published form, and thus establishes its seniority. Sometimes the authority and date are placed in parentheses e.g. (L., 1758), which indicates that the species was first described by Linnaeus but that subsequently it has been placed in a different genus. Often the date is omitted in abbreviated forms.

Although taxonomists strive to give all this information, for practical purposes in archaeology it is usually sufficient to refer to the scientific name (in the above example *Clupea harengus*) but if several species of fishes are discussed a reference to the nomenclature used in a recent and reputable faunal list will establish without ambiguity the source of the names used.

Family names always end with the suffix 'idae'. They begin with a capital letter but are not italicized. Thus Clupeidae is the scientific name for the herring family. In informal usage clupeid (as in clupeid fishes), with a lower-case initial, is a useful and acceptable form.

Biologists will be aware of these conventions; but they may not be aware of some of the finer points of archaeological stratigraphy. Perhaps the greatest problem for the biologist entering the archaeological arena is to understand the concept of residuality. In the perfect archaeological site the most recent material would be found in the uppermost layers and the oldest in the lowest, with a continuous gradation of material between. Sadly, this is rarely what excavators find. The general rule is that the more recent material will be in the uppermost layers, however often very ancient pottery may be found in modern layers. The reason for this is not difficult to explain: people dig holes. Imagine the medieval invader finding the ruins of a Roman site. He may first erect a flimsy shelter, throw away broken pots, animal bones and other rubbish on the ground surface. Some of this may become trampled into the Roman layer just below the turf. More serious mixing of material will occur when he digs a cesspit or starts robbing the footing of a Roman wall. Pottery and other rubbish will fall into these features or material may be deliberately dumped into them. As a result medieval and Roman material will become mixed. This will be obvious to a pottery expert who can recognize Roman and medieval pottery forms, but Roman and medieval cod or herring are identical. Clearly it is essential that there is excellent communication between excavators and bone specialists to ensure that only securely dated material is used to provide information on the distribution of species in time.

Other facts that should be communicated to the person studying fish bones include the location of the site and its soil type, details of the methods used to recover fish bones, and the nature of the deposits which contained the bones. Ideally, the animal bone specialists should be involved with the planning of the excavation and be encouraged to suggest which parts of the site are most likely to produce informative material. Visits are invaluable for understanding the site in its context and seeing the methods, style and practical limitations of excavation.

The diversity of fishes

Most recent estimates of the number of different kinds of fishes known vary from 20,000 to 22,000 species. The precise number is impossible to establish at the moment, and will be for several decades, because systematic ichthyology is an active field with new species being described every year, and reviews of existing literature and specimens removing some species founded in the past, as they are found not to be distinct. Simultaneously the list of recognized species is both increasing and decreasing, but the nett result is a small but steady increase in species, and Nelson (1984) estimates that there will be found to be possibly 28,000 species of fish extant. Even at the present upper level of 22,000 species there are more recognized kinds of fishes than there are of the sum of all mammals, birds, reptiles and amphibians. Not surprisingly, the sheer number of species which could come to the attention of the archaeologist is one of the major problems.

However, these 22,000 species are not evenly distributed between the major groups of fishes, or geographically or spatially throughout the seas and fresh waters of the world. The most striking disparity is in their classification, for while about 21,000 species are bony fishes (Osteichthyes), the remaining 1,000 are spread between three classes, and most of these are the cartilaginous fishes (Chondrichthyes), which include the sharks, skates and rays. The remainder are the primitive jawless fishes belonging to the superclass Agnatha. Even within the bony fishes, one order (the Perciformes) includes nearly 8,000 species, in contrast to four orders which each contain only a single species (figures from Nelson, 1984). Because of these disparities in numbers it is pointless to discuss each order in turn so the remainder of this chapter comprises a discussion of those orders (and families in some cases) which have relevance to zooarchaeology. Orders in the succeeding pages can be recognized by the ending -iformes.

Jawless fishes
Class Myxini
   Myxiniformes – Family Myxinidae (hagfishes) (fig. 2.1a). About 32 species; marine; mainly in the temperate zones of both hemispheres. Not known to have been exploited for food. Skeleton weak cartilage – no hard parts.

Class Cephalaspidomorphi
   Petromyzontiformes – Family Petromyzontidae (lampreys) (fig. 2.1b). About 41 species; freshwater and marine; migrate to rivers to breed.

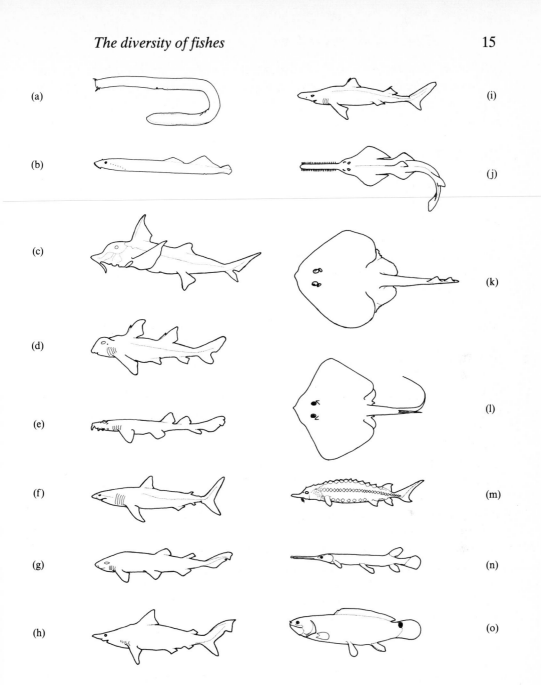

2.1   The diversity of fishes – Myxiniformes to Amiiformes

Mainly in temperate zones of the northern hemisphere, but also southern
S. America, Australia and New Zealand. Occasionally exploited as food.
Skeleton of weak cartilage; only hard parts are horny buccal teeth.

Cartilaginous fishes
Class Chondrichthyes
  Subclass Holocephali
         Chimaeriformes (chimaeras and ploughnose chimaeras) (fig. 2.1c).
About 24 species mostly deep-sea fishes except for the southern hemisphere
family Callorhynchidae. Skeleton cartilaginous; hard parts are characteristic
tooth plates. Probably never exploited by man as food.
    Subclass Elasmobranchii (sharks, skates and rays)

      Superorder Selachimorpha (sharks)
All sharks have cartilaginous skeletons, but in most (especially the large
species) the skeleton is heavily impregnated with calcium; the skeletal
elements thus look like bone in modern specimens. Under natural conditions
these elements often disintegrate into small calcified units (see chapter 6).
Their vertebral centra are distinctive for the group and sometimes diagnostic
for the species. However, other hard parts such as jaw teeth and specialized
scales (see pp. 81–6), and in some families fin spines, are frequently characteristic for species determination.
    Shark teeth are very common in geological deposits, e.g. Tertiary clays,
and may be confused with recent archaeological material. Early fossil shark
teeth also sometimes appear as contaminant material in Pleistocene or early
Holocene deposits where these are physically close.
    Four orders of which three are possibly relevant.
         Heterodontiformes – *Family Heterodontidae* (horn sharks) (fig.
2.1d). Eight species in Indian and Pacific Oceans especially southern hemisphere. Unlikely to be exploited.
         Lamniformes – *Family Orectolobidae* (carpet sharks) (fig. 2.1e).
About 28 species in tropical and warm temperate oceans, many living in
shallow water, maximum length 4 m, most smaller.
         Family Lamnidae (mackerel sharks) (fig. 2.1f). About ten species
in open seas of all oceans. Large, active (and dangerous) sharks; unlikely to
be exploited except by specialist fisheries.
         Family Scyliorhinidae (dogfishes and cat sharks) (fig. 2.1g). About
90 species mostly in shallow tropical and temperate seas; attaining 1.5 m in
length. Some species easy to capture and used for food.
         Family Carcharhinidae (requiem and whaler sharks) (fig. 2.1h).
About 50 species in temperate and tropical oceans, occasionally in tropical
rivers and lakes, in inshore and offshore waters. Most are 4–5 m in length;

some are aggressive and dangerous to man. The smaller species have been widely exploited as food.

    Squaliformes – *Family Squalidae* (spurdogs and dogfish sharks) (fig. 2.1i). About 70 species, some being relatively small (up to 2 m); temperate and tropical oceans. Many species have a prominent spine in front of each dorsal fin. The shallow-water species are easy to catch and have been widely used for food.

    Superorder Batidoidimorpha (skates and rays)

    Rajiformes with eight families of which three are possibly relevant. Like sharks they have calcium deposited in their cartilaginous skeletons, but jaw teeth and scales, which may be strongly modified, are characteristic.

    Family Pristidae (sawfishes) (fig. 2.1j). Six species, mainly marine but entering rivers; mostly in tropical areas. Attain 6 m in length. Teeth on saw blade, and minute jaw teeth are distinctive.

    Family Rajidae (skates) (fig. 2.1k). About 200 species, about half of them living in shallow seas; found in all oceans. Most are about 1 m in length, some much larger. Shallow-water species are relatively easy to capture.

    Family Dasyatidae (stingrays) (fig. 2.1). About 90 species, most living in the sea, especially tropical and sub-tropical seas; a few occur in fresh water. (In north-eastern South America a family of stingrays – the Potamotrygonidae – live in rivers and lakes.) Some live in shallow water and can be simply captured, but have a dangerous, envenomed, serrated spine on the tail – which is also characteristic.

Bony fishes
Class Osteichthyes

    Acipenseriformes (sturgeons and paddlefishes) – *Family Acipenseridae* (sturgeons) (fig. 2.1m). 23 species, mainly freshwater but some migrate to sea to feed; northern hemisphere in temperate areas. Some grow to large size (4 m). Skeleton mainly cartilaginous; hard parts include characteristic bony scutes and sculptured head bones.

    Lepisosteiformes (gars) – *Family Leipsosteidae* (gars) (fig. 2.1n). Seven species. Fresh and brackish water, and occasionally marine (in Caribbean). Extant species confined to eastern North America, Central America and Cuba. Largest species 3 m. Skeleton ossified; characteristic hard parts, heavy ganoid scales, and opisthocoelus vertebral centra (see fig. 7.11).

    Amiiformes – *Family Amiidae* (bowfin) (fig. 2.1o). One species. Freshwater in eastern North America; maximum length about 90 cm. Skeleton ossified, vertebrae concave at each end, higher than wide. Probably not much used for food, but easy to capture.

Anguilliformes (eels) – *Family Anguillidae* (freshwater eels) (fig. 2.2a). 16 species. Freshwater but also estuaries and coastal waters. Eastern North America, Europe, eastern Africa, south-east Asia, eastern Australia, New Zealand. Attain 1.5 m. Valuable food fishes in some areas. Jaws and vertebral centra distinctive.

Family Muraenidae (moray eels) (fig. 2.2b). About 110 species. Marine eels of tropical and warm-temperate areas, mostly found in shallow water; all oceans. Maximum length 3.0 m. In tropical regions flesh often toxic (ciguatoxin); possibly not often eaten. Jaws characteristic.

Family Congridae (conger eels) (fig. 2.2c). About 100 species. Marine eels of Atlantic, Indian and Pacific Oceans, temperate and tropical. Some species are eaten. Jaws and vertebral centra distinctive.

Clupeiformes (herrings and tarpons) – *Family Clupeidae* (herrings, sardines, shads) (fig. 2.2d). About 190 species. Mostly marine, some migrating into fresh water (shads), worldwide, mainly coastal. Maximum length 75 cm. Often extremely abundant and an important food resource; the most important fish family to the modern fishing industry. Bones very fragile; vertebral centra are probably the most common fish remains on post-Roman European sites but due to their small size are only recovered by sieving.

Cypriniformes

An order of entirely freshwater fishes living only in North America, Africa and Eurasia. Distinguished by toothless jaws, special tooth-bearing pharyngeal bones (see p. 91 and fig. 7.6e, f), and four modified anterior abdominal vertebrae. Six families of which two are relevant.

Family Cyprinidae (carps and minnows) (fig. 2.2e). About 2,000 species. Living in fresh waters of North America, Africa, Europe and Asia. Maximum size about 2.5 m, most less than 30 cm. Important food fishes in inland areas.

Family Catostomidae (suckers) (fig. 2.2f). About 60 species. Fresh waters of China, north Siberia, North America. Maximum length about 1 m; most are much less. Potentially food fishes in inland areas. Pharyngeal teeth very numerous, but in one row.

Characiformes

An order of freshwater fishes living in Africa (about 176 species), South and Central America, northwards to Mexico (abou⁺ 1,150 species). Most have elaborate and distinctively toothed jaws; the pharyngeal bone is present but is not so specialized as in the carps and suckers. Ten families are recognized; perhaps four are relevant to the archaeological context.

Family Characidae (characins and tigerfish) (fig. 2.2g). Central and South America and Africa, mostly small but some of 1 m in length.

Family Citharinidae (fig. 2.2h). African fishes, some of which attain 80 cm.

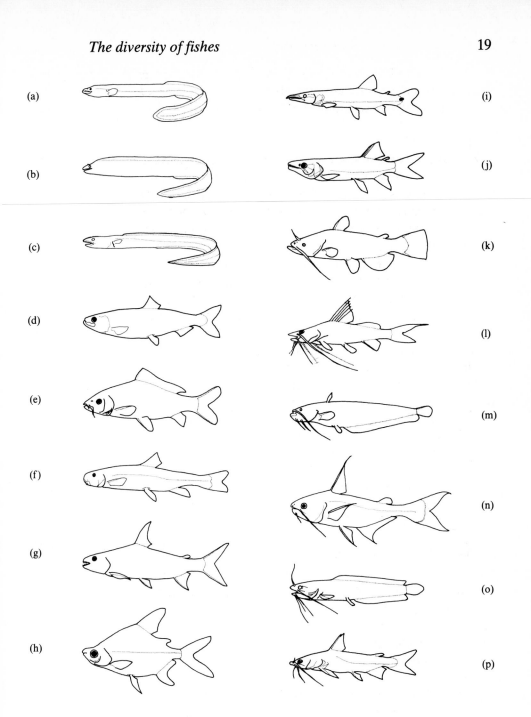

2.2 The diversity of fishes – Anguilliformes to Siluriformes

Family Ctenoluciidae (pike-characids) (fig. 2.2i). Panama and South America, where there are four species, one of which attains 1 m.

Family Hepsetidae (pike characin) (fig. 2.2j). West and Central Africa, with a single species attaining about 40 cm in length.

Siluriformes

An order of mainly freshwater fishes which contains about 2,200 species in 31 families. Perhaps six are relevant in this context. Many catfishes have strong spines at the front of their dorsal and pectoral fins, and some have finely sculptured cranial bones; they also have fused anterior abdominal vertebrae.

Family Ictaluridae (North American catfishes) (fig. 2.2k). North American lakes and rivers; about 45 species, some growing to 1.5 m, most much smaller. Important food fishes.

Family Bagridae (bagrid catfishes) (fig. 2.2l). Fresh waters of Africa and Asia with about 200 species. Some are used as food.

Family Siluridae (sheatfishes) (fig. 2.2m). Fresh water in Europe and Asia; about 70 species. Largest species is *Silurus glanis* in Europe, at 5 m; most are much smaller. Some are used as food fishes.

Family Pangasiidae (fig. 2.2n). Fresh waters of southern Asia. About 25 species, the largest, *Pangasianodon gigas*, attaining 2.5 m in the R. Mekong. This and other species are food fishes.

Family Clariidae (fig. 2.2o). Fresh waters of Africa, Middle East and southern Asia. About 100 species, some with accessory breathing organs which allow them to survive out of water, making transport to markets easier. Used as food.

Family Ariidae (sea catfishes) (fig. 2.2p). Marine; tropical and sub-tropical areas. About 120 species. Important food fishes.

Salmoniformes

An important group of food fishes, which are mainly concentrated in the northern hemisphere, and are mostly freshwater fishes, although many migrate to the sea to feed. They include some 15 families, of which four are relevant. In general salmoniforms have rather poorly ossified bones, which often do not preserve well in the soil. Although tooth-bearing bones are distinctive, their otoliths are usually minute, and the vertebral centra are pierced. They also have numerous intramuscular bones.

Family Esocidae (pikes) (fig. 2.3a). Fresh waters of the northern hemisphere; about ten species, several being large and important food fishes.

Family Osmeridae (smelts) (fig. 2.3b). Migratory, marine and freshwater fishes; northern hemisphere only, mainly in coastal areas. 11 species. Important food fishes despite a maximum length of 40 cm.

Family Galaxiidae (galaxiids) (fig. 2.3c). Fresh water and migratory to the sea; New Zealand, southern Australia, southern South Africa and South America. Maximum length 58 cm; most around 20 cm, but despite this valued food fishes.

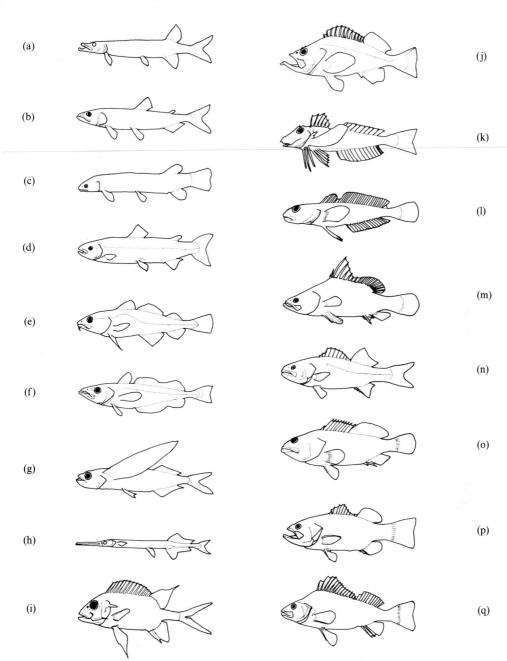

(a)

(b)

(c)

(d)

(e)

(f)

(g)

(h)

(i)

(j)

(k)

(l)

(m)

(n)

(o)

(p)

(q)

2.3   The diversity of fishes – Salmoniformes to Perciformes (Percidae)

Families Salmonidae and Coregonidae (salmons, trouts, charrs, whitefishes) (fig. 2.3d). Fresh water and migratory to the sea to feed. Occur in northern hemisphere only, often in Arctic regions. Maximum length 1.5 m; most less than 1 m. Highly important food fishes.

Gadiformes
Important food fishes in the temperate North Atlantic; with one freshwater species, the burbot, *Lota lota*, occurring across most of northern North America, Europe and Asia. Seven families, mostly living in deep water but two are relevant in this context.

Family Gadidae (codfishes) (fig. 2.3e). Marine with one freshwater species. Most abundant in North Atlantic, but also occurring off southern South Africa and New Zealand. About 50 species living in inshore waters, a few on the shore. Lengths range from 2 m to 15 cm. Dominant in European coastal sites.

Family Merlucciidae (hakes) (fig. 2.3f). Marine, offshore and coastal waters; about seven species in the Atlantic, eastern Pacific, and off New Zealand. Growing to 2 m, mainly in deep water, but locally caught for food.

Cyprinodontiformes
A large order of some 800 species, which includes the minute killifishes and live-bearers, such as the guppy, *Poecilia reticulata*, but also flying fishes and garfishes, which are relevant here.

Family Exocoetidae (flyingfishes) (fig. 2.3g). Marine, surface-living especially in tropical and sub-tropical Atlantic, Pacific and Indian Ocean; about 50 species. Can be captured in quantity using special methods.

Family Belonidae (garfishes) (fig. 2.3h). Marine fishes, especially in tropical and warm temperate seas; some species live in fresh water. About 30 species. Surface-living, but can be caught by specialized fisheries. Distinctive features: elongate toothed jaws, and green bones in some.

Beryciformes
A large order of mainly deep-water fishes with about 14 families; only one is relevant in the present context.

Family Holocentridae (squirrelfishes) (fig. 2.3i). About 60 species of marine fishes confined to tropical waters of the Indian, Pacific and Atlantic Oceans. Mostly nocturnal and crepuscular in their habits and often red coloured, they live in relatively shallow water on reefs. Possibly incidentally captured and used as food.

Scorpaeniformes
A large order of over 100 species in 20 families. Many are small, but some are large and used as food. Possibly only three families are relevant.

Family Scorpaenidae (scorpionfishes) (fig. 2.3j). Marine tropical and temperate seas, about 300 species. They include some venomous species living in shallow water on reefs in the tropical Indo-Pacific, and many temperate (mainly North Pacific) rockfishes (genus *Sebastes*). Several are easy to capture, and are eaten.

Family Triglidae (searobins, gurnards) (fig. 2.3k). Marine tropical and temperate seas, living on the bottom often in shallow water. Maximum length is 1 m; most are much smaller. About 80 species. Distinguished by the sculpturing on the head bones.

Family Cottidae (sculpins, bullheads) (fig. 2.3l). Marine fishes, most abundant in the North Pacific, also occurring in the North Atlantic, and freshwater fishes in the northern hemisphere. About 300 species known. Many live in shallow fresh and salt water and can be captured easily. Distinctive features include prominent head spines.

Perciformes

The largest order of fishes, containing about 150 families and 7,800 species. They occur in fresh and salt water, and include many important food fishes. Typically, they have spines in the fins (as well as branched rays), two dorsal fins, a spine and five, or fewer, branched rays in the pelvic fins. The pelvic fins are placed forward close to the head, and the scales, when present, are ctenoid. Most species have fewer than 30 vertebrae, which are strongly built and ridged. The following summary of potentially relevant families omits many on account of the numbers involved.

Family Centropomidae (snooks and Nile perch) (fig. 2.3m). Marine in tropical Atlantic and Pacific Oceans, and fresh water especially in Africa. Maximum length 2 m. Potential food fishes locally.

Family Percichthyidae (basses) (fig. 2.3n). Marine, brackish (and freshwater in Australia and North America) in tropical and temperate areas. Includes the European seabass, *Dicentrarchus labrax*, an important food fish, and many large 1–2 m long basses in tropical seas. Upper gill cover with only two spines.

Family Serranidae (sea basses, groupers, and sea perches) (fig. 2.3o). Marine tropical and temperate seas. About 370 species, most of which are moderately large, and some huge (up to 3 m). Most are predators and relatively easy to catch as they live in shallow seas, and many are important food fishes.

Family Centrarchidae (sunfishes) (fig. 2.3p). Fresh waters of North America. About 30 species including the black basses, *Micropterus* spp.; often abundant in inland waters, catchable and potentially food fishes.

Family Percidae (perches) (fig. 2.3q). Fresh waters of northern hemisphere. About 140 species, several of which are potential food fishes including the yellow perch, *Perca flavescens*, and walleye, *Stizostedion vitreum*, of North America, and their Eurasian relatives, the perch and zander.

Family Carangidae (jacks, pompanos, scads) (fig. 2.4a). Marine fishes of all tropical and temperate seas. About 140 species of active, predatory fishes, common in coastal waters; many are important food fishes. Most have enlarged, spiny scutes on the lateral line.

Family Lutjanidae (snappers) (fig. 2.4b). Marine fishes of the tropical Atlantic, Indian and Pacific Oceans. About 180 species, many living in shallow coastal waters. Strong teeth in jaws. Important food fishes in tropics.

Family Sparidae (sea-breams, porgies) (fig. 2.4c). Marine fishes of Atlantic, Indian and Pacific Oceans; growing to a maximum length of 1.2 m. Distinguished by specialized jaw teeth. Important food fish, especially in tropical and temperate zones.

Family Sciaenidae (drums, croakers) (fig. 2.4d). Marine fishes in all oceans, particularly attracted to estuaries; also in fresh waters of Middle America. About 200 species, some of them growing to 1.5 m. All are potentially good food fishes. Particularly large sagittal otoliths are distinctive.

Family Cichlidae (cichlids) (fig. 2.4e). Freshwater fishes particularly abundant in Africa; also occur in Central and South America, Middle East to India (where found in brackish water). Grow to 80 cm; most around 30 cm; about 700 species. Important as food in inland regions.

Family Mugilidae (grey mullets) (fig. 2.4f). Coastal marine and brackish waters in tropical and temperate seas; also fresh water in tropical areas. Grow to about 90 cm; some 70 species. Potential food fishes.

Family Labridae (wrasses) (fig. 2.4g). Marine fishes in all tropical and temperate oceans, approximately 500 species, many small, but some growing to 3 m. Used as food. Jaws and pharyngeal bones with distinctive shapes and dentition aid identification.

Family Scaridae (parrotfishes) (fig. 2.4h). Marine fishes of tropical and warm temperate oceans, often close inshore. About 70 species, some attaining 2 m, many moderately large. Potentially food fishes near tropical reefs. Teeth in jaws and pharyngeal dentition distinctive.

Familoy Acanthuridae (surgeonfishes) (fig. 2.4i). Marine; all tropical seas. About 76 species, some growing to 60 cm. Common in coral reef areas, feeding on encrusting algae. Jaw teeth are distinctive, as are the sharp spines in the sides of the caudal peduncle.

Family Scombridae (tunas, mackerel) (fig. 2.4j). Marine, all tropical and temperate oceans. About 48 species, some huge, attaining 4 m, most in excess of 1 m. Mostly in the open sea, but making seasonal coast-wise migrations. Valuable food fishes throughout history. Skeleton curiously soft and not preserving well; otoliths minute.

Pleuronectiformes

Approximately 500 species of flatfishes are known in six families. Almost all are bottom-living fishes which have adapted to benthic life by turning on their sides and having both eyes on one side. The jaws are also often unequally developed. Two families are relevant in the context of the archaeologist. Dis-

3

ASPECTS OF FISH ECOLOGY

Introduction
There is both archaeological and historical evidence that many human cultures have exploited fish as food. As fishes live in an environment alien to man and have not, until the twentieth century, been extensively cultured for food, there must be special reasons why they have been so widely exploited.

One may be that fishes are very numerous and in general are of moderate size and thus represent a significant food source. Because of the very great numbers of species and the generally very high fecundity of fish, they are abundant in almost all aquatic habitats. Great fecundity implies both extremely high numbers of juvenile and immature fishes and also heavy losses during these stages. One of the factors involved in this high mortality is predation. The fact that fishes, unlike the majority of mammals, live in a three-dimensional habitat, which is capable of supporting both a greater number of species and a greater biomass than most terrestrial environments, results in more food being available to predators in an aquatic habitat than elsewhere.

Moreover, there are factors peculiar to fishes which may make them more vulnerable to capture. Even the most cursory comparison between the brain of a fish and that of a mammal will show fundamental differences related both to life style and to the animal's perception of its surroundings. In fishes those parts of the brain which are best developed are the olfactory and optic lobes (the former much more than the latter in sharks and skates). In fishes the regions of the brain involved with memory and learning are poorly developed when compared with the mammalian brain. Although fishes can be trained to respond to repeated visual and olfactory stimuli, the process of learning is slow compared to that in mammals. A fish's world is one of strong sensory perception, with instant reaction, relatively little acquired knowledge and no cogitation. These factors, which are positive advantages to the fish in its natural environment, leave it at a disadvantage when hunted by man.

As a result, baited hooks and traps of very simple design are sufficient to secure many kinds of fishes, which are attracted to bait by their often very sensitive olfactory organs. In coastal waters the tidal rise and fall of the sea level permits fishes to exploit the intertidal zone to feed and this makes them vulnerable to shore-line traps and barriers designed to lead the fish retreating with the falling tide into a water-filled pound from which they can be collected. Neither the construction of traps nor manufacture of hooks requires a high level of technology. In addition, marine fishes (chiefly the smaller species) are susceptible to capture by hand in the intertidal zone, so that technology is never a limiting factor.

A substantial number of groups of fish have adopted a survival strategy of schooling. These are predominantly surface and open-water fishes such as herrings (family Clupeidae), jacks (family Carangidae), mackerels and tuna (family Scombridae), and in fresh water carps and minnows (family Cyprinidae), characins or tetras (family Characidae) and cichlids (family Cichlidae), but many others form schools at some stage during their lives. While schooling has clear survival value to the species, it can in some circumstances be of negative value. With only slightly elaborate means of capture, such as floating nets or seine nets, or natural poisons, it is possible to capture enormous numbers of fish in a short space of time.

Even in circumstances when a large quantity of fish has been harvested, more than required for immediate consumption, the surplus is relatively easy to preserve. The stockfish of Norwegian fishermen was plain dried cod, *Gadus morhua*, gutted and hung in the cold, dry spring weather with plenty of wind and sunshine (Cutting, 1955). In less sunny, more humid areas, the flesh would quickly decompose with this treatment, so preservation was aided by salting. 'White fish', that is those which do not have oily flesh, could be preserved by salting and drying, or salting and smoking. Those with oily flesh (for example, herring, tuna, salmonoids) could be preserved by salt pickling, or salting and smoking. Fermenting fish, using a minimum of salt, was another means of preservation, used in Scandinavia for both herring, *Clupea harengus*, and salmon, *Salmo salar* (Norsander, 1984), as was the well-known Mediterranean garum, which used both salt and herbs, made from the waste from gutted fishes, especially large tuna (Ponsich and Tarradell, 1965), but which also was manufactured locally from small clupeid fishes, such as sprats and herring (Bateman and Locker, 1982), or sardines (Wheeler and Locker, 1985), although virtually any small fishes with oily flesh could be employed (Flower and Rosenbaum, 1958).

The value of such treated fish was not merely that a seasonal glut could be preserved for leaner times, but that the product could be transported. While such transport could have been of limited significance in early communities, it led to the development of a fishing industry in the Mediterranean in Classical times and in northern Europe in the medieval period.

Wild fish populations
Natural communities of fishes fluctuate continuously and often irregularly in both species composition and in the size and age ranges of their constituents, from a variety of causes. The abundance of food is a prime factor in the migrations of fishes of the kind which lead to the seasonal gluts mentioned

above. It may also have a profound influence on the age-structure of a population of fishes, in that variation of food resources in the early stages of growth can be reflected in the numbers and the individual sizes of fishes for a considerable period of years. Some knowledge of the food available to fishes and their feeding relationships is therefore desirable for a wider understanding of what might be expected of a stock of fishes.

Every food organism is part of a chain relationship, but the chain is not a simple link-to-link relationship but rather an interlinking mesh of prey, predators, saprophytes and parasites, each ultimately dependent on other organisms for sustenance and survival. Moreover, when the various levels at which the food web exists and the relative positions of predators and prey, carnivores, herbivores and omnivores are considered, it is clear that the relationship is three-dimensional, forming a pyramid, the apex of which is usually occupied by the largest carnivore or top predator. Such a pyramid illustrates the complexity of food relationships through various levels of dietary specialization and also shows the decreasing biomass at each higher level of the pyramid with the top-level predator having the lowest biomass.

Green plants form the base of the pyramid in water, mostly relatively simple algae, which, nourished by inorganic matter (mainly nitrates and phosphates), bind the energy of the sun into plant cells. Although the most noticeable algae in the sea are the wracks, thongweeds and kelps (usually known as seaweeds), these play a relatively small role in the food web, being virtually a dead-end in the food chain, although a few animals feed on them and shelter amongst their fronds. The minute single-celled algae which drift near the surface of the water, in the photic zone, are, however, all-important. This phytoplankton, comprising mostly diatoms and flagellates, has a very short individual life span but reproduces at a great rate, usually simply by division of one cell into two. The rate of reproduction is therefore geometrical and this confers an enormous advantage, in that the algae can quickly respond to seasonal sunshine.

The algae are known as primary producers and form the first trophic level of the food pyramid. The second trophic level is occupied by herbivores, chiefly small crustaceans, mainly copepods, but also young crustaceans, mollusc larvae and post-larval fishes, which together form the zooplankton, which floats near the sea's surface. A third trophic level comprises the carnivores, which prey on the herbivores, many of which may also be part of the zooplankton. This level is composed of several tiers of fishes and larger animals such as squids, cetaceans, birds and man, all of which prey on animals smaller than themselves (fig. 3.1).

The cycle is completed by the excretions of the varied predators and the dead bodies of those animals and plants which escaped being eaten falling to the bottom, to decompose as a result of bacterial action, eventually to provide the basic nutrients required to set the process going again.

The three main aquatic habitats, lakes, rivers and the sea, all share these basic processes, but the detailed relationships in each are extremely complex and specific to the habitat. In freshwater habitats insect larvae are of particular importance at both second and third trophic levels and occupy several tiers of the third level, where larger larvae eat smaller larvae before being eaten by larger vertebrate animals. Rivers have a considerable allochthonous supplement, especially in their headwaters, where terrestrial insects and plant debris commonly fall into the water and the former at least are eaten by fishes. Allochthonous nutrients affect rivers in their lower reaches, not least near human habitations where excreta and organic waste are disposed of into the water, providing enrichment which in moderate quantities stimulates primary productivity. Stimulation of primary production may be deliberately achieved, as in the very long-established pond culture of fishes of the family Cyprinidae in India and South-east Asia by siting latrines and pig stalls above the pond and by keeping ducks on the water. This is particularly effective as several carps (exceptional amongst large fishes) feed mainly at trophic levels one and two.

As a broad generality the complexity of the food pyramid is less in cool climates, perhaps because the fauna is less rich than in tropical regions. In addition, primary productivity is lower in higher latitudes and is strongly seasonal, spring sunshine leading to a burst of phytoplankton growth, sometimes after several barren months. This in turn suggests that biomass (the totality of animals or plants) at each level will be lower overall than in a comparable tropical area.

In addition, the biomass of each trophic level is always lower than that of the prey organisms of the animals of that level. This is due to the low rate of food conversion from one stage to the next. The figure of 10% is often used as a general conversion rate (meaning that 1 kg of phytoplankton will support 100 g of herbivores and 10 g of carnivores). Many fishes can improve on this conversion rate, particularly young ones, and some can attain 50% for a short period when they are growing fast and food items of the right size are available. The biomass of fish produced is, in addition, much greater for species which are close to the primary producer level. This is the reason why several Asiatic carps and the milkfish, *Chanos chanos*, are widely used in pond culture in Asia, some African cichlid fishes have been spread around the tropical world for cultivation, and also accounts for the clupeid fishes (herrings and sardines) and anchovies forming such important marine fisheries.

A simple example of the consequences of the biomass decreasing at each trophic level can be cited from the unpublished data of Sir Joseph Banks's fishing parties on the River Witham, Lincolnshire, England, over the period 1788–96. He recorded year by year the total weight of 'whitefish' (almost all cyprinid fishes and thus low on the trophic levels), and of perch (a higher-level predator) and pike (the highest-level fish predator). His figures for weights for the nine years were 'whitefish' 5581 kg, perch 275 kg, pike 349 kg, and although the numbers of 'whitefish' were not recorded there were only 299 pike captured compared to 990 perch (reflecting the greater size of the former when full grown).

This example illustrates the degree of selectivity exercised in capturing large pike in Danish sites, where considerable numbers have been reported (e.g. Noe-Nygaard, 1983). It also points up an aspect of the relationship between man and exploited fish (or other animal) populations, in that specialization on high trophic levels prey may exhaust that food resource (simply because its biomass is comparatively smaller). At a low level of exploitation no problems ensue, but at increased levels the prey diminishes in biomass although not necessarily in numbers, as more small fish may replace fewer large fish, but the effects on the protein available to the human population may be traumatic.

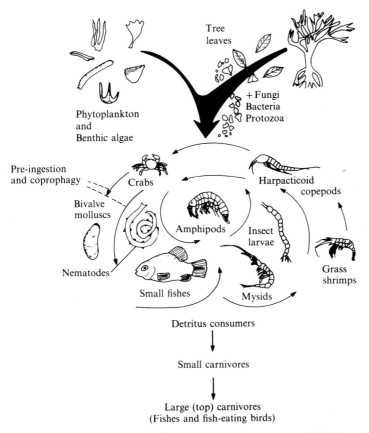

3.1   The flow of energy and materials through several trophic levels in an estuary in Florida. The complex central portion illustrates the use of detritus from faecal material. (From K. H. Mann, 1982. *The ecology of coastal waters – a systems approach*. Blackwell, Oxford.)

To a limited extent the age structure of a natural population of a fish species can be likened to a broad-based pyramid. The apex of the pyramid comprises those individuals of the greatest age and thus usually the largest size. Because of the effects of senescence, disease, parasites and predators, these large old fish are few in number. Below them in the pyramid come the younger mature fishes, which form the mainstay of the population, being fecund and very numerous, while below these are the immature fishes, which are more numerous still. The pyramid base is extended seasonally by the sequential appearance of larvae, post-larvae and juveniles after the spawning season. The age pyramid also represents the numerical abundance for the species, but not the biomass, for clearly the total weight of the year-classes varies and attains a maximum in the middle ranges. It can be represented graphically by an elongate kite shape with the youngest fish at the foot and the maximum width above the vertical mid-point.

However, such a model would be revealed only by analysis of all the fish of one species in a confined water such as a lake. Elsewhere the structure would be masked by the distribution of different year-classes in different parts of the habitat, by migration, by the tendency of fishes of similar size to school together, and in many predatory fishes by their dispersal through the habitat to form individual territories. Moreover, the structure of the population represented by either age or size is unlikely to be revealed by primitive fishing techniques, which must necessarily be designed or employed to give the maximum yield per unit of effort for the species, the season or the habitat.

Faunistic zones
Fishes are distributed around the world unevenly but reflect the geological history of the continents and the oceans. This is most noticeable with freshwater fishes which, with certain exceptions, are confined to the continental land masses by the barrier of the sea.

Freshwater fishes can conveniently be divided into three main groups: primary freshwater fishes, which are physiologically incapable of surviving exposure to salt water and are therefore confined to the fresh waters of the landmass in which they have evolved; secondary freshwater fishes, which can tolerate salt water even though individually they may never be exposed to it. The third group can conveniently be called migratory fishes, and these are physiologically adapted to survive in both salt and fresh water; most individuals will be exposed to both media in the course of their lives.

These divisions are recognized only in bony fishes. The cartilaginous fishes (sharks, skates and rays) are marine animals. Sharks and sawfishes are exceptionally found in fresh water and then only in large tropical rivers and their associated lakes. A very few stingrays occur in tropical rivers and most of these are marine species which have penetrated from the sea. The Potamotrygonidae, stingrays which live in the fresh waters of northern South

America, are the only exception to the rule that cartilaginous fishes are marine, for they spend all their lives in fresh water.

The best-known, and most widely distributed, primary freshwater fishes are the carp-like fishes, order Cypriniformes, which are widely distributed in North America, Eurasia and Africa (but are absent from South America, Madagascar and Australia, their absence being possibly more significant than their occurrence). Most of these belong to the family Cyprinidae, but the small loaches (family Homalopteridae + Cobitidae) occur only in Eurasia and northern Africa, while the suckers (family Catostomidae), which are large and have been used as food fishes, are found principally in North America as well as China and north-east Siberia. Another important primary freshwater fish group is the order Characiformes, which occurs in South and Central America and tropical Africa. Although most are quite small fishes (they include the beautifully coloured tetras of the tropical aquarium), some are large enough to be used as food. In this, however, they are less important than the catfishes (order Siluriformes), which are also mostly primary freshwater fishes – only two families, Plotosidae and Ariidae, are found in the sea. Catfishes of the family Ictaluridae are abundant in North America (south to Guatemala); the Bagridae and Clariidae occur widely in Africa and Asia; the Pimelodidae, Doradidae and Callichthyidae all occur in South America. In general catfishes occur mostly in tropical and subtropical rivers (Europe has only two species, one of which is severely restricted in range) and they occur on all major continents and large land masses in these regions, although the Australian species all belong to the Ariidae and Plotosidae and are therefore secondary freshwater fishes.

Other primary groups of freshwater fishes in North America include the sunfishes (family Centrarchidae), the perches (Percidae) and pikes (Esocidae), the latter of which also live in temperate Eurasia. Lungfishes are representatives of ancient groups and live in South America (Lepidosirenidae), Africa (Protopteridae) and Australia (Ceratodontidae). Africa and tropical Asia have the gourami suborder Anabantoidei, the spiny eels (Mastacembelidae) and snakeheads (Channidae) in common.

Secondary freshwater fishes are widespread through all tropical rivers and include the cichlids or tilapias (Cichlidae), which are abundant in Africa and Madagascar, and occur also in South and Central America, as well as in coastal regions of India. They also include a number of potential food fishes such as grey mullets (Mugilidae), theraponids (Teraponidae), and some basses (Dicentrachidae). All the Australian freshwater fishes (with the exception of the lungfish and the baramundi, *Scleropages* sp.) belong to secondary groups, as do all the fishes of New Zealand without exception.

Naturally, these precise distributions have been obscured by human activity and particularly in the case of freshwater fishes there have been many introductions of exotic species. Thus, certain tilapia species (Cichlidae) have been released in tropical fresh waters in virtually all major landmasses, and European fishes such as carp have been introduced to temperate areas, especially North America, Australia and New Zealand, as have trout, *Salmo trutta*, while the rainbow trout, *Salmo gairdneri*, originally native to the Pacific drainage of North America, is now widespread in temperate fresh waters worldwide. Most of these introductions have been made in the late historical period (although the spread of the carp, *Cyprinus carpio*, from eastern Europe predates this period) and as such are of limited interest to the archaeologist, although an awareness of introductions to a local fish fauna and the possibility that the composition of the native fauna might have been affected would be useful background information to the archaeologist.

Marine fish families or larger groupings tend to have much wider distributions than freshwater fishes and many are limited in their range only by temperature barriers, which may no more than restrict migration from one ocean to others. There are therefore difficulties in analysing marine fish distribution in the same way as that for freshwater fishes. However, a discussion based on broad marine habitats possibly has more relevance to the archaeologist's needs than one based on biogeographical principles. It is convenient to divide marine fishes into the following three groups, littoral (= shore), inshore and offshore, because exploiting each group demands different levels of technology.

Littoral fishes are those which live between high- and low-tide levels (and can practically be extended to below low-tide mark at wading depth). The species represented vary from ocean to ocean and between temperate and tropical zones. Polar and near-polar regions have very few species which live on the shore, and then mainly in the warm season, but in Arctic seas certain codfishes, like the Arctic cod, *Boreogadus saida*, and the cottid fish, *Myoxocephalus scorpius*, living close inshore, can be captured by simple line fishing. The Arctic cod lives literally at the edge of the polar ice. However, the resident fishes are supplemented by species which migrate seasonally into Arctic rivers to spawn, most notably the Arctic charr, *Salvelinus alpinus*, which moves through coastal waters. The capelin, *Mallotus villosus*, a member of the order Salmoniformes, also comes close inshore in the warm season to spawn, in places such as Newfoundland and Labrador, actually spawning on the shore in huge schools, which are very easily exploited, using minimal technology. Antarctic seas have few landmasses comparable to those of the northern hemisphere, the largest being the Patagonian region of South America. Here, as in southern Australia and New Zealand, migratory fishes comprise the southern hemisphere 'trouts' (family Galaxiidae) and in New Zealand and Australia the 'smelts' of the family Retropinnidae. As in the northern hemisphere, truly littoral fishes are scarce in high latitudes but representatives of the family Bovichthyidae occur on the shore, and close inshore are representatives of the families Cheilodactylidae (known as morwongs in Australia) and Latridae. The seas on the southern tip of South America contain a number of representatives of the Antarctic fish family Nototheniidae.

Temperate ocean shores and shallow seas are inhabited by a wide range of fishes, although because of the nature of the shore they are often small fishes. Typically, blennies (Blenniidae), klipfishes (Clinidae) and gobies (Gobiidae) are characteristic of these habitats but there are a large number of eels (Anguillidae, Congridae and Muraenidae), sculpins (Cottidae) – but only in the northern hemisphere – and some scorpionfishes (Scorpaenidae) and wrasses (Labridae) which also occur there. Flatfishes of various families (order Pleuronectiformes) may be abundant chiefly on sandy shores, as are members of the cod family (Gadidae) in the northern Atlantic.

Tropical shores are inhabited by many of the families of fishes which occur in temperate zones, especially blennies, gobies, moray eels, wrasses and scorpionfishes, but also by more tropical forms such as damselfishes (Pomacentridae), silversides (Atherinidae), and rabbitfishes (Siganidae). The shore fauna may be enhanced locally by the great richness of fish life associated with coral reefs. This illustrates a generality that littoral fish faunas are specialized and localized, and are heavily dependent on physical conditions, such as the nature of the substrate (coral and rock provide suitable cover, sand very little, pebbles none at all), exposure to strong winds and waves, which inhibit the development of algal cover, and a legion of other factors. The fishes available on the shore to a community with a low technology are a product of the immediate physical geography of the area, its climate and biological factors. The potentiality of such a habitat can be assessed only with a knowledge of the local fauna.

Inshore fish faunas are more varied than even the littoral faunas. The Indo-Pacific fauna is by far the richest and contains most of the families and many of the genera which are represented in the tropical eastern Atlantic and the Caribbean and western Atlantic. In all three tropical regions, areas where coral reefs occur are very rich in species, but the eastern Atlantic is relatively poor in coral (as is the South American Atlantic coast because of turbidity and low salinity from the Amazon). The vast majority of coral reef fishes are relatively small, typical examples being the butterflyfishes (Chaetodontidae), damselfishes, wrasses, blennies and gobies, but the coral reef fauna also includes some large species, amongst them some parrotfishes (Scaridae) and groupers (Serranidae). Fishes haunting the edge of the reef tend to be much larger and include sharks, barracuda (Sphyraenidae), small tunas (Scombridae), jacks (Carangidae), groupers, sea-breams (Sparidae) and snappers (Lutjanidae).

The extremely rich Indo-West Pacific fish fauna diminishes in variety in the eastern Pacific to form the Eastern Pacific Region or Panamanian Region. This region is separated from the West Pacific by a wide stretch of deep water with few intervening islands (unlike the remainder of the tropical Pacific). In general its fish fauna is less varied and some groups which are widely distributed through the ocean are poorly represented there; its fauna has much in common with that of the Caribbean.

Tropical regions which have sparse coral have a less diverse fauna, but one which is nevertheless important. Drums or croakers (Sciaenidae), marine catfishes (Ariidae), sea-breams, flatheads (Platycephalidae), threadfins (Polynemidae) and numerous sharks, sawfishes (Pristidae), and stingrays (Dasyatidae), are locally abundant.

In temperate seas the inshore fish fauna is less varied still but is frequently as productive in terms of available fish as tropical seas. The North Atlantic inshore fauna is well known for the numbers of codfishes and flatfishes (both Pleuronectidae and Bothidae) represented in it, together with skates (Rajidae) and small sharks. The southern parts also have numbers of sea-breams, wrasses, red mullets or goatfishes (Mullidae) and grey mullets (Mugilidae), all of which are common in shallow water and are moderately easy to catch with simple fishing methods. The North Pacific's temperate region also contains cod family representatives, as well as pleuronectid flatfishes, but has strong representation of the scorpionfish family Sebastidae in the rockfishes (redfishes in Europe), and unique groups such as the greenlings (Hexagrammidae).

Fishes living offshore, mainly in surface waters over the continental shelf (although some live close to the sea bed), can only be successfully exploited by communities with a high level of technology. This is particularly true of the pelagic species, such as members of the herring family (Clupeidae), which usually live in vast schools near the surface and are found in all temperate and tropical oceans. In general, they are not vulnerable to simple fishing techniques such as hook and line, or trapping, and their capture requires some kind of boat, extensive nets (and concomitant ropes, floats and weights), and considerable manpower. However, they have been exploited by small communities quite successfully, as was shown by historical accounts of shore-seining for pilchards, *Sardina pilchardus*, in Cornwall when the fish came close inshore (Couch, 1865).

Clupeids, such as herrings and pilchards, are migratory fishes making regular seasonal journeys to spawning or feeding grounds. Other pelagic fishes, such as tuna (Scombridae) and some jacks (Carangidae), also make regular seasonal migrations and despite their pelagic life style have migratory routes which take them in close proximity to land. There is ample evidence, as, for example, from the site at Franchthi in the Greek Argolid that an extensive fishery for blue-fin tuna, *Thunnus thynnus*, had been developed by a society with low technology (Wheeler, unpublished data). Some of these tuna are estimated to have been in excess of 50 kg weight.

Various species of tuna and jacks occur world-wide in warm-temperate and tropical oceans, as do dolphinfishes (Coryphaenidae), various billfishes (Istiophoridae) and large sharks (mostly carcharinids); all perform migratory movements of some extent and may become available locally for exploitation.

More advanced fishing techniques also open access to stocks of fishes living in deeper waters on the continental shelf. In the North Atlantic the cod can be captured close inshore, but in general larger fish live in deeper water; therefore improvements in fishing technology can result in a significant increase in the weight of fish captured. Moreover some species, such as ling, *Molva molva*, and hake *Merluccius merluccius*, become available to fisheries only with the development of boats, lines and hooks. These examples drawn from European Atlantic species must have parallels in other areas, such as the North Pacific, where a specialized fishery for Pacific halibut was developed, and in the central tropical Pacific, where comparable fisheries for the escolar, *Ruvettus pretiosus*, and other large pelagic species were known.

The study of fish remains from archaeological sites can be made considerably easier and more informative if these remains are interpreted with knowledge of the local fauna and the life style of the most abundant potential food fishes in the area. Close liaison with local fishery workers or ichthyologists will often produce such information, and many parts of the world are covered by local faunistic publications which will yield some information on locally abundant fishes. Where neither source of information is available, the archaeologist should collect details of catches and obtain specimens from fishermen or in local fish markets (which would also provide comparative material for a collection of fish skeletons).

4

METHODS OF RECOVERY

Introduction

In the past archaeologists collected animal bones (including fish remains) in a rather haphazard manner. A few nineteenth-century excavators were extremely conscientious in making bone collections, but many archaeologists neglected environmental evidence of all kinds. Some appear to have collected bones only when other forms of evidence were sparse. Often only whole bones were kept and invariably few small bones were found. As a result many important sites were inadequately investigated, and irreplaceable deposits removed without detailed study.

Recent work on assemblages of animal remains from archaeological and natural deposits has demonstrated the need to employ sieving techniques if representative samples of animal remains are to be recovered. Several experiments have highlighted how much material is lost if hand collection is the only means of recovery. For example, Payne (1972), Barker (1975), Wheeler and Jones (1976), Clason and Prummel (1977), Spencer (1979) and Levitan (1982) have shown that small bones are overlooked by excavators collecting material by hand. Furthermore, sieving experiments have made it clear that there is a bias in hand-recovered material favouring the bigger bones of large animals (fig. 4.1). Few fish bones are large enough to be collected by hand and so sieving, at least as an adjunct to careful trowelling, is essential to obtain representative assemblages of fish remains.

This does not mean that sieving is the only method by which fish remains should be recovered from layers, for it is impractical to sieve all deposits on most sites. Hand collection (fig. 4.2) and sieving must be carried out in a complementary manner in order to obtain the optimum amount of information from an archaeological investigation. The problem therefore is to decide how much to sieve and what should be collected by hand. Both these questions may involve sampling. Much has been written in recent years on the theoretical basis of sampling in archaeology, e.g. Mueller (1975) and Cherry *et al.* (1978), and approaches to collecting material have varied considerably. It is clear that no single sampling strategy can be applied to all sites. Flexibility in sampling is essential if the strategy is to fit the research objectives and the amounts of time and money available.

There are probably as many views on the details of sampling as there are workers active in the field. However, all would agree on two points: first, that

38

4.1 Above: Medieval fish bone assemblages from 16–22 Coppergate, York, recovered by trowelling excavated soil. Two species are present, both represented by large bones. Below: An adjacent sample, recovered by sieving, revealed the bones of six species. (Photographs by R. Hunter; copyright Department of Biology, University of York.)

the purpose of sampling is to obtain a representative quantity of the remains lying in the deposits; secondly, that every site is unique in requiring its own sampling strategy. Thus the final decision concerning the method chosen to sample a site and the amount to be processed depends on the nature of the site, its soil, the density of bones and the information required.

In order to illustrate these points it is simplest to describe briefly some sites recently sampled for fish remains. Shell middens of Mesolithic date on Oronsay (Inner Hebrides on the north-west Scottish coast) were examined by a team from the University of Sheffield, England. Fish bone investigations were undertaken by Wilkinson (1981) to learn as much as possible about the Mesolithic way of life. Three procedures were used to collect fish bones: they were recovered by hand from trenches; the fills of these trenches were wet-sieved on one-eighth inch (roughly 3.1 mm) aperture mesh sieves; finally column samples were collected from the trench walls of some sites while up to four samples (each roughly 4 kg weight) were taken from pits at the Oronsay site of Cnoc Coig. These were dried and sieved through 2 mm and 1 mm meshes, and the resulting fractions sorted.

Another Scottish coastal site, rather later in date, in dune sands at Freswick (Caithness) has been investigated by a team from the Universities of Durham and York, England. Here the work was carried out at the request of the Scottish Development Department (SDD) in order to assess the nature of the eroding midden. The positions of trenches were limited both by the SDD's insistence that excavation should be concentrated at the cliff edge, the area of greatest erosion, and by the topography of the links, which made the removal of huge dunes impractical. From trial observations on the site it was clear that small trenches would produce enormous quantities of fish remains. The smallest trench that would reveal sufficient information on the nature of the deposits was judged to be 4 × 2 m. A central 50 cm wide strip in each trench was divided into 1 m lengths. The two outer 75 cm wide strips were excavated by hand, the excavators collecting bones and other finds while also examining the stratigraphy. The amount of sediment collected in a sample was limited to roughly 50 kg (i.e. 1 m × 50 cm × approximately 2 cm) so that each could be transported in 500-gauge polythene sacks. Seven trenches were excavated in this manner. As a result thick layers yielded several samples in a vertical sequence. New sample numbers were assigned at every observed change in the deposits. All these bulk samples were wet-sieved using 1 mm aperture mesh. In addition small columns (25 cm square) were taken from the sides of each trench. These were sieved using 500-micron aperture sieves in order to check whether materials were missed by the bulk-sieving method using 1 mm mesh.

Sampling midden deposits at Freswick was relatively simple as the layers tended to be large deposits, sometimes 25 cm thick and extending for several

4.2 Concentrations of medieval fish remains from Norwich, UK, recovered *in situ*. Above: The larger articulated vertebrae are from the caudal region of cod, *Gadus morhua*; the small vertebrae are from herring, *Clupea harengus*. Below: Two sets of herring remains; articulated vertebrae and fin rays are visible. (Photograph by M. Sharp; copyright Norfolk Archaeological Unit.)

metres. There was little obvious variation within each layer. A sample from one area was quite likely to give results similar to a sample of the same layer in another part of the site. Preliminary observations at Freswick show that all the trenches were dominated by the remains of large numbers of adult cod, ling and saithe, while medium-sized individuals occurred in most areas. Small saithe bones and otoliths were also widespread. Other fish remains occurred in small numbers and did not appear to be concentrated in any of the midden layers. Differences were, however, noted in the condition, colour, and degree and nature of fragmentation of the bones from the various cliff trenches.

Substantial remains of domestic buildings and other structures were also revealed at Freswick Links. The strategy for sampling these parts of the site was completely different from that used on the cliff-edge midden. The highly complex and variable stratigraphy meant excavation using the block sample method (as used in cliff-edge trenches) would have cut indiscriminately across walls and other features, mixing material from two or more deposits – an occurrence equally appalling to excavators and environmental archae-ologists. Consequently, layers were selected for sampling. These can best be described as 'judgement' samples. That is, the excavators and environmental archaeologists jointly agreed that some layers were more likely to produce valuable evidence than others. For example, the ashes from around hearths were carefully collected as they were likely to contain charred grain and other food remains. By contrast, after trial investigations showed little to be present, the clay bases of hearths were not extensively sampled, on the grounds that they contained few informative remains. This approach is empirical, based on experience and common sense.

A similar approach was adopted at the 16–22 Coppergate site in central York. Here a deeply stratified site proved to contain waterlogged organic deposits up to 7 m deep, dating from the Roman period to the post-medieval era. The bulk of the deposits were laid down during the Anglo-Scandinavian period (AD *c.* 850–*c.* 1100). The site contained remains of four separate long, narrow tenements, each comprising buildings and a large yard. The buildings closest to the street have been interpreted as domestic accommodation and shops, while the structures behind them are thought to have been used as workshops.

A small number of fish bones was collected by hand from the deposits during the course of the excavation. Although some attempt was made to take columns through the whole sequence of the deposits, the stratigraphy was so complex and the composition of layers so variable that judgement sampling was the only practical method. Some kinds of deposits, principally house floors and pit fills, were identified as those most likely to yield interpretable assemblages of remains, and sampling concentrated on these kinds of features. Three kinds of samples were taken. A large number (over 200) of bulk samples, usually at least five buckets of trowelled soil, were collected. No bone was collected by hand from the bulk samples. They were wet-sieved on 1 mm aperture mesh and yielded the majority of the fish remains. In addition 'general biological analysis' samples weighing between 5 and 10 kg were taken, primarily for laboratory analysis of insect and plant macrofossils (fish bones were present in most in small numbers). The third category of sample was 'spot finds'. These were localized concentrations of small bones noticed by excavators. The bones and the surrounding soil (usually 1 kg or less) were collected.

This three-tiered strategy provided ample material for post-excavation investigations on assemblages of animals and plants from within and around the various buildings. In addition, it has been possible to make comparisons between different tenements. A random sampling procedure would have examined many layers which were unlikely to contain interpretable groups of fish bones. Random techniques assume that all layers or areas of the site are of equal importance. Anyone who has excavated urban sites will realize that material is rarely distributed randomly over a site, and that some layers are more important than others.

These approaches contrast starkly with that used by some workers on the mainland of Europe. For example, at Haithabu, Schleswig, West Germany, excavations were carried out by mechanical excavators skimming off thin layers of deposit across the whole site (Lepiksaar and Heinrich, 1977). This method of excavation prevents detailed attention being paid to stratigraphy. Samples were selected at random and washed to remove soil. The chief advantage of this approach was that untrained staff could be used to collect and process samples. However, the material so gathered did not relate to particular features or kinds of deposit, e.g. structures or tenements. Nevertheless, this technique produced a large number of fish bones, which were examined and ably reported by Lepiksaar and Heinrich.

It is important to recognize that, although an archaeozoologist may be primarily interested in the animal remains on the site, other kinds of evidence will be essential to understanding their exploitation and the economy and environment of the site as a whole. Thus, it is desirable that the sampling strategy takes into account the various kinds of artefactual, industrial and environmental evidence. In practice the technique most generally used is to bulk-sieve large soil samples to 1 mm. Although some classes of evidence are lost through 1 mm meshes (e.g. most insect remains, pollen grains and parasite ova), small bones, mollusc shells, larger seeds (including most cereal grains), mosses and a host of artefacts will be retained. The best sampling strategy requires both bulk and small samples to be collected from the site. The following guidelines are produced for general consideration.

Developing a sampling strategy

It is not possible to set down rules giving the quantities of soil to be processed and a sieve mesh size that will be applicable for use on all sites. However, the following points should be borne in mind both prior to and during excavation of the site.

It is usual for excavators to seek advice from a number of specialists before removing the first sod or digging out the most modern drain. Specialists are also often called to excavations to give advice during the dig. These consultations are designed to ensure that excavation produces the most cost-effective combination of structural, artefactual and environmental data in order to reconstruct as complete a picture as possible of the life and conditions on the site during its occupation. During these discussions a strategy for sampling the deposits is likely to emerge. This will take into consideration a number of aspects. Earlier work at the site may have provided information about certain aspects of the site and its inhabitants and it may be decided to concentrate on others. It is important to gauge how the excavation fits into the regional, temporal and cultural context.

If earlier work has taken place, probably at best a few hand-collected specimens will have been studied. Occasionally it will be clear that the fish remains from the site are from the same species, and occur in the same relative abundance as those from a contemporaneous site a few miles away. Under such circumstances it is unlikely that further work will discover much that is new unless there were major cultural differences between sites. The main reasons for this are that fish populations and fish exploitation are usually correlated within a small geographical area, and that the remains that are preserved in archaeological deposits are in any case a small fraction of the material consumed at a site (see chapter 5). Although fish bones are intrinsically interesting and very beautiful, it is not possible to justify the collection and detailed examination of all bones from all sites. The constraints of time and finance which beset all disciplines cannot be ignored.

Assuming that bones are preserved in the excavated deposits and that the decision to sample fish bones has been taken before the excavation, how then do we best proceed? The next stage is to draw up a list of questions that can be posed and decide which are the most important.

Points involved in establishing an excavation strategy

      General
1   What species are present?
2   Are they freshwater or marine fishes (or both)?
3   Are the different species spread evenly across the site or are fish remains concentrated in particular areas or periods of occupation?

      Specific
4   Were the cod (for example) from this site different in size from those at site X?

5 Is there any evidence for fish processing on the site?
6 Does the nature of the faunal assemblage tell us anything about the methods of exploitation or fish processing?

In order to answer these questions intelligently, it is important that the excavator and the fish bone worker should frequently discuss the site and the results of each other's work. Information must flow between them.

It should be clear that flexibility is an important element in the development and execution of a successful sampling strategy. It is possible to go onto a site with a preconceived plan, e.g. to sieve to 1 mm 5% of every context excavated. Such an approach may yield as much information as a more flexible one, but it is much more likely to produce endless groups of fish bones which are almost identical and to under-sample the few deposits crucial to the accurate interpretation of the site.

A most useful technique is to sieve a series of small samples (10 litre or one bucketful) of material and identify the bones from each sample, paying particular attention to the number of taxa present in each sample. An experiment of this kind was carried out in the early days of the sieving programme at the excavation of Coppergate, York, as a student project. Twenty bucketfuls of this deposit were collected by site workers, only large stones being removed from the samples. The samples were processed using the modified Sīrāf bulk sieving apparatus. After drying, the samples were sorted. The results are presented in table 4.1.

The 20 bucketful samples yielded a total of 17 fish taxa. Herring and eel occurred in all 20 samples while cod and haddock were present in 17. By contrast, gurnard, perch and scad were each present in only one sample. All samples produced at least four different kinds of fish and one contained nine taxa. From the results of this experiment, it was judged that a sample size of five bucketfuls (approximately 45 litres, weighing roughly 50 kg) was optimum. The maximum size was more difficult to determine for, had more samples been processed, the total of 17 taxa almost certainly would have been exceeded. On the basis of this experiment and constant monitoring, bulk samples of 50 to 100 kg were routinely processed. This experiment provided a useful starting-point for determining how much sediment needed to be processed.

The selection of samples for environmental analysis
During an excavation it is better to collect too much material than too little. Fish remains can always be archived if they have proved to be relatively uninformative. Once an excavation closes no more material can be obtained. However, it is unwise to collect soil samples blindly, and the following paragraphs are intended to reduce the collection of uninformative soil samples.

Large (more than 5 kg) soil samples should be collected only after three basic criteria have been satisfied. First, there should be evidence that the layer contains fish remains. The best way to establish the presence of small bones is to take a trial sample (1–2 kg) and sieve it on a fine-meshed sieve (500 micron) on site, or in a nearby laboratory, at an early stage during the excavation of a feature.

Secondly, there must be a reason for collecting the material. Questions must be posed. Perhaps the most common question archaeologists ask is, 'What kinds of fish are present and what can you say about them?' As more work is done so the sorts of questions being addressed become more specific. It is now common to hear the following questions being posed: 'What methods were used to catch these fish?' or 'How common are freshwater fishes at this site?' Doubtless more specific queries will be investigated in future.

The third criterion concerns resources. It is important to ensure that funds and specialists will be available to study the material before samples are collected and packaged and to consider what facilities are likely to be necessary to answer questions generated on site, especially if unexpected features appear. It is impossible to predict precisely what will be found, but consultation with other excavators and specialists working in the same area may provide invaluable background information. Ideally, specialist advice should be sought on as many aspects of the site as possible before digging commences and, if they are not on site, specialists should remain in close contact during the course of the excavation.

Occasionally, completely unexpected discoveries will be made, for example, substantial layers of charred grain and large concentrations of small bones, and rapid decisions are necessary. As a general rule, as much of the complete sediment should be collected as is practical, and advice sought as soon as possible concerning its treatment. If large stones or other bulky inclusions are removed from a deposit prior to treatment, their weight and volume should be recorded in order that the concentrations of fish remains can be calculated with reasonable accuracy.

The most difficult aspects of sampling are to decide what and how much to collect. Clearly, each excavation will pose its own problems and will require its own sampling strategy. For example, if information is sought concerning diet, all animal bone and shell should be collected by hand from trowelled soil. Rubbish pits and bone dumps should receive careful attention. It is important to sieve large amounts of the soil to recover species which are sparsely distributed in the deposits and are too small to be collected by hand. Cesspits should be sampled for food remains.

As a general strategy, when there is an abundance of bone-rich contents, attention should be focussed on those deposits which are likely to have been laid down during a short period. Some deposits can be shown to have accumulated over a relatively brief period and are therefore likely to contain

Table 4.1. *Establishing an excavation strategy*

Presence/absence data for layer 18256, Coppergate, York
(1 present, 0 = absent)

Bucket	Fish taxa identified																	Total
	1	2	3	4	5	6	7	8	9	10	11	12	13	14	15	16	17	
A	0	1	1	0	0	0	0	0	0	0	1	1	0	0	1	0	0	5
B	1	1	1	0	0	0	0	0	0	0	0	1	0	0	0	0	0	4
C	0	1	1	0	0	0	1	0	0	0	1	1	0	0	0	0	0	5
D	0	1	1	0	0	0	0	0	1	0	1	1	0	0	1	0	1	7
E	0	1	1	0	0	0	0	0	0	0	1	1	1	0	0	0	0	5
F	1	1	1	1	0	0	1	0	1	0	1	1	0	0	0	0	0	8
G	0	1	1	0	1	0	0	0	0	0	1	1	0	0	0	0	0	5
H	0	1	1	0	0	1	1	0	1	0	0	1	0	0	0	1	0	7
I	0	1	1	0	1	0	1	0	1	0	0	0	0	0	0	0	0	5
J	0	1	1	0	0	0	0	1	1	0	1	0	0	1	0	0	0	6
K	0	1	1	0	0	0	0	0	1	0	1	1	0	0	0	0	1	6
L	0	1	1	1	0	0	0	1	1	0	1	1	0	0	0	0	0	7
M	1	1	1	1	0	0	1	0	0	0	1	0	0	0	0	0	0	6
N	0	1	1	1	0	0	0	0	0	0	1	1	0	0	0	0	0	5
O	0	1	1	0	1	0	0	0	0	0	1	1	0	0	0	0	0	5
P	0	1	1	1	0	1	0	0	1	1	1	1	0	0	1	0	0	9
Q	0	1	1	0	0	0	0	0	1	0	1	1	0	0	0	0	0	5
R	0	1	1	1	0	0	0	0	1	0	1	1	0	0	0	0	0	6
S	1	1	1	0	0	0	0	0	1	0	1	1	0	0	0	0	0	6
T	0	1	1	0	0	0	0	0	0	0	1	1	0	0	0	0	0	4
Total	4	20	20	6	3	2	5	2	11	1	17	17	1	1	3	1	2	

Key to fish taxa
1	Elasmobranch	10	?Gadidae
2	Herring	11	Cod
3	Eel	12	Haddock
4	Pike	13	Gurnard
5	Salmonidae	14	Perch
6	Smelt	15	Mackerel
7	Cyprinidae	16	Scad
8	?Cyprinidae	17	Flatfish
9	Gadidae		

only small amounts of residual material. Pit-fills and house floors are two types of feature likely to fulfil these criteria. However, some classes of archaeological site yield only faunal remains that are dated to phases spanning hundreds or thousands of years. This is particularly true for material from prehistoric excavations but to reject this material would be folly.

Deposits built up gradually over a long period may be used to detect long-term environmental changes. Slowly filled ditches and natural accumulations of peat and lacustrine deposits are probably the most informative for such investigations and fish remains can add to the pattern of change deduced from analyses of plant and insect remains. Other slowly accumulating deposits such as ancient garden soils and dumps of material laid down prior to building construction are often excavated in towns but yield little information. Such layers usually contain large quantities of residual material (objects, bones etc. reworked from older deposits). While Roman pottery can be readily distinguished from medieval wares, fish bones cannot be dated by eye.

On most excavations it is necessary to collect only soil monoliths (intact columns of sediment) to extract fish bones when groups of articulated bones are suspected to be present and careful laboratory 'excavation' is practicable. However, when they are found articulated, bones should receive special attention. They should be collected as a single unit. Occasionally, specialist advice from palaeontologists or archaeological conservators may be needed if they are to be lifted and packaged correctly. For most purposes, a carefully collected bag (or other suitable container) of soil is sufficient.

The mechanics of collecting soil samples

Materials

Clean trowel, hand-shovel, spade and bucket (if necessary)

Black spirit-based waterproof felt-tip marker

Strong (350 or 500 gauge) polythene bags (45 × 60 cm) or plastic tubs

Nylon (or similar synthetic) string

Plastic 'Tyvek' labels (pieces of 'Permatrace' or similar plastic drawing film punched with a hole with suffice in emergency)

Clean dustbins, intact clean polythene agricultural fertilizer sacks or other suitable containers for bulk samples

Sample form/book and pencil to record details of sample

Method of sampling

Clean the area to be sampled; be vigorous if area has been exposed for more than two hours or so.

Large samples (5–10 kg) should be double-bagged in strong (350–500 gauge) polythene bags with one 'Tyvek' or plastic label facing outwards between the bags and another label tied round the neck of the external bag.

Bulk samples (50+ kg) should be placed in clean strong bins, or double-bagged using 500 gauge polythene bags. (Clean intact fertilizer bags are useful for this purpose.) Two labels should be completed, one placed in the sample and one securely tied to the container. If they have to be carried more than a few metres, it is best to divide bulk samples into subsamples weighing no more than 25 kg, for carrying large and heavy loads is dangerous, particularly over rough or slippery terrain.

Complete sample form, including a sketch of the sampled area and surrounding features, coordinates and north arrow.

Normally, nothing should be removed from the sampled material. Occasionally it may be necessary to exclude large stones or small-finds. This information, including volumes and weight where relevant, should be noted on the sample form.

Notes: always write labels with black, spirit-based, waterproof felt-tip marker, or in waterproof Indian ink. Soft black pencil may be acceptable on some kinds of label. Avoid ball-point pens, fountain pens and coloured felt-tip markers.

Never recycle bags from one set of samples and thoroughly wash bins before re-use.

Storage of samples

The time between collecting a sample and processing it for fish remains should be kept to a minimum. However, it is often impossible to process all the material during the excavation and samples need to be adequately packaged and stored in order to prevent deterioration. Most samples are best stored in conditions as similar to burial on site as possible. For temperate regions dark, cool conditions with a fairly high relative humidity are appropriate; for arid regions the humidity should be low. The conditions of storage are designed to slow down biological decay – the main enemy of ancient animal and plant remains in soil samples. Covering stacks of samples with sheets of black polythene reduces light levels. The addition of moth balls to the outer bag of double-bagged samples is recommended to prevent insect colonization. Ideally, samples should be stored in sample order sequence on shelves. Easy access to the samples is, of course, necessary.

Practical methods of recovering bones from deposits

Fish bones may be collected from archaeological deposits by a variety of techniques. The simplest is to collect bones by hand during the excavation as the deposits are trowelled away. Bones collected in this way are normally processed through the 'Finds Department' of an excavation. If they are well preserved they may be carefully washed, dried, marked and bagged together with mammal and bird bones. If the bone is friable, as is often the case, it is best to allow the bones to dry in the air and to brush off soil particles gently. Special techniques need to be used to extract bones from breccia and similarly intractable deposits. A useful review of techniques used for separating isolated teeth and bones of small vertebrates has been given by Ward (1984).

The bags used to package animal bones may be made of strong paper or polythene. Self-sealing 'snap-top' bags are often preferred. If polythene bags are used, it is essential that the bones are thoroughly dried before they are bagged. Damp material will cause condensation in the bags and encourage the development of moulds.

Frequently an excavator will notice a small group of fish bones concentrated together within a layer. They may be too small to collect individually without a great deal of time being spent. In these cases excavators should be encouraged to collect all the bones together with the soil from the immediate area. These finds can be termed 'spot finds'. They often consist of sections of partly articulated vertebrae or groups of fin rays and their associated supports.

Sieving

An assemblage of hand-collected bones typically contains only large bones from large fish. However, most deposits contain small remains, perhaps from small fishes as well as large ones. For example, otoliths may be present and they are potentially more informative than larger, more noticeable elements like branchiostegal and fin rays. In order to collect smaller fish remains some kind of sieving is necessary.

Before discussing details of the techniques that can be used to sieve archaeological bone-rich deposits, it is important to consider the mesh size needed. In general, the finer the mesh used the more fish remains will be recovered, but as a corollary the amount of time and money needed to process samples increases. On-site processing takes a small fraction of the time needed to study, record and report on the bones and it is essential to consider the amount of time needed to process material in the post-excavation phase, particularly when expensive specialist time is involved.

In one experiment it took 30 minutes to sieve 100 kg wind-blown sand to 1 mm (Jones, 1983a). To sieve the same quantity to 10 mm would have taken less than five minutes.

However, it is sorting the sieved residues that takes an enormous amount of time. Sorting can either be selective, i.e. collecting only bones which are considered identifiable, for example, collecting jaw bones, vertebrae and a selection of the more robust elements but passing over small fragments of broken bone, ribs and fin rays, or it can be comprehensive, i.e. collecting all fragments. The latter strategy is possibly only justifiable when inexperienced personnel are sorting, for then all bones should be collected. The final cost of sorting makes it imperative to decide the mesh size, although the nature of the deposit strongly influences the choice of sieving technique. As a general rule sieving to 1 mm is probably most appropriate. Coarser meshes allow many small bones to pass through, while finer meshes retain unwanted mineral material and fragmented fish remains. Sieving can be carried out with either wet or dry deposits.

Dry-sieving is only practical if the deposits are totally free from moisture. In temperate regions dry sand-dune deposits are the only kind that can be successfully dry-sieved to 1 mm. Damp sand deposits will pass through 10 mm mesh, but other sediments e.g. loam, clay-based layers etc., do not readily pass through sieves even when artificially dried prior to sieving. In arid parts of the world dry-sieving is carried out routinely on many excavations. Payne (1972) gives drawings of a frame used to dry-sieve deposits.

Wet-sieving involves the use of water to wash the soil on meshes. Two fundamentally different approaches have been devised to achieve this objective. Most techniques shower water onto a mesh or tower of sieves, gradually disaggregating the lumps of soil and separating the soil components into similarly sized fractions. Descriptions of this kind of sieving have been published by Payne (1972), Guerreschi (1973), Jones (1983a) and Mantle *et al.* (1984). The simplest kind of wet-sieving procedure involves clipping 1 mm mesh to a garden sieve. The soil sample is placed on the mesh and water played onto it until all the fine soil particles have washed away. Alternatively, a basket constructed from weld-mesh can be lined with 1 mm aperture nylon mesh and soil washed by shaking the basket in the running water of a stream. These processes are extremely simple to set up and ideal for checking deposits to see what they contain. They are not recommended as a routine method for processing bulk samples as these simple mesh-covered baskets are heavy and can be extremely messy to use; furthermore they require large quantities of water which may not always be available.

The 'Cambridge froth flotation tank' (Jarman *et al.*, 1972) may be used to collect fish bones. However, it was designed principally to extract animal and plant remains which float, e.g. charred plant remains and small gastropod mollusc shells. To collect heavy materials, the sample residues from the bottom of the tank are washed on screens as a second stage in the operation.

The modified Sīrāf tank

A second technique has been developed to process bulk samples. Here the soil is suspended by the mesh within the tank of water; the most commonly used device utilizing this approach is the 'Sīrāf' tank (Williams, 1973) and its derivatives. Experiments testing the efficiency of the 'Sīrāf' tank and a device using the showering principle have recently been published by Jones (1983a) and Mantle *et al.* (1984). Jones showed that 15 kg of wind-blown sand samples could be processed in five minutes, while a similar weight of clay-rich deposit took 12 minutes to process. Mantle *et al.* (1984), sieving on 250 micron aperture mesh, principally to recover charred plant remains, rejected the 'Sīrāf' tank in favour of a system that achieved a rate of about 15 litres of fine silt and clay per hour. These reports demonstrate that where large-scale sieving is to be carried out it is worthwhile experimenting to determine the optimum method for local soil conditions.

However, over the last few years the modified 'Sīrāf' tank has emerged as probably the most suitable, and certainly the most commonly used, device for collecting a range of materials, such as small bones, artefacts, and other remains (including charred seeds) from archaeological deposits. 'Sīrāf' tanks have been used on a large number of urban and rural excavations in Europe and western Asia to process many tonnes of soil, varying from wind-blown sand to boulder-clay and waterlogged organic deposits. Moreover, they are portable, and easy to construct and repair. For these reasons details of construction and operation are given below.

The modified 'Sīrāf' tank is derived from David Williams's design (Williams, 1973) and has been described by Kenward *et al.* (1980) (figs. 4.3, 4.4). Several years' experience have shown that the original design can be improved by fitting a 10 cm diameter drain plug to facilitate emptying.

4.3   The modified Sīrāf tank in use at the Environmental Archaeology Unit, York University. (Photograph by Keith M. Buck, courtesy York Archaeological Trust.)

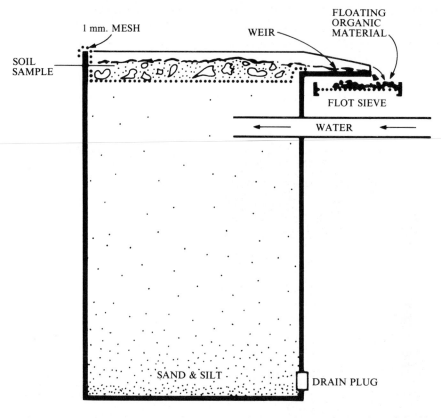

4.4   Diagrammatic view of modified Sīrāf tank. (From the original by
R. Hunter.)

Recent work has demonstrated that flot collection is most efficient if the inlet
pipe is positioned beneath the weir rather than opposite it.

Siting the tank
(a) In the field
The empty tank is relatively light (approximately 20 kg) and fairly portable,
and is best set up on level ground. Three factors influence its siting: the availability of the water supply, proximity to the deposits to be sieved, and the
disposal of fine soil particles and dirty water from the tank after washing. If
water is not available from a mains supply it may have to be pumped from a
stream or reservoir. The tank is capable of processing large volumes of soil,
and it is therefore wise to position it as near to the excavation as possible in
order to reduce the labour required to move samples. Ideally, the tank should
be sited where water will drain away and where sediment can be dumped
without causing inconvenience or annoyance. When the drain plug is
removed to empty the tank, the mixture of soil and water will spread to cover

a considerable area (approximately 10 m^2). The sand and silt can either be shovelled away or be left as a layer. As water may be flowing over the weir for several hours a day, the area surrounding the tank may become water-logged unless adequate drainage is available. Duck-boarding can help reduce this problem.

(b) In the laboratory
While the tank was designed for field work, it can successfully be used indoors. A room which will not suffer from occasional spillages of water and soil should be selected, for splashes of muddy water are inevitable. The drain plug should be fastened securely and tested for leaks before the tank is used. Generally, it is necessary to empty the tank by siphoning out the water and then shovelling out the fine sediment – a messy job.

Water supply
Water may be taken from a mains supply, pumped from a stream or lake, or pumped from a settlement tank connected to the system. The flow of water is regulated by means of a gate valve on the inlet pipe. Water pressure from a domestic mains supply is usually sufficient to carry floating debris over the weir. (If the water flow is too rapid, sand and other coarse inorganic material may be carried into the flot sieve and block the mesh, leading to spillage.)

When water is in short supply, a system of settlement tanks and a pump can be used to recycle water. One settlement tank should be placed below the weir; it will collect most of the larger suspended particles passing through the flot sieve. A second tank, fed from the upper part of the first settlement tank, will receive water carrying only very fine particles. Water from this second tank is suitable for pumping back to the modified 'Sīrāf' tank. Whenever water is pumped, great care must be taken to ensure that contamination of samples does not occur. This is best achieved by covering the intake hose with fine (300–500 micron) mesh.

Sea water can be used when no other is available but the samples obtained should be washed thoroughly in fresh water at the first opportunity.

It may be necessary to seek permission from the local water authority to pump water from natural streams. In addition, care should be taken to incorporate settlement tanks so that the water returned to the watercourse is clear. Excessive silt can cause environmental problems to fisheries and is unlikely to be well received if silt contaminates drinking water further downstream.

Fitting the mesh and sieve
The tank, mesh and sieve must be checked to ensure that they are thoroughly clean. The water supply hose is connected to the inlet pipe and the drain plug

closed securely. While the tank is filling with water, the weld-mesh support for the nylon mesh is positioned. Two of the hooks of this support are positioned on the rim at either side of the weir, and the basket pushed into the body of the tank. The mesh (usually 1 mm aperture) is secured upon the weir using the V-shaped rod, and fold-back clips are used to anchor the mesh to the rim of the tank. It is necessary to pleat the mesh at the rim in order to allow the support mesh to take the weight of the soil. Two spring clips are bolted onto the weir with brass screws and wing nuts. The flot sieve is positioned beneath the weir with the spring clips and a steady stream of water is established.

For most purposes the 1 mm mesh and flot sieve should be used. However, if a layer contains charred plant remains or other small material, a 500 micron aperture mesh and flot sieve should be employed to ensure that small seeds are collected. Because very large amounts of soil residue will be collected by a 500 micron mesh, it is wise to limit its use to a minimum. It is necessary to sort both the flot and the residue for all kinds of remains, for some bones and scales will float and much charred plant material will fail to float.

Recording and labelling

A record sheet is completed and four waterproof labels are marked (with a black spirit-based waterproof felt-tip pen) with the site code, context number and sample number. A separate code is used to distinguish the residue and flot (R and F respectively have been found to be convenient). Particular attention should be paid to recording accurately the volume and weight of soil processed, the aperture of the mesh and flot sieve, the nature of the sediment and evidence of modern contamination (for example, living insects and air-borne seeds).

Washing soil samples

If water is freely available, it is preferable to maintain a constant flow of water over the weir during washing. Where the supply of water is limited, once the tank is full of water, it is possible to wash samples by using water inter-mittently to flush away any floating material. When water is flowing steadily through the sieve, a bucket of soil is introduced onto the nylon mesh, care being taken to avoid losses by splashing. The lumps of soil are gently dis-aggregated by hand, so as to minimize mechanical damage to fragile remains. Large stones should be cleaned and set aside. Floating debris is encouraged into the flot sieve by the manual generation of small waves at the water surface. During washing, notes are made of the nature of the sample, includ-ing the size and types of stone; particular attention is paid to any possible modern contaminants, for example, airborne seeds or live insects. The pro-cess continues until all the fine sand, silt and clay has been washed through the nylon mesh, leaving only clean residues.

Removing the flot

The flot sieve should be emptied when about one third of its mesh area is covered with flot, to avoid blockage and subsequent spillage. If the sieve needs emptying before the whole sample has been washed, the V-shaped rod which clips the mesh to the weir is removed and lodged so that the portion of mesh lying on the weir is raised free of the water, thereby preventing further flow of flot. The flot sieve is removed, briefly drained of excess water, and emptied onto a labelled tray by inverting the sieve and giving it a sharp tap on the tray. If drying facilities are not immediately available, the flot can be labelled and temporarily wrapped in kitchen foil which is punctured with pin pricks to allow water to drain and evaporate. It is recommended that two labels be placed with each packet of flot. Often a small amount of flot will adhere to the sides of the mesh. This can be rinsed to one side of the sieve and emptied as outlined above; this process is repeated until all the flot is removed. The sieve can then be replaced into the stream of water, the V-shaped clip replaced and washing continued. The flot sieve should be thoroughly cleaned after each sample has been washed to avoid cross-contamination.

Paper towel was once widely used to package flot but cannot be recommended as small pieces of paper often adhere to the flot particles. Furthermore, packets of flot wrapped in kitchen towel will begin to sprout moulds and produce unpleasant smells if left in a confined place for more than a few weeks. Flot samples should be air-dried as soon as possible but gentle warmth in an oven will speed up the process.

Removing the residue

Judging the moment to remove the residue from the tank is only possible after a little experience. There is a tendency amongst inexperienced operators to stop the washing process before the residues are completely clean. All the particles on the mesh should appear spotlessly clean and all lumps of sediment should have disappeared before the residue is removed.

The residue is removed while the flot sieve is in position beneath the weir. The spring fold-back clips are removed from the rim of the tank, and the mesh gently agitated to free any material trapped by surface tension. Particles of charcoal, charred grain etc., can be readily removed by dabbing the mesh on the surface of the water. Floating particles will then be carried over the weir and into the sieve. When most of the flot is cleaned from the mesh, the V-shaped clip is removed and the four corners of the mesh gathered together. The mesh is removed from the tank, allowing free water to drain into the tank. If clean water is available, it is desirable to rinse the soil residues. The residue is then tipped onto a drying tray and two labels placed with it. Alternatively, the residue can be tipped into polythene bags and dried later. The residue can remain damp for a few weeks before it begins to deteriorate, although steps should be taken to air-dry (or if necessary oven-dry) the samples as soon after washing as possible.

Frequently, it is impossible to wash all fine soil particles from soil residues. This may be because the sediment adheres to the larger sediment particles (e.g. clay soils) or it may be that the staff washing samples have prematurely removed the sample from the washing tank. Under these conditions it is highly desirable that the residues are rinsed before they are set to dry.

Emptying the tank, cleaning and maintenance

When all the material from a context has been washed, and the residue and flot removed, the tank is emptied by removing the drain plug. At first a cylindrical plug of soil will gradually emerge from the plug-hole and suddenly a rush of soil and water will follow. After all free water has drained from the tank the remainder of the soil is pushed through the plug-hole with a spade. Soil is most rapidly emptied from the tank by regulating the water flow into the tank with the drain plug removed. When all the soil has been flushed out, the drain plug is fitted and the tank refilled with water.

The nylon mesh rarely requires more than a vigorous shake to free it from any small particles of residue. When waterlogged samples are washed, fine pieces of plant material may become tangled with the nylon mesh. These can be removed by allowing the mesh to dry and brushing them off.

Very little routine maintenance is needed to ensure a long life for the modified 'Sīrāf' tank. The most vulnerable part is the drain plug, which should be thoroughly greased before the tank is used and at weekly intervals thereafter. If the tank is to be stored for any length of time it should be thoroughly washed, drained and the threaded parts greased.

Processing the washed soil samples

Final drying of the samples is best done by spreading residues onto clean trays and letting them air dry. This is best done indoors, where wind will not disturb the samples or introduce contamination. If this is done out-of-doors, labels must be carefully fastened to the trays. Once dry, the residues can be bagged and stored, or sorted.

If an experienced fish bone analyst is available on site, fish remains may be separated from those of amphibians, reptiles, birds and mammals. However, this should not be done by inexperienced workers or without prior consultation with the person who will study and report on the bones.

Sorting is best accomplished in a laboratory. Comfortable seating and adequate lighting are essential. All too often there is pressure to sort material on-site in order to reduce the amount of material to be processed during the post-excavation phase. Sorting on-site is often difficult to supervise properly and important remains may be missed.

Soil residues usually consist of a vast mixture of different kinds of animal, vegetable and inorganic substances occurring in a wide size range. To sort such samples it is best to sieve the residues into fractions of similar size classes. If a 1 mm mesh was used for washing, the residues may be most readily sorted if they are sieved to 5 and 2 mm. This allows the largest finds to be collected from the 5 mm sieve, and most of the small material from the 2 mm sieve, leaving the finest material on the 1 mm sieve. In practice, the 1 mm sieve may often only contain small bones of the same species collected on the larger meshes. It therefore may not always be necessary to sort all fractions of the sieved residues. Like sampling soil deposits, it is impossible to state precise quantities to be sorted. Empiricism must form the basis for these decisions.

Rather than sort soil residues by sieving and picking out the various kinds of material, some workers have experimented with flotation procedures on soil residues. Streuver (1968) described a process where bone and plant remains were separated from the 'light fraction' (presumably equivalent to the flot) by using a solution of zinc chloride with a specific gravity of 1.62. More recently, Bodner and Rowlett (1980) determined the density of materials in washed soil residues and by using a solution of ferric sulphate (specific gravity 1.6–2.1) separated bone fragments from gravels. These and similar dense medium flotation techniques may help to reduce the time spent sorting samples.

The most informative remains

So far the discussion has considered methods of collecting bones from washed soil residues. A most important aspect of this part of the process is to decide which bones should be collected for detailed analysis. Anyone with experience of dealing directly with fish remains from archaeological excavations, or who has read fish bone reports, will be aware that many fish bones cannot be readily identified, particularly when the material is fragmentary. There is no easy answer to the question 'Which bones should I collect?'

The answer will depend on several factors, the most important being the resources available for the study and the value given to very detailed work. Many workers identify only a limited range of bones. Leach (1986) maintains that, after 16 years of work on archaeological fish bones from the Pacific region, five parts of the cranial anatomy are the most useful for identification. These bones are: the dentary, articular, quadrate, premaxilla and maxilla. In addition, certain other 'special bones' have been found to be characteristic of particular species, genera or families. Typical examples of these bones and some of the fish families represented are as follows (scombrid nomenclature updated following Collette and Nauen [1983]):

Specialized spines	– Elasmobranchs, Balistidae, Aluteridae, etc.
Basipterygium	– Balistidae
Scutes	– Carangidae

Pharyngeal clusters – Coridae, Labridae, Scaridae
Bucklers   – Acanthuridae
Teeth   – Nemipteridae, Elasmobranchs, Balistidae
Vertebrae   – Elasmobranchs, Istiophoridae, Xiphiidae, Scombridae
Caudal peduncle   – Istiophoridae, Xiphiidae, Scombridae

For Europe and North America a small number of other bones should be added, in particular: some vertebrae, the prevomer, otoliths, basioccipital and the opercular. Hyomandibulars, cerato- and epihyals, posttemporals, supracleithra and cleithra are also highly distinctive in many fishes. However, some workers collect and identify most bones in a fish's skeleton. For example, at Eketorp, Sweden, Hallström (1979) identified almost all the bones of herring including the five infraorbitals (nos. 1, 2, 3, 4 and 5), the lateral radials (nos. I, II and III) and hypurals (nos. 1, 2, 3, 4 and 5). This kind of detailed work is rarely possible because of limitations of time, and it is doubtful whether the effort involved warrants the extra knowledge obtained thereby.

It should be stressed that selecting the identifiable material from the processed soil residues is extremely difficult, requiring considerable experience with archaeological fish remains. Experienced workers will readily recognize a fragment of premaxilla in an assemblage of highly fragmented material. Inexperienced workers will pass over it completely unaware of what they have missed.

The sorted bones are best stored in permanently labelled, appropriately sized polythene bags or stiff paper envelopes.

If there is sufficient interaction between fish bone workers and excavators, the fish remains recovered from a site will rarely need to be subsampled, for all that has been collected will have been judged important and worthy of detailed consideration. This ideal, however, is sometimes not attained and subsampling excavated material may be necessary.

Occasionally, excavators find and collect bones without discussing their importance and may eventually present an extremely large number of relatively uninformative remains for identification and comment. Similarly, unusually rich deposits consisting mainly of fish bones may be revealed. In both these circumstances, subsampling the collected material may be necessary. More often the fish remains have been recovered together with other biological material and the fish bone specialist will be presented with the totality of the excavated fish material and will have to devise a method for coping with the remains.

Three strategies are used by fish bone workers faced with large assemblages of material. Some examine every fragment in great detail and record the kind of bone, its measurements (where appropriate) and identify the species. The site of Eketorp is an example of extremely thorough, meticulous work (Hallström, 1979). With this approach a large amount of information is recorded that adds little if anything of relevance to the interpretation of the site. The second approach, which is very cost-effective, is to select from the assemblage the most informative bones and concentrate on measuring and identifying those.

For example, Olsen (1967), when faced with the formidable task of reporting on several thousand hand-collected bones from Varanger-Funnene, northern Norway, decided to examine 20 selected bones from members of the cod family. He chose the dentary, articular, premaxilla, maxilla, palatine, ectopterygoid, quadrate, hyomandibular, prevomer, parasphenoid, opercular, preopercular, subopercular, interopercular, ceratohyal, epihyal, post-temporal, supracleithrum, cleithrum and the postcleithrum. He ignored other elements and judged that 'It would be quite impossible, within a reasonable amount of time, to identify all the osteological material' (1967: 164).

The third subsampling procedure is relevant where a large quantity of homogeneous material is recovered. Two examples can be cited where sub-sampling was employed without apparent distortion of the results. A large deposit of small herring family bones from Roman layers at the Peninsular House site in London were reported by Bateman and Locker (1982). On the basis of subsamples, they calculated the total number of fishes present and demonstrated the homogeneity of the material. Likewise Wheeler and Locker (1985) used subsamples of the mass of fish bone, scales and sand in Roman amphorae recovered from a shipwreck at Randello, Sicily, to estimate the species composition and size of the sardines, *Sardina pilchardus*, which dominated the samples. This kind of sampling strategy is particularly applicable where the material is very rich. However, care must be taken not to bias the results by taking too small a subsample, or by using a sampling strategy without careful inspection of the whole sample to ensure that it is homogeneous.

Where excavators and fish bone workers have a close understanding of the potential and limitations of their material and are aware of each other's sampling requirements, cost-effective sampling strategies emerge.

5

TAPHONOMY

Introduction

In the early 1970s Payne and Uerpmann published their critiques of methods used in osteoarchaeology and elucidated the difficulties of dealing with archaeological bone assemblages (Payne, 1972; Uerpmann, 1973). Although they were writing principally for workers studying mammal bone assemblages most, if not all, of the points made are relevant to fish bone workers. They pointed out that it is never possible to recover all of the bone debris from a site, no matter how careful and how extensive the excavation may be. There is always an unknown quantity which is not collected. Factors affecting this missing quantity are the consumption of meat beyond the limits of the site, the consumption and removal of bones by dogs, the use of bone as a raw material, the acidity or alkalinity (pH) of the soil and weathering of bone.

In recent years much attention has been focussed on this 'missing quantity', which has developed into a field of study in its own right: taphonomy. This can be defined as the process during which an organism becomes incorporated into an archaeological or natural deposit and becomes a specimen in a museum or environmental archaeology laboratory. The term was coined by a palaeontologist who was trying to understand groups of fossil bones and realized that many factors influenced which bones survived and where those bones were deposited. In archaeology taphonomic factors begin as the animal is slaughtered (or a fish is caught) and include butchery practice, the effects of cooking and ingestion, the effects of weathering, trampling and damage by scavengers, possibly movement by water or as a component of soil, and burial in archaeological layers. In addition to taphonomic factors, it is widely recognized that the process of excavation and the methods of recovery influence what is available for study because not only may animal remains be damaged during excavation, but a large amount of material may not be recovered and the assemblage be very biased.

Taphonomy has become increasingly important in archaeology as bone workers have attempted to understand how the material arrived at the site as opposed to simply describing what they have found. Steenstrup (1862) recognized that the weaker parts of mammal skeletons were consistently underrepresented in bone assemblages from Danish Mesolithic midden sites. He examined collections of bones from contemporary Eskimo middens and fed bones to dogs to see what was destroyed. A series of papers by Brain (1967,

61

1969, 1981) explored bone samples from Hottentot villages and modern carnivore dens and concluded that representation of the various antelope skeletal elements at the Makapansgat site was typical of any bone assemblage 'chewed-over' by carnivores. Binford (1981) discussed in great detail the kinds of carnivore damage that can be seen on bones. He also studied marks made by Nunamiut Eskimos as carcasses were skinned and butchered. Furthermore, Binford examined the element distribution of mammal bone assemblages from wolf kill sites, dog yards and human-derived contexts. More recently Payne and Munson (1985) described a series of experiments where squirrels and goats were fed to large dogs. These important contributions have helped to show that the pattern of element distribution seen in many bone groups is not caused directly by man and that some of the conclusions drawn by early workers concerning how animal populations were exploited are now untenable. As yet, little work on bone damage, patterns of fragmentation, butchery marks or element distribution has been carried out for assemblages of fish remains with the exception of that of Jones (1984a; 1986a), who examined fish bones ingested by man and fed to a pig and to dogs.

Innate factors influencing bone survival
There are two factors which influence whether a bone, otolith or scale will survive in archaeological deposits. The first is the nature of the material forming the hard tissue. The second is the treatment the carcass received in the period between being captured and its remains studied.

Some kinds of hard tissues found in fish are more resistant than others. As we shall see in chapters 6 and 7, fishes do not all produce skeletons of the same material. Most mineralized cartilage does not persist in a recognizable form in soil, ultimately breaking into small prismatic particles, which superficially resemble grains of sand once the collagen and other organic material has been destroyed. Within the bony fishes, not all produce the same number of bones, and some species have tougher, more resistant bone than others.

The jawless fishes (agnathans) have rarely been recorded in archaeological deposits despite the use of fine-meshed sieves. Horny teeth, identified as those of river lamprey or lampern, *Lampetra fluviatilis*, have recently been recovered from medieval deposits at Coppergate, York (Jones, 1986c). Elasmobranchs are usually represented only by dermal structures (denticles, teeth and spines) or vertebral centra. Even within the teleosts, bones are not all of equal robustness. Some fishes produce bones which are extremely fragile, for example the boxfishes (Ostraciontidae), sunfish, *Mola mola*, and lumpsucker, *Cyclopterus lumpus*. Rather more robust in general are the bones of the salmon family (Salmonidae) and the mackerel, *Scomber scombrus*, and tuna, *Thunnus* spp., but these are often recovered as broken fragments on archaeological sites. The pike, *Esox lucius*, the carp family

(Cyprinidae), the cod family (Gadidae), the perch family (Percidae) and other spiny-finned fishes have strong bones which often survive well in archaeological deposits.

In addition to differences in the mechanical properties of hard tissues between families of fishes, there is considerable variation in the robustness of elements within a single species. This of course is related to the function the elements perform in the animal's skeleton. Element analysis is not often fully published but in those reports where it is given (e.g. Lepiksaar and Heinrich, 1977) it is clear that some elements are well represented while others are rarely present. It must be stressed that element analysis is rarely undertaken because many workers do not attempt to identify all elements while others are not sufficiently familiar with all the elements of the species present to give such data.

Although fish bone is noticeably more fragile than mammal or bird bone, little work appears to have been carried out on its mechanical properties. An undergraduate thesis examining ribs from several European fishes (Chasler, 1972) established that they were less able to withstand bending forces than is mammal bone. More recent simple experiments (Jones, forthcoming) have shown that fish bone is less resistant to mechanical damage than mammal bone. Pieces of modern adult cod parasphenoid and modern adult sheep metacarpal were trimmed to $20 \times 2 \times 2$ mm and placed in an end-over-end tumbler with rounded limestone pebbles. After a few hours in the tumbler the fish bones had begun to fall to pieces while the sheep bones were only slightly polished. This simple experiment verifies the intuitive belief that fish bone is not very resistant to attrition.

Environmental factors influencing bone survival
Important factors influencing which fish remains survive in archaeological deposits are the physical and chemical environments of the bones once the fish has been caught and the kind of sediment surrounding fish remains. Archaeological sites on acid substrates rarely produce fish remains. Neutral and alkaline soil conditions are conducive to fish bone survival. However, otoliths rarely persist except in base-rich deposits, such as alkaline shell sands.

While the soil pH is probably the major factor influencing bone survival, the nature of the sediment burying ancient remains is also important. Layers composed mainly of mineral particles are more likely to cause post-burial abrasion than layers rich in organic debris. Stratified waterlogged sites often produce fish remains that are exceptionally well preserved, for here delicate bones were rapidly buried and cushioned by large volumes of organic refuse, which protected the remains from mechanical damage.

An understanding of these inherent biases has helped to dissuade many fish analysts from drawing from their data elaborate and probably false conclusions. As a result, many recently published fish bone reports concentrate on the presence and absence of species and the numbers of identifiable elements recovered rather than attempt to estimate the calorific value of the fish consumed.

After this brief discussion of the innate and environmental factors influencing which fish remains survive on archaeological sites, it is appropriate to examine how the activities of past populations may have affected bone survival. As illustration, a hypothetical example of a small population, perhaps a couple of households settled on a new site close to the sea, is considered.

Steps in taphonomy
Catching and selecting fish
The local fish population comprises numerous species, some abundant, others scarce, some living close to the surface and readily caught using nets, others living in deeper water, which can best be caught by hook and line. Other species may be taken using traps or lines set at low tide and a small amount of fish may be collected from the shore after storms or having been left by carnivores. Several species will not be available as food because they are small or rare in the area. Some species may be taken only under exceptional circumstances, for example by divers.

Experienced fishermen do not set off to 'see what they can catch' in the way that a small boy may approach a stream or rock pool with a hand-net. Example and experience have taught them when particular species are common and seasonally abundant and in prime condition. Taboo and custom prejudice them in favour of some species and against others for no apparently logical reason. An excellent example of this has recently been published by Meehan (1983), showing how Australian aborigines choose shellfish in a way that does not necessarily reflect their availability. Smith (1981) has shown that certain Amazonian fish species are not eaten because of local taboos. In addition, fishermen discard from their catches species or size classes considered to be unpalatable or poisonous; thus all the animals caught are rarely landed.

It is clear that we are unlikely to learn much about the total population of fish by studying archaeological material alone. However, by combining the archaeological evidence with data from carefully selected modern ecological studies, a picture of the unfished 'target' population may be reconstructed.

There is perhaps less need to rely on modern studies if the animals exploited by man are considered, i.e. those species caught and landed, for usually only a small number of species (usually less than 40) is involved. However, taphonomic factors may bias what is deposited. When fish are caught, their bones may be broken accidentally (this damage is unlikely to be noticed in archaeological material). Occasionally jaws are split at their symphysis to facilitate removing swallowed hooks (dentaries of large gadids with chop marks at the symphysis occur in European assemblages).

Processing fish on land

What happens to fish from the point of landing is governed by many factors. A few species are provided with sharp or poisonous spines. Many catfish (*Synodontis* sp.) spines present in an assemblage of fish bones from Karnak-North, a monumental temple of the New Kingdom near Luxor, Egypt, had been deliberately broken. Wall paintings from the Tomb of Akhouthotep and Tomb Ti confirm that fishermen broke off pectoral spines from *Synodontis* (Driesch, 1983). Scales may fall or be deliberately removed from fish. Today in Britain, large dermal denticles of the thornback ray, *Raja clavata*, are sometimes removed using carpenters' pincers but more often only the 'wings' of the fish are landed (the rest of the body being discarded at sea). Universally, envenomed spines are removed as soon as the fish is caught; in Europe this is seen with the weeverfishes (Trachinidae) and stingrays, *Dasyatis* sp.

After this initial superficial treatment, designed to make the flesh less dangerous to handle, fish may be consumed fresh. Much, however, is processed by smoking, drying or pickling and eaten later. Fresh or preserved fish may be decapitated, gutted or filleted, all processes which can, but do not always, fragment or leave marks on bones. At waterside sites, accumulations of fish remains may be found which will reflect these activities. For example, large numbers of head bones and small numbers of vertebrae may indicate that animals were decapitated and the flesh taken elsewhere. Occasionally cut marks on the head bones will suggest how the head was removed and whether the skeleton was filleted.

Cut marks

An attribute of some fish bone assemblages is the presence of knife marks and chopping marks on particular bones. While it is not always easy to distinguish knife marks from the tooth marks of scavengers gnawing bones, close scrutiny of modern knife- and tooth-marked bones, perhaps using a scanning electron microscope, can greatly assist in distinguishing the two kinds of damage. It is important to remember that knife marks do not always occur on fish bones even when knives are used in gutting and filleting. Knife contact with bone blunts the blade and so fishmongers try to avoid such contact.

Often knife and chop marks are restricted to a small number of elements for each species in an assemblage. By considering where these bones lie in the fish, it may be possible to deduce something of the way fish were processed. The most obvious features to interpret are clear transverse chop marks on vertebrae, indicating that the vertebral column was divided into sections or steaks.

The commonest marks in European assemblages are knife marks on cleithra, although postcleithra and posttemporal bones of large gadid fishes may also be found with knife marks (see Colley, 1984b). It is most probable that these marks were made during filleting because fish skeletons prepared from filleted specimens often display these marks. Careful observation of contemporary fishmongers may show how these marks are made.

When a large gadid fish is being filleted, the most commonly used technique is to lay the cleaned fish on one side with the head pointing towards the filleter's free hand. The pectoral fin is lifted to prepare for the first cut. This incision is made roughly diagonally across the fish just behind (caudally) the lifted fin, drawing the knife as far towards the roof of the cranium as possible to the supraoccipital or frontal ridge. This action can cause the knife to cut the posttemporal or supracleithrum. The next cuts, usually executed as a series of alternating knife strokes towards the tail and head, separate the fillet from the neural and haemal spines of the vertebrae along the length of the vertebral column. This series of strokes can make fine cut marks on the lateral surface of the cleithrum, branchiostegal rays and very occasionally the vertebrae.

Another bone which has been observed to have fine cut marks is the opercular bone of large cod. Such marks may be caused when a large hook or cord is threaded through the operculum to facilitate carrying freshly caught fishes. Other explanations for these marks are, of course, possible.

Bones may be marked when the gills are being removed or a deeply embedded hook taken out. Dentary bones may be chopped at or near the symphysis in an attempt to retrieve a deeply swallowed hook. Bones of the oromandibular and hyoid regions may be marked by the action of extracting the tongue.

Wilkinson (1979) described cut marks on material from Exeter and suggested that they may have resulted from the 'splitting' of the fish in preparation for salting or drying.

There is considerable potential for learning more about the way fish were processed by considering any signs left by a knife or cleaver. By careful examination, perhaps combined with experimentation, this potential will be realized.

Consumption of fish

Eventually the fish are eaten, often at a settlement site. This may, for example, be a short-lived camp or an intensively occupied cave, a town or monastery. It is at this stage, at the site of consumption, that some of the most important agencies affecting the survival of fish remains operate. It is also the kind of site most likely to receive archaeological scrutiny, for here is where people lived, made artefacts and left the most varied evidence of their life styles. Here the fish was prepared for consumption, during which descaling, gutting and butchery were important processes. Perhaps the most important are the effects of cooking in softening bone. A recent experiment (Jones, forthcoming) showed that cod, haddock and hake bones which had been boiled for two hours were much more vulnerable to mechanical damage than bones from the same fish which were boiled for only 30 minutes or bones which had not been boiled at all. Fish may be cooked whole or filleted or cut into small pieces. If filleted, the skeleton may be boiled for soup or fed to dogs or pigs. The fish is eaten, some bones may be discarded and trampled onto the floor, whilst others may be swallowed and passed with faeces. A small amount of fish is likely to have putrefied before it is eaten, and may have been thrown onto the rubbish heap where dogs, chickens, pigs and other animals could have chewed or ingested it. Eating fish, whether by man, dog, rats or pig, destroys and damages bones (Jones, 1986a). Discarded fish remains may be trampled, dug up, thrown into moving water or pits. All these processes abrade bones.

Post-depositional changes

Finally bones are buried. Within the deposits fish remains may be safe from further destruction (if, for example, the soil is alkaline); alternatively, fish remains may be subject to chemical and mechanical erosion (see above). It is clear that the bones that become part of archaeological deposits are likely to be a small and probably biased sample of those brought onto the site.

Taphonomic processes have not yet ceased to operate, for the methods used in excavation affect what is recovered. Depending on the techniques used to recover small remains, some bones have a better chance of being recovered than others. Many layers are excavated by picking and shovelling the deposits into a wheelbarrow. Finds are collected as they become apparent to those shovelling or to the person emptying the barrow. It is not difficult to understand why few fish bones are noticed under these conditions. Very few fish bones are large enough to be collected under such conditions of excavation. (Although there are few excavators who would knowingly shovel out and throw away a deposit rich in small bones, layers containing low concentrations of small bones are frequently treated in this manner.) The decision to shovel away a layer is often made without considering evidence from sieving trial samples.

Large bones of big fish (usually over 1 m long) can be collected by trowelling deposits. Here, however, recovery is much more 'operator-dependent'. That is, some people are more likely to collect small bones than others. This has been noticed by, amongst other, Levitan (1982) at excavations at West Hill, Uley, Gloucestershire, UK, where experiments were carried out to examine the rate of bone recovery for a group of excavators.

Sieving techniques (see chapter 4) have been developed to redress biases caused by differences in excavation technique and the abilities of excavators. However, seldom is it practical (or desirable) to sieve all of the bone-bearing deposits from a site.

The final factor affecting what is examined is human error. Bags are mislabelled, boxes of bone mislaid, and poor storage conditions may cause material to be lost or damaged after the excavation has ceased. Every effort should be made to guard against mistakes and carelessness. Recording systems (see chapter 8) should be designed to accommodate some human error, but methodical working procedures, care and conscientiousness are the best guards.

Processing fish: decapitation, filleting

Fish processing is an enormous subject and much has been written concerning the methods used to prepare fish for consumption. Cutting (1955) outlined the history of fish processing from ancient to modern times while Burgess *et al.* (1965) have carefully documented the principles used today to salt cure, smoke, dry and freeze fish. An interesting account of fish preserving in Britain and elsewhere is given by Anderson Smith (1883), while Ross (1883) and Walker (1982) detail fish curing and preservation in Scotland. Much has also been written about fish processing in other parts of the world.

When fishes are processed for immediate consumption or prepared for a method of preservation, bones are sometimes modified, but many fish, including large specimens, can be processed without leaving knife cuts or marks of other bladed instruments. For example, haddock can be prepared for the 'Eyemouth cure' or 'Finnan cure' by being opened with a knife, after which the viscera are removed from the body cavity, causing no damage to bones. With one movement, the head, with the gut still attached, is separated from the body. This is achieved by passing the forefinger and thumb of one hand round the 'neck' of the fish and seizing the head in the other. The vertebrae are dislocated at the base of the skull by a straight backward jerk. A final sharp pull ensures that the muscles and skin of the cleithrum region are detached from the base of the skull (Ross, 1883). In this process no knife marks are made on bones and the cleithrum remains with the body. Large fish can also be beheaded without a knife. Small fish, for example herring, are rarely decapitated, gutting being the only preparatory process carried out when they are pickled. Fish guts often contain large numbers of bones of species recently ingested. Midden deposits may contain bones, usually small ones, of fish discarded with the guts of large species.

While decapitation can be carried out without leaving traces on bones, filleting may leave marks. If the knife is sharp but not pointed the bones are less often cut. The commonest sites for such cuts are the cleithrum, supracleithrum and posttemporal. Medieval cod cleithra from the site at 1–5

Aldwark, York, UK (Jones, 1985) have been found to bear identical marks to modern ones obtained from fish filleters at Grimsby, Humberside, fish-market.

Fish are often split – that is, the right and left sides of the body divided along the length of the vertebral column – in order to lay the flesh flat. This is carried out after gutting and may be done with the head on or off. Rarely are vertebral processes damaged by filleting. Sometimes the splitting process involves removing a considerable length of the vertebral column: usually the abdominal vertebrae are cut out, leaving only caudal vertebrae with the flesh.

There are many more elaborate ways of preserving fish for later consumption. Some techniques cause considerable damage to fish. In North Africa small fish are prepared for sale by pounding them entire in a wooden mortar and drying them in the sun in large lumps (Anderson Smith, 1883). Fish sauces, sometimes prepared from whole fish, were important in Classical times and details of their preparation have been discussed by Badham (1854) and others.

What happens to the bones when fish are eaten?

The effects of animal digestive systems on fish bones are another important influence on which bones survive in archaeological deposits. In order to investigate this topic, two experiments were carried out. In the first a dog was fed two red snappers, *Lutjanus campechanus*, by Sebastian Payne and Pat Munson and bones examined after digestion (Jones, 1984a). This experiment provided clear evidence that in excess of 80% of the identifiable bones of medium-sized fish disappeared when whole fish were eaten. It also demonstrated that considerable damage can be caused to fish bones when they are ingested. Crushed bones, particularly vertebrae, are frequently found in archaeological deposits. While it is possible that trampling or other processes may cause such damage, it is perhaps more likely that crushing and fragmentation occurred as the fish were ingested and digested. The experiment with the dog indicates that mechanical damage is not the only problem. It appears that a large number of bones can be dissolved during digestion.

A further experiment was carried out to assess the effects of the digestive systems of man and three associated mammals, dog, pig and rat, which are known to have lived together on many sites in the past. Pigs, rats and dogs are today important disposers of waste in settlements where little attention is given to such matters. (Many details of these experiments were published by Jones, 1986a.)

Four species of fish were used (herring, mackerel, plaice and haddock); all are small to medium-sized fishes, which can be readily ingested with little chance of bones lodging in the oesophagus. The experiments were carried out during the period November 1983 to July 1984 with the assistance of the animals' owners. With the exception of a few haddock bones, all were readily ingested and swallowed. Faeces were collected and carefully washed to recover bones. These were identified as if they were an archaeological assemblage, i.e. counting the most distinctive elements (for example, jaw bones and vertebrae), while excluding ribs, branchiostegal rays and uncharacteristic broken fragments from bone counts.

The mammals selected for this experiment were: an adult European male human; an adult female pedigree Wessex saddleback pig; adult white laboratory rats (Wistar strain); and an adult cross-bred collie dog.

The man ate a grilled kipper (a traditionally smoked North Sea herring, *Clupea harengus*). All bones were swallowed, although only after thorough mastication. Faeces were collected for the following seven days. In order to establish that all fish residues had passed through the gut, marker foods (sweet corn and unpitted olives) were swallowed during the period of faecal collection. The faeces were thoroughly stirred in a bucket of water and washed onto 500 micron aperture meshed sieves. The process was repeated until all faecal components were completely disaggregated, whereupon the residues were air-dried and sorted for fish bones.

Three rats, housed individually in cages, were fed young plaice, *Pleuronectes platessa* (total length 13 cm), and young herring (total length 12 cm). All the bones were ingested with 48 hours of feeding. All the bones of the flatfish and the young herring were consumed, no recognizable fragments being recovered from faeces. Later other rats of the same strain were fed the head and backbones of herring 27 cm long. The adult herrings were not completely eaten because there was concern that the fish might begin to decompose, making the environment of the animal laboratory unpleasant. As a result the remains of the fish were removed after 48 hours. It was clear that, had the fish been left for longer, or had more than one rat had access to each fish, all the bones would have been consumed. No recognizable fragments were recovered from the faeces. Rats must be regarded as major destroyers of fish bones on ancient occupation sites where they are indigenous or introduced.

The pig eagerly bolted a fresh gutted herring and a mackerel, *Scomber scombrus*; mastication was minimal. The pig was housed in a small stone-built shed, which opened onto a grass lawn. An electric fence was used to confine the pig. The fenced area contained a small amount of old, dried, pig faeces, which was thoroughly cleared to the perimeter of the paddock. During the period of collection the weather remained dry, so no faeces were lost through disaggregation by rain. Collections were made at 12-hour intervals for the first five days and daily for the last two days. Disaggregation of the faeces was slow and laborious, not to say odorous, and was carried out in the presence of many thousands of dung beetles and flies. It was accomplished by repeated stirring in hot water in a 20 gallon capacity tank, the suspension being decanted through 500 micron sieves. As the animal was kept out of doors in

Table 5.1. *Bone survival following consumption of fish by four species of mammal*

Mammal	Pig		Dog		Man	Rat	
Species ingested	Herring	Mackerel	Herring	Haddock	Herring	Herring	Plaice
Total length (cm)	25.5	35.5	27.3	32.5	24	15	12
Gutted weight (g)	150	370	140	260	135	50	10
Bones rejected	0	0	0	6	0	0	0
Number identifiable fragments in faeces	7	7	9	10	2	0	0
Number unidentifiable fragments	4		19		13	0	

a paddock, where it also ate large quantities of grass during the period of the experiment, partly digested grass remains formed the bulk of the faeces. A satisfactory method of separating the grass fragments from the denser bone and other ingested matter (mostly soil, eggshell, small stones and seeds) involved allowing the floating fraction to pass through an outlet placed towards the top of the tank. The disaggregated grass fragments were collected on a 1 mm aperture sieve, dried and sorted to check for fish bones. No bones were recovered from the floated fraction.

The dog was fed a herring and a small haddock, *Melanogrammus aeglefinus*. Both fish were gutted, lightly fried and mixed with the dog's cereal-based feed. This mixture was readily ingested. However, shortly after swallowing, there was a brief period of coughing and regurgitation. Most of the fish was reingested over the next ten minutes but a small amount was left in the feeding bowl overnight. After 24 hours the bones remaining in and around the bowl were collected and labelled 'rejected'. Faeces were collected for the following seven days. Bones were collected by washing the faeces on 500 micron aperture meshes in a continuous flow of hot water. The air-dried residues were sorted for fish bones. Table 5.1 shows the mammals involved and the fish eaten in this experiment.

It is clear that a large number of bones which might be expected to have survived passage through the mammalian guts were absent. All gave broadly

Table 5.2. *Proportional survival of fish bones following ingestion by four species of mammal*

Mammal ingestor	Pig		Dog		Man	Rat	
Species ingested	Herring	Mackerel	Haddock	Herring	Herring	Herring	Plaice
Approx. number identifiable bones in whole skeleton	80	53	80	80	80	80	80
% survival all bones	9	13	12	3	11	0	0
% survival whole vertebral centra	3	3	7	0	0	0	0

similar results – only a small number of recognizable bones were recovered and in the experiment with rats none survived.

Although the rat experiment was the only one carried out under controlled laboratory conditions, there is little chance that any faeces containing fish bones were not examined. There is no chance that any bones were lost from the human faeces and every effort was made to ensure that none were lost from the pig or dog faeces. It is also extremely unlikely that bones were over-looked or lost during the washing and sorting process.

The numbers of bones that survived have been expressed as a percentage of the number of identifiable bones for the experiments with man, dog and pig. The number of identifiable bones was determined by summing the number of vertebrae and the more resistant diagnostic head bones. The classification of bones as 'identifiable' is necessarily somewhat arbitrary. A more objective index of survival has been determined by computing the percentage of whole vertebral centra that were recovered. This includes crushed vertebrae where the centrum was intact. Table 5.2 shows the results of these calculations.

When the percentages are calculated (table 5.2), a maximum of 13% of the expected bones was found to have survived. The results of the percentage survival for whole vertebral centra show the man destroyed all the vertebrae. The pig passed 3%, while the vertebrae survived slightly better in the dog. These differences are probably related to the amount of mastication and the length of the gut in the three species. The man thoroughly chewed the herring in order to swallow a rather unconventional morsel. This probably fragmented most, if not all, of the vertebrae. The pig did not appear to chew the fish but, because it possesses a long digestive tract, the bones were adversely affected by enzymes and acid. The dog, which apparently did relatively little damage by chewing the bones and possesses a relatively short gut, passed most bones (fig. 5.1). No bones survived the rat's teeth and digestive system.

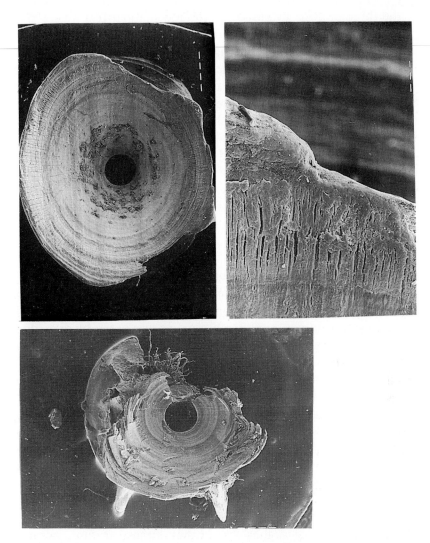

5.1   Animal damage to bones. Top left: Modern herring, *Clupea harengus*, SEM micrograph of vertebral centrum recovered from dog faeces (lowest scale bar = 100 microns). Top right: SEM micrograph detail of margin of same centrum. Note erosion of the margin as a result of digestion (lowest scale bar = 10 microns). Below: SEM micrograph of centrum partly eaten by rat (left scale bar = 100 microns). (Photographs by A. K. G. Jones; copyright Department of Biology, University of York.)

The kinds of bones which survived these experiments are of interest. In the red snapper experiment the quadrate had the best survival rate (50%) in faeces. This element, one from a herring and one haddock, gave one of the best survival rates in these experiments showing that the quadrate is amongst the most robust bones in fish skulls. The quadrate is covered by layers of other bones and muscle which probably protect it from enzyme attack. One of the three otoliths swallowed in the red snapper test was recovered. Both haddock otoliths were recovered from the dog faeces although their highly polished surfaces showed that digestive juices had attacked them.

However, some bones (e.g. the palatine) which survived in the red snapper experiment did not survive the second experiment. Clearly further experiments are necessary to assess which bones survive and which disappear during digestion. Future work should concentrate on the effects of scavengers of the bones of large fishes.

More work needs to be carried out before an accurate picture can be established of the survival potential of each bone of the species found on archaeological sites. These experiments seem to show that a large number of bones from small and medium-sized fish (up to 35 cm total length) do not survive passage through the mammalian gut.

Implications for archaeology

These experiments demonstrate the degree of loss of fish remains as a result of ingestion. However, it must be pointed out that these fish bones have been passed through one gut only. On some sites it is possible that at least some human excrement containing fish remains was eaten by pigs, dogs or other scavengers. Domestic animal faeces were probably also ingested by scavengers. Presumably any bones that survived the first digestion would have been vulnerable to destruction by the second.

Some archaeological deposits consist largely of material that has been through a mammalian gut. Samples of fish bones from latrine and cesspits are often crushed in a manner identical to the bones recovered from these experiments (fig. 5.2). These experiments indicate that the recovered assemblage is a small sample (probably less than 10%) of the bones swallowed. Many archaeological assemblages of fish bones do not provide evidence that they have been eaten. Under such circumstances it is impossible to estimate what percentage has survived. However, scavengers probably did eat food waste, faeces and other domestic refuse, so causing a large but unquantifiable amount of the potentially identifiable fish remains to be lost from the archaeological record.

The validity of many of the calculations applied to assemblages of archaeological fish remains must be questioned, particularly for urban sites. Calculations of minimum numbers of individuals or the meat weights contributed

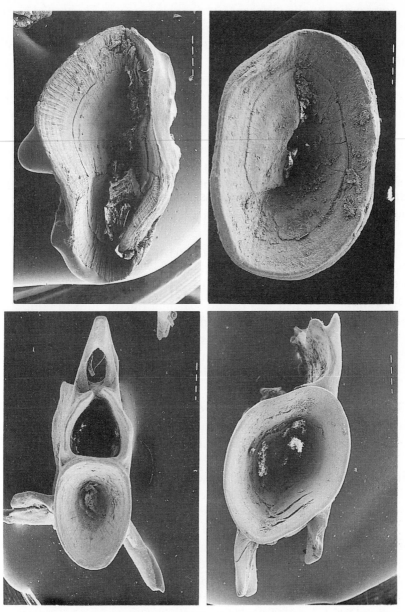

5.2   Effects of mastication on fish bone. Above: SEM micrographs of herring,
Clupea harengus, vertebral centra; left: a modern specimen from human faeces
(note the considerable crushing caused by mastication); right: from tenth-century
latrine pit at 16–22 Coppergate, York (note comparable damage). Below: SEM
micrographs of eel, *Anguilla anguilla*, vertebral centra from tenth-century latrine
pit at 16–22 Coppergate, York; left: note the asymmetry of the transverse
process; right: note asymmetry of the centrum (lowest scale bars = 100 microns).
(Photographs by A. K. G. Jones; copyright Department of Biology, University
of York.)

to human diet by the different species present in archaeological assemblages must be seen against the likelihood that the bones considered are but a minute, and no doubt heavily biased, sample of the animals brought onto the site in antiquity.

Perhaps it is better to adopt a more conservative approach to the data, considering primarily the range of small to medium-sized fish taxa present in the different phases of occupation, paying some, but secondary, heed to the number and kinds of identified fragments. This approach will reveal major changes in the kinds of fish exploited and, in combination with detailed information on the provenance of the bones, show how they were distributed about the site. Regrettably, at the moment there seems no alternative to presenting a somewhat subjective impression of the importance of the various species. This approach will no doubt disappoint some but it is true to the data.

The results of a range of recent experiments demonstrate that fish bone readily disintegrates as a result of the processes which occur on human occupation sites. Eating fish, whether by man or synanthropic animals, cooking fish, trampling on fish waste, and seasonal fluctuations in temperature and humidity all cause fish remains to disappear from the archaeological record. There is little doubt that enormous loss of fish remains has occurred at most occupation sites and the fish remains preserved in, and recovered from, deposits are a very small sample of those originally discarded.

With this in mind, it is perhaps not surprising that there is frequently a discrepancy between osteological evidence and that obtained by analyzing carbon isotopes (^{12}C and ^{13}C) in human bone to investigate the diet of past populations. Tauber (1986) determined the relative amounts of ^{12}C and ^{13}C in human bones from Denmark and Greenland, ranging in time from approximately 7000 BC to the present day, to assess the roles of marine and terrestrial animals as food sources. This work indicated a change from terrestrial to marine sources at roughly 6000 BC. Later his data show a return to terrestrial foods at about 4000 BC. This finding was at variance with previous estimates of food supplies in the Late Mesolithic based on the amounts of bones and shells found in midden layers of Danish Mesolithic sites. In part, the discrepancy may be related to the failure of past generations of archaeologists to sieve sufficient of the midden deposits to recover fish remains. However, even if sieving is carried out, it is clear that the bones of large terrestrial mammals, being more resistant to decay than those of fishes, are overrepresented in the archaeological record when compared to fish remains.

Animal occupation on sites
Man was, no doubt, responsible for the accumulation of most assemblages of fish remains recovered from archaeological sites. However, other agencies

Table 5.3. *Processes involved in the formation of archaeological fish assemblages*

Process	Activities affecting bones	Resulting assemblage
Live population of fish comprising several species, some small and some large, some common, some rare	Scavengers and decomposers	Natural death assemblages, uninfluenced by man
1 Fish caught by fisher-folk (some bones may be damaged)	Few bones may be broken, some scales may be lost	Collection of fresh whole dead fish
2 Selection at site of capture (inedible, poisonous or unesteemed fish discarded)	Few bones may be broken, some scales may be lost	Selected assemblage of fresh fish
3 Fish landed (gutting may take place, perhaps decapitation)	Entrails containing small fishes, heads discarded	Middens at coastal, lakeside, or riverside location
Fish taken to market	Gutting, filleting, dividing into steaks	Middens at population centres
Fish acquired and cooked	Gutting, filleting, divided into steaks, eaten, some bones may be discarded	Waste thrown out or dumped in pits
Waste discarded	From tables or in faeces	Waste thrown out or dumped in pits
Scavengers ingest bones	Crushing, fragmentation, chemical digestion	
Weathering and trampling	Crushing, fragmentation, chemical digestion	
Bones in archaeological site		
Bones recovered		
Bones recorded		

can also cause fish remains to be incorporated into archaeological deposits. At sites close to large fish populations, whether inland or coastal, birds and other piscivores can drop fish bones, which may become mixed with human occupation debris. Birds and otters often deposit bones in selected locations and local concentration can build up. On a small island in the Firth of Clyde, Scotland, an area of limestone roughly 20 square metres in extent yielded an assemblage of approximately 50 fish bones, consisting of gadid otoliths, vertebrae, jawbones etc., when carefully examined for fish remains. Observations of the site showed it to be used by gulls, the bones being the more resistant part of regurgitated pellets. Similar scatters of fish remains can be found at many locations and it is not difficult to envisage such naturally deposited material becoming incorporated into the accumulating sediments on an abandoned human occupation site.

Abandoned human occupation sites provide shelter for other species. Caves and abandoned buildings are often occupied by animals which may pass bone-rich faeces or bring in fish carcasses for consumption. Examples have been given in chapter 1.

Movement of bones by natural forces
Small bones can be carried considerable distances by the wind and waves. Small numbers of bones may thereby be cast onto occupation sites. Seasonal flooding can strand small fish on sites and 'rains' of small fishes, although rare, are well documented.

Natural agencies depositing fish bones rarely produce substantial concentrations of the kinds of fish preferred as human food. However, archaeological reports occasionally refer to species that are unlikely to have been eaten and some of these bones may have been deposited by agencies other than man.

Testing for non-human bone accumulations, be it bird accumulations or wind-transported material, may be achieved by examining a small area near the excavation, where other traces of archaeological activity are absent. Assessing the natural background bone in sediments should be part of the excavation strategy. Careful scrutiny of the species list should provide a clear indication of the origin of the assemblage.

6

ANATOMY OF AGNATHANS AND CARTILAGINOUS FISHES

Skeletal remains

The agnathans are not really fishes: they stand apart from the two main groups (cartilaginous fishes and bony fishes), separated by an even greater distance than, say, birds are from reptiles. However, they are moderately large and live in water and are thus usually thought of as fishes. Their most obvious characteristic is that they lack jaws (Agnatha is formed from A = without, gnathos = jaws), while all other fishes have jaws. They form two distinct zoological classes, the hagfishes and the lampreys (see pp. 14–16), but possess several features in common, notably a cartilaginous skeleton and a neurocranium (brain case) and olfactory, optic and otic capsules; they also lack fins with skeletal supporting elements. The cartilage which comprises the skeleton is not mineralized and is soft – it is therefore unlikely, except under exceptional conditions, to survive in archaeological sites.

Both hagfishes and lampreys feed in an unusual manner (lacking jaws to engulf their prey). Hagfishes, which are marine animals, eat bottom-living invertebrates but are best known for their habit of boring into dead or captured fishes in a net or on a line and virtually hollowing out the victim until only skin and bone remain. They do this by means of a muscular tongue with four rows of keratinized teeth, which are in opposition to a cartilaginous dental plate in the roof of the pharynx. These keratinized sharp teeth are the only hard structures of the hagfish and thus might survive in the archaeological context. However, hagfishes live in moderately deep water and produce enormous quantities of slime; they certainly would not appeal to anyone as food and probably have never been eaten.

Lampreys also have keratinized teeth in species-specific numbers and arrangement and have a considerable number on the inside of a sucker disc and on their muscular tongue. As adults, some of the larger species of lampreys feed by attaching themselves to a bony fish and then, rasping away the skin and underlying muscle, they suck the blood of the victim. Their keratinized teeth are the only hard parts that may be preserved and then only under special conditions. Lampreys are slimy, eel-like creatures which, despite their unprepossessing appearance, have been extensively eaten either fresh or salted in North America, Europe and New Zealand. Young specimens and small species have also been well regarded as bait for bigger fishes.

79

The cargilaginous fishes comprise three main groups, the chimaeras (see p. 16), the sharks, and the rays and skates. As their group name suggests, their skeletons are formed of cartilage, but as they grow it becomes mineralized, and as they have well-developed jaws they have strong teeth, which are often characteristic of the genus and sometimes species. Cartilage is a hard gristle composed of protein and toughened by fibres. The chondrocranium (which is open at the top surface), gill arches and fin supports are usually plain cartilage, but where the skeleton has to bear heavy loads, such as the jaw bones of sharks in particular, parts of the pectoral skeleton and vertebrae, the cartilage is reinforced with an external layer of apatite (a mixture of calcium phosphates and carbonates) formed by many small interlocking plates. The vertebrae of these fishes have to withstand different stresses from those experienced by the jaws and have calcified struts within the body of the centrum (fig. 6.1).

In practice it seems that this means of strengthening the centra leads to better survival as archaeological or subfossil remains. The vertebral centra of sharks and rays appear as simple cylinders, strongly concave at both articulating ends, with lengthwise struts alternating with deep lacunae. Some specimens tend to resemble a bobbin with concave ends, perhaps where the centrum was only lightly strengthened. Both sharks and rays have large numbers of centra: for example in 25 species of the genus *Carcharhinus* the mean number ranged from 119 to 235 (Garrick, 1982); in general they decrease uniformly in diameter from head to tail, but there are striking variations in the length of the centra, which sometimes increase in the middle of the body to twice the length of the anterior and posterior centra. Many years ago Goodrich (1930) showed that many species of sharks and rays had distinctive patterns of calcification within the centrum. These patterns have been explored more recently by George Desse, first in a wide survey of the characteristic structures of sharks and rays (Desse and du Buit, 1971) and later applying the technique to archaeological elasmobranch vertebral centra in G. Desse (1984; Desse and Desse, 1976). Using radiography to reveal the internal structure, Desse and his co-workers claim to be able to identify vertebral centra to species. This aspect of work with elasmobranch centra merits further study.

6.1   Vertebral centrum of a shark, the smooth hound, *Mustelus asterias*. Left: lateral view; centre: cross-section showing calcified struts; right: anterior face (note the spinal foramen in the centre, which pierces the centrum). (Bar scale 1 cm.)

Teeth

The bodies of all sharks, skates and many rays are rough to the touch, especially if the hand is run over the skin from tail to head. This roughness is due to the presence of dermal denticles (skin teeth) embedded in the epidermis. The teeth in the jaws are dermal denticles which have become modified in shape and position to play a different role, that of food capture. However, they still have the basic structure of the dermal denticles, each comprising a central core of dentine, pierced by a pulp cavity containing blood vessels and nerves, while covering the dentine is a layer of enameloid tissue.

Where the teeth differ from those of mammals is that they have no roots and are not attached to the jaws, but lie within the gum, joined at their bases by very tough fibrous membrane. Also unlike mammals they do not retain their teeth through life but are constantly shedding the oldest, outer teeth, which are replaced by others newly developed inside the gum. Tooth replacement thus takes place in a linear fashion, much like an escalator or moving staircase (fig. 6.2a).

The teeth vary strikingly with the preferred diet or feeding habits of the fish. Thus, many of the requiem sharks (family Carcharhinidae) have more or less triangular teeth in both upper and lower jaws. The upper jaw teeth are equal-sided triangles in the centre of the jaw, but gradually become oblique towards the angle of the mouth, the point of the tooth leaning towards the angle; all the cutting edges are serrated (fig. 6.2c). In the lower jaw the teeth are more pointed, with concave cutting margins and with finer serrations along the edges. Many sharks have long dagger-like teeth, sometimes with distinct smaller cusps at their base (e.g. the sand shark, *Eugomphodus taurus* – fig. 6.2a), sometimes with no cusp at all (e.g. the mako shark, *Isurus oxyrhinchus*) and others with two cusps either side of the median one (e.g. the South African dogfish, *Scyliorhinus capensis*). Others have very oblique teeth with a moderately large cusp at one end followed by a series of smaller cusps (e.g. the tiger shark, *Galeocerdo cuvier*, fig. 6.2f, and the six-gilled shark, *Hexanchus griseus*, fig. 6.2d). By contrast, some sharks have flattened teeth in the jaws, notably the horn sharks, *Heterodontus* sp., where the teeth in the sides of the jaw are flat, and ten times broader than those in the centre (fig. 6.2b). Skates are perhaps less diverse in their dentition and have much smaller teeth in relation to their body size, but even then there is great variation: species such as the thornback ray or roker, *Raja clavata*, have only slightly pointed teeth, but the shagreen ray, *Raja fullonica*, has long, slender, pointed teeth. Sexual dimorphism in tooth form is exhibited in both sharks and skates, but has not been intensively studied, but in the North American Atlantic species the barn-door skate, *Raja laevis*, for example, and in the European roker, females have teeth with only a blunt, small central cusp, while males of equal size have long sharp cusps (fig. 6.3a).

Rays and their relatives likewise have very variable teeth. The sawfishes, *Pristis*, in addition to the massive teeth on the rostrum (fig. 6.4a), have minute jaw teeth with smooth surfaces similar to those in the sting-rays, *Dasyatis* sp., which are densely crowded in the jaws (fig. 6.3d). In contrast the cow-nosed rays, *Rhinoptera* sp. (fig. 6.3c), and the eagle-rays, *Myliobatis* sp. (fig. 6.3b) have relatively few flattened plates, arranged in a mosaic pattern, a large one at the centre, smaller ones slotting in at the edges. The oldest of these are frequently worn away, for these fish eat hard-shelled molluscs such as oysters and clams.

To summarize this discussion of elasmobranch teeth, from the archaeologist's viewpoint there is no doubt that they can be of value in establishing which species are represented on a site. However, they do not

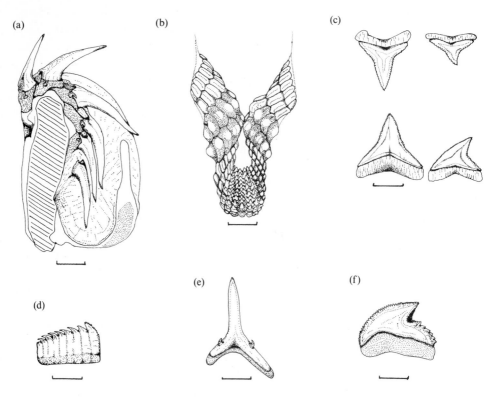

6.2   Shark teeth, showing tooth succession and variation in shape. (a) Sand shark, *Eugomphodus taurus*, showing tooth succession in lower jaw.
(b) Japanese bullhead shark (horn shark), *Heterodontus japonicus*, showing both tooth succession and variation of tooth shape in the lower jaw. (c) Requiem shark, *Carcharhinus* sp., teeth from near the midline and the side of the jaws (upper and lower). (d) Six-gilled shark, *Hexanchus griseus*, lower jaw tooth.
(e) Sand shark, lower jaw tooth. (f) Tiger shark, *Galeocerdo cuvier*, lower jaw tooth. (Bar scales 1 cm.)

represent an easy tool to use, as their morphology varies between species, sometimes between the sexes of the same species, to some extent with the size of the fish, and in other cases between upper and lower jaws, and with their position on the jaw. This last vitiates against using them for size estimation other than in the crudest of categories, for quite small teeth can come from the sides of the jaws of even very large sharks.

Dermal structures

We have already seen that virtually the entire skin surface of the elasmo-branch fishes is covered with dermal denticles (the only exceptions are the electric-rays, sting-rays, eagle-rays and mantas, while some skates have bare patches on the body). These denticles have the same structure as the jaw teeth already discussed, with dentine internally covered by a layer of hard enamel. The denticles have a broad, calcified base, fixed in the dermis by fibres, and are backwardly pointing tooth-like structures which cover virtually the whole body. Most of the denticle is hidden from view, being embedded in the dermis and surrounded by epidermis (the outer layer of the skin). Denticle shapes are very variable from species to species. Some are narrow with a single pointed cusp (e.g. the spurdog, *Squalus acanthias*),

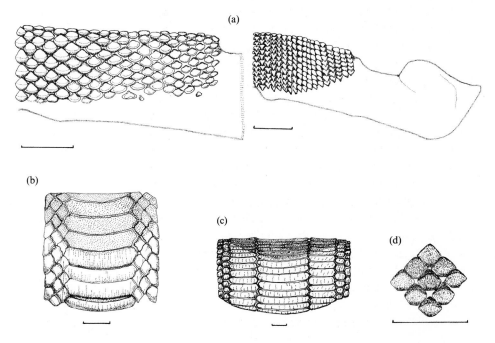

6.3   Teeth in skates and rays. (a) Thornback ray, *Raja clavata*, lower jaw (female on left, male on right). (b) Eagle ray, *Myliobatis aquila*, lower teeth. (c) Cow-nosed ray, *Rhinoptera javanica*, lower teeth. (d) Stingray, *Dasyatis centroura*, lower teeth. (Bar scales 1 cm.)

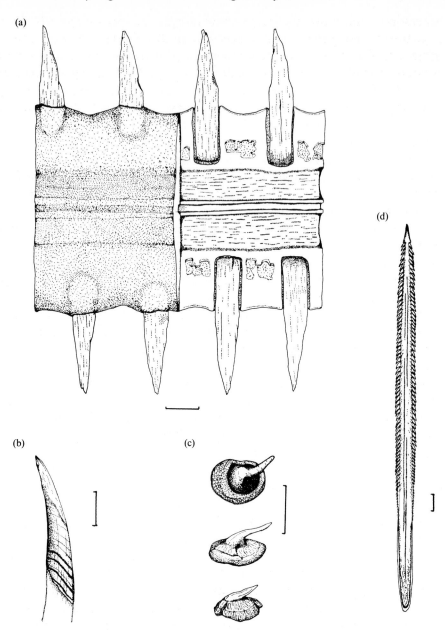

6.4   Modified dermal denticles in cartilaginous fishes. (a) Section of rostrum of
sawfish, *Pristis* sp., dorsal surface removed to show tooth base (right).
(b) Spurdog, *Squalus acanthias*, dorsal fin spine. (c) Thornback ray, *Raja
clavata*, enlarged 'bucklers' from mature female. (d) Stingray, *Dasyatis* sp., tail
spine. (Bar scales 1 cm.)

others have three pointed cusps, the central one being longest (e.g. some dogfishes or catsharks, family Scyliorhinidae), while others are broad and flattened, almost heart-shaped and have faint ridges down their long axis (smooth-hounds, *Mustelus* sp.). Denticles vary a little from place to place on the body of the fish and also suffer from erosion of the tip as the fish ages. They are not regularly replaced (as are the jaw teeth) nor do they grow in size, but are replaced by identically sized denticles after injury. Dermal denticles survive well in archaeological sites but as they are small are usually only recovered in finely sieved samples. They offer a useful means of identification provided appropriate reference material is available. Although most ichthyological text books illustrate the denticles of one or two species of elasmobranch there is no atlas of shark denticles.

The skates, and some sting-rays, have more variable dermal denticles than sharks. Generally the body surface feels rough to the touch, with small denticles the points of which are nearly vertical and are simple spikes, but they are not regularly arranged. However, most have very much larger denticles along the mid-line of the back with a considerable hooked spine on each. In these the basal part of the denticle is appropriately enlarged to provide a firm anchorage. Some skates have very large thorns scattered over the back, and in some cases on the underside. The European roker, or thornback ray, *Raja clavata*, is one such, in which the spine is set in a massive, hard, rounded base – they are known as bucklers and are not infrequently sorted as exotic plant seeds, buttons or other small finds when recovered (fig. 6.4c). The thorny skate, *R. radiata* (known as the starry ray in the British Isles), is another, but this has strong ridges running from the base of the spine towards the tip. Several species of sting-ray (for example, the Indo-Pacific ribbon-tailed ray, *Taeniura lyma*) develop large button-like denticles down the middle of the back as they reach maturity.

The sting-rays (family Dasyatidae) have a long, serrated-edged spine rooted in the tail (fig. 6.4d), which is also present in the families Potamotrygonidae and Myliobatidae. Not infrequently, two or more spines may be present on the same fish, usually when the replacement spine has grown before the oldest one is shed. These also are modified dermal denticles. They have been used extensively as weapons by primitive societies, especially in tropical regions where these sting-rays are abundant. (In live fish the spines are equipped with venom-producing tissue, and wounds from them are extremely painful. Fatalities have occurred in the Pacific Islands when a fisherman has stepped onto a large buried ray and has been stabbed in the thigh or abdomen.)

The teeth in the saw of the sawfishes, *Pristis* sp., are also distinctive specialized denticles (fig. 6.4a). They are deeply embedded in sockets in the cartilage of the rostrum. The teeth are lanceolate, with a convex, leading edge but concave hind edge. They vary in number with the species, and in size with both age and wear.

Somewhat similarly shaped spines, but longer, thinner and curved, occur in the tissues of the dorsal fins in many of the small sharks of the family Squalidae. A very abundant North Atlantic species, the spurdog, *Squalus acanthias*, lives in shallow water in large schools and is easy to catch; similar species occur world-wide in temperate regions. Its fin spines (fig. 6.4b) occur singly in front of each dorsal fin and the enamel covering is very persistent in the archaeological context. There is some evidence that seasonal growth can be detected in the enamel structure (Holden and Meadows, 1962), so that there is the possibility of relating archaeological recovered spines to known ages (and thus size) of fish, but the work on recent sharks is far from conclusive. Spurdog spines are alleged to have been used as awls or chisels in prehistoric Denmark (Noe-Nygaard, 1971). However, it has to be borne in mind that these fin spines show signs of wear at the tip during the life of the shark; not all worn spurdog spines have necessarily been used as artefacts.

Spines similar to those found in the family Squalidae occur in the dorsal fins of the horn-sharks (*Heterodontus* sp.). Some species, such as the Port Jackson shark (*H. portusjacksoni*), occur in relatively shallow water in southern Australian seas. It is possible that such fin spines might be recovered in archaeological sites.

To conclude this discussion of the teeth and dermal structures of elasmobranch fishes, it must be said that they offer the only certain method of identifying to species these cartilage-skeletoned animals. However, there are so many variables involved in their use that they are not the facile tool that casual contact might suggest.

7

THE BASIC ANATOMY OF
BONY FISHES

The fish skeleton

The skeleton of bony fishes differs from that seen in the lampreys, sharks, skates and rays in that it is composed of bone not cartilage. This is immediately obvious to anyone who has prepared fish skeletons (or even eaten fish) for it is possible to cut (or even chew) through the skeletal supports of a skate accidentally, whereas those of a cod will stop the sharpest knife.

For convenience here the fish skeleton can be divided into two main parts, the head skeleton and the axial skeleton (fig. 7.1). The head bones are in turn composed of several systems: firstly, the neurocranium or brain case, which houses and protects the brain and surrounds the olfactory, optic and otic capsules and organs; secondly, the system of bones which are concerned with securing food, principally the bones forming the jaws but also parts of the gill arches (fig. 7.1b); and thirdly, the combined hyal and branchial systems which form the throat of the fish, its gill arches (fig. 7.1c) and gill covers. The axial skeleton is essentially a series of vertebrae forming the vertebral column or spine. At its termination in most fishes is a caudal fin (tail fin), attached by linking bones to several other fins. The main function of the vertebrae is to give firm attachment for the muscles of the body which provide the motive power when swimming. They also give support to the body of the fish and provide a cavity for the viscera, by means of attached ribs in the abdominal region. Further discussion of the parts of the skeleton is deferred, as some systems are of greater significance to the archaeologist then others. The pectoral and pelvic fins and their skeletal supports (fig. 7.1d) form part of the appendicular skeleton, although they are often closely associated with the head.

It is clear that bone is strong so as to serve its several functions, but fish bone is light relative to mammalian bone. This is one of the strategies adopted by fish to reduce their weight in relation to mass so as to conserve energy. (The lightness of fish bone has an advantage to the archaeologist sorting miscellaneous animal bones; the comparative weight of mammal bone quickly leads to a 'feel' for fish bone without detailed examination. Fish bone also often has a fibrous or 'woody' appearance.) Bone is composed of an organic fibrous compound of mainly collagen, hardened with inorganic salts of calcium phosphates and carbonates in the form of apatite. The collagen fibrils run in groups parallel to one another so as to form fibres, and the apa-

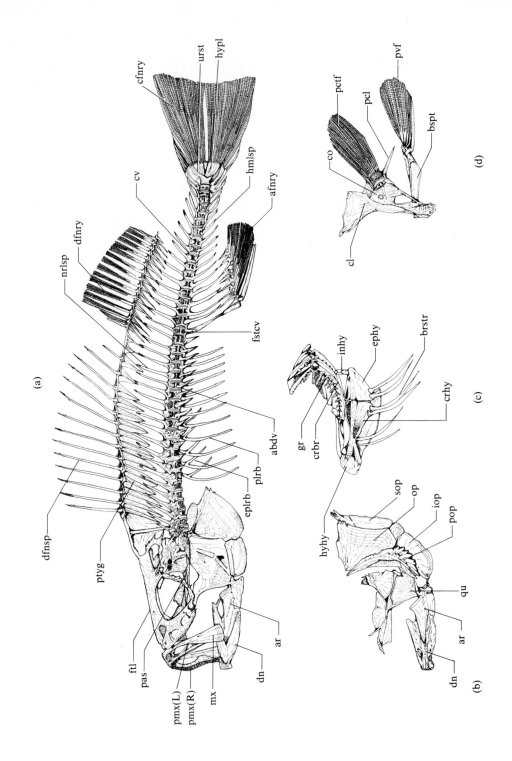

(a)

cfnry
urst
hypl
cv
hmlsp
afnry
dfnry
nrlsp
fstcv
abdv
plrb
eplrb
dfnsp
ptyg
ftl
pas
pmx(L)
pmx(R)
mx
dn
ar

(b)

sop
op
iop
pop
hyhy
qu
ar
dn

(c)

inhy
ephy
brstr
gr
crbr
crhy

(d)

pctf
pvf
co
pcl
bspt
cl

tite crystals lie close to and are firmly attached to the fibrils. The strength of fish bone lies very largely in the presence of internal supporting struts where, because of the concentration of fibres and apatite, support to the thinner bone is provided. Fish vertebrae have a light structure, usually with struts running horizontally to provide support; virtually all are biconcave and their structure is quickly recognized as typical by anyone handling large quantities of mixed vertebrate bone.

Fishes are remarkable in that they have the capacity for sustained although diminishing growth throughout their lives. Thus, members of any one species can be of different sizes depending on their age and environmental conditions, even after sexual maturity (which in mammals and birds causes the cessation of physical growth). This indeterminate growth in fishes has numerous important applications for archaeologists (see chapter 9), and means that the bones are constantly increasing in size (although growth in

7.1   Perch, *Perca fluviatilis*. (a) Whole skeleton (elements of the left side of head and the branchial and pectoral and pelvic fin skeletons removed). (b) Left suspensorium. (c) Branchial skeleton (left side). (d) Left pectoral and pelvic fin skeleton.

List of abbreviations

abdv	abdominal vertebra	hmlsp	haemal spine
afnry	anal fin ray	hyhy	hypohyal
ar	articular	hypl	hypural
brstr	branchiostegal ray	iop	interopercular
bspt	basipterygium	inhy	interhyal
cfnry	caudal fin ray	mx	maxilla
cl	cleithrum		
co	coracoid	nrlsp	neural spine
crbr	ceratobranchial		
crhy	ceratohyal	op	opercular
cv	caudal vertebra		
		pas	parasphenoid
dfnry	dorsal fin ray	pcl	postcleithrum
dfnsp	dorsal fin spine	pctf	pectoral fin
dn	dentary	plrb	pleural rib
		pmx	premaxilla
ephy	epihyal	pop	preopercular
eplrb	epipleural rib	ptyg	pterygiophore
		pvf	pelvic fin
ftl	frontal		
fstcv	first caudal vertebra	qu	quadrate
gr	gill raker	sop	subopercular
		urst	urostyle

fishes is often strongly linked to the seasons). New bone is laid down principally at the edges of existing bone, as can be clearly seen in a flat bone like
the opercular which, when it is held up to the light, shows a succession of light
and dark zones as growth has varied seasonally. As new bone is produced
three-dimensionally, however, so the opercular grows thicker as well as
wider.

The fins of bony fishes are composed of spines and soft (or branched) rays,
in both cases joined by a fin membrane to the neighbouring spines or rays.
Spines, which are straight bony rods usually sharp at the tip, only occur in the
more highly evolved groups (from the Beryciformes onwards in chapter 1)
and may form the first dorsal, or part of the dorsal fin, the first few elements
of the anal fin, and in many fishes the outer element of the pelvic fin. The
remaining elements in the dorsal, anal, pelvic and all the pectoral and caudal
fin rays are branched rays (lepidotrichia), which are segmented along their
length, dumb-bell shaped in cross-section, and usually branched. These are
considered to be modified scales in origin, and each is composed of two, one
from each side of the fish, and joined together in the mid-line (hence the
dumb-bell shape in cross-section). Certain less highly evolved groups such as
carps (order Cypriniformes) and catfishes (order Siluriformes) (see chapter
1) have a spine in the dorsal, anal and pectoral fins in some species, but these
are highly specialized soft rays (lepidotrichia), as is seen in the heavy dorsal
spine of the carp, *Cyprinus carpio*, which has a groove in the mid-line (and in
archaeological material may be split into its component halves).

Head bones

The head bones of bony fishes form an elaborate puzzle of smaller bones,
either articulating with or fused to one another in a highly complex manner
(fig. 7.1). They are very numerous compared with those in mammals and
birds. Their names are thus frequently unique to fishes. However, it is by no
means necessary for the archaeologist to be able to name or recognize more
than the most distinctive bones which can be identified without doubt to
species, or at least species groups. The following account is therefore
empirical and practical. Its bone nomenclature follows Harder (1975). A
wider survey of fish skulls was given by Gregory in 1933.

Jaws and other tooth-bearing bones

The jaws and their articulating bones are paired. The most conservative
across the bony fishes as a whole are the dentaries which, meeting at a
symphysis, anteriorly form the lower jaw (fig. 7.1b). In most groups – the
carps (family Cyprinidae) are a major exception – the upper edge of the
dentary bone bears teeth, although their number and shape are highly
variable. Posteriorly, the dentary is attached to the articular, which typically
has a narrow anterior end which slides into the V-shaped notch of the dentary

to form a firm base for the whole lower jaw. The rear end of the articular is broad, rounded and has a deep articulating notch to which the quadrate attaches to form the joint on which the lower jaw pivots in the vertical plane.

The upper jaws are usually composed of two bones (fig. 7.1a). The edge of the jaw, from the tip of the snout posteriorly, is formed by the premaxilla, typically an elongate bone with teeth on one edge and a complex articulating surface at the anterior end. Many fishes have protrusible jaws and in these there is an ascending process at the anterior end which, sliding forward, allows the upper jaw to swing outwards. The maxilla articulates to the anterior end of the premaxilla but internally. The maxilla lies above the premaxilla to the side of the jaw, acting as a hinge when the jaws are swung open. In many of the more generalized groups of fishes, e.g. Salmoniformes, the maxillae are toothed and are much longer than the premaxillae, but in higher fishes, e.g. Perciformes, the maxillae are toothless and are of comparable length with the premaxillae. In the order Anguilliformes (eels) the premaxillae are greatly reduced in size and fused with the mesethmoid at the anterior end of the neurocranium and each upper jaw is formed solely from the maxilla.

It is fundamental to their survival that fishes should capture food without the species being involved in inextricable overt competition with other fishes. The jaws and their dentition have thus evolved in many often highly characteristic ways. The four (sometimes three) essential bones forming the jaws therefore usually offer the best chance of accurate and quick identification for the archaeologist (see figs. 7.3 and 7.4 for comparison of these bones within one family, the Gadidae, and the related Merlucciidae, which occur frequently in European archaeological sites).

Other toothed bones within the gape of the fish are the paired palatines which lie in the roof of the mouth, usually parallel to the premaxillary but set well in. They are typically toothed. The prevomer, however, is an unpaired bone lying in the mid-line of the roof of the mouth anterior to the palatines and just behind the maxillae or premaxillae. It too has teeth, often conspicuously large teeth, which lie in species-specific patterns (see fig. 7.5 for a selection of prevomer bones in gadiform fishes).

Toothed bones of the pharyngeal region
Within the throat of the fish a series of complexes of cartilage bones forms the outer margins of the buccal cavity. Essentially they are the gill arches (fig. 7.1c), in most fishes four on each side, which can be seen if the gill cover is raised as U-shaped structures with the soft, bright red (because they are blood-filled) gills lying on their outer sides. These gill arches are formed from several elements, the hyobranchial, ceratobranchial and epibranchial, while joining each pair together at the base of the throat are three basibranchials, and beneath the base of the cranium the pharyngobranchial. In most perci-

form fishes there are teeth on the inner (pharyngeal) surfaces of most of these bones. Most notably the gill arches have finger-like gill-rakers, which have teeth along their sides. The gill-rakers are cartilaginous and do not survive in archaeological sites but the minute teeth might do so and be recovered by fine sieving. Unfortunately such teeth are quite indistinctive.

In the dorsal side of the pharynx, associated with the pharyngobranchials, are the suprapharyngeal plates, which are flattened cartilage bones, heavily toothed on the ventral surface. An equivalent set of toothed bones lies on the underside of the pharynx, associated with the basibranchial and either side of its posterior termination; these are the infrapharyngeal plates (fig. 7.6). Although they are cartilage bones, both suprapharyngeals and infra-pharyngeals are heavily calcified and sometimes persist in archaeological sites; they are useful bones for confirming species identity but secondary to jaw bones.

However, in some groups of fishes these upper and lower pharyngeal bones are highly specialized, in response to the diet of the fish, and are much larger, stronger and more distinctive than in the majority of fishes. The strengthening of the infrapharyngeal complex involves fusion of the two plates with part of the basibranchial, but the suprapharyngeals are usually represented by two enlarged bones. These are highly distinctive in the wrasses (family Labridae) and parrotfishes (Scaridae) (fig. 7.6h and i) and within a fish fauna are often species-specific in shape and dentition. Such elaborate dentition is a response to their diet of hard-shelled animals, mainly molluscs in the case of the wrasses and coral in the case of the parrot fishes. Similar but less extreme development of the pharyngeal bones can be seen in African cichlid fishes (Cichlidae) and American sunfishes (Centrarchidae) in which mollusc-feeding groups of species have strong, blunt teeth in compari-son with those which feed on soft-bodied food.

Two important groups of fishes, the suckers (Catostomidae) and the carp family (Cyprinidae) (fig. 7.6e–g) have characteristic and distinctive pharyngeal bones with teeth, but these are different in origin from those

7.2   Cod, *Gadus morhua*, head (exploded view). List of abbreviations:

ar	articular	op	opercular
dn	dentary	pl	palatine
ecp	ectopterygoid	pmx	premaxilla
enp	entopterygoid	pop	preopercular
hyo	hyomandibular	pot	posttemporal
mpt	metapterygoid	qu	quadrate
iop	interopercular	sop	subopercular
la	lacrimal	sor	suborbital series (5)
mx	maxilla	st	supratemporal series (4)
na	nasal	sym	symplectic

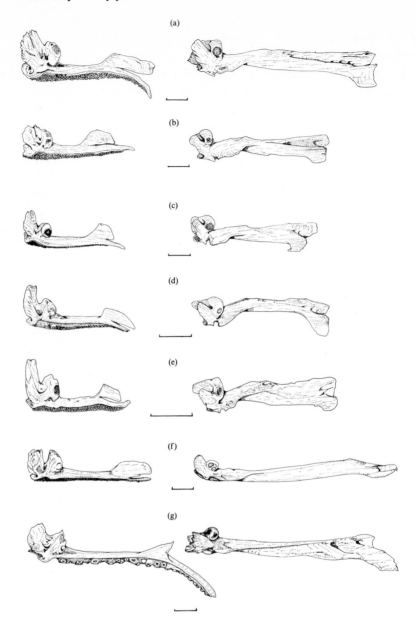

7.3   Premaxilla (left) and maxilla (right) bones of members of the order
Gadiformes. (a) Cod, *Gadus morhua*. (b) Pollack, *Pollachius pollachius*.
(c) Coalfish (pollock in North America), *Pollachius virens*. (d) Whiting,
Merlangius merlangus. (e) Haddock, *Melanogrammus aeglefinus*. (f) Ling,
Molva molva. (g) Hake, *Merluccius merluccius*. (Bar scales 1 cm.)

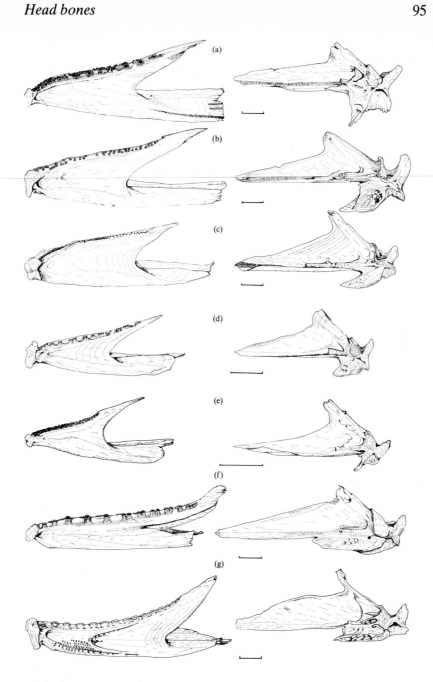

7.4   Dentary (left) and articular (right) bones of members of the order
Gadiformes. (a) Cod, *Gadus morhua*. (b) Pollack, *Pollachius pollachius*.
(c) Coalfish, *Pollachius virens*. (d) Whiting, *Merlangius merlangus*.
(e) Haddock, *Melanogrammus aeglefinus*. (f) Ling, *Molva molva*. (g) Hake,
Merluccius merluccius. (Bar scales 1 cm.)

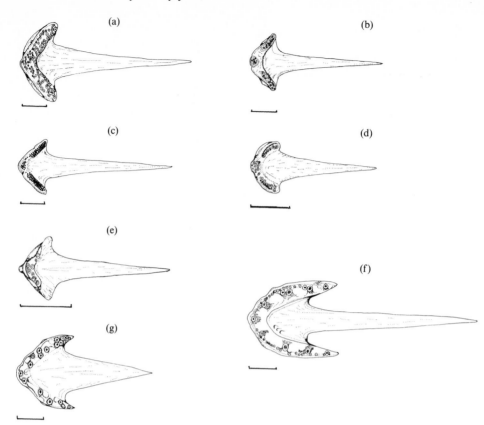

7.5   Prevomer bones of members of the order Gadiformes. (a) Cod, *Gadus morhua*. (b) Pollack, *Pollachius pollachius*. (c) Coalfish, *Pollachius virens*. (d) Whiting, *Merlangius merlangus*. (e) Haddock, *Melanogrammus aeglefinus*. (f) Ling, *Molva molva*. (g) Hake, *Merluccius merluccius*. (Bar scales 1 cm.)

already discussed, being modified from the fifth pair of ceratobranchials. In both groups – also in the smaller, related loaches (Cobitidae) – the pharyngeal bones lie behind the gill arches and frame the gullet entrance. The teeth are attached to the bones in one, two or three rows (Cyprinidae) and have very variable but species-specific shapes and numbers, depending on the preferred diet of each species. The suckers have a single row of numerous, comb tooth-like pharyngeal teeth (fig. 7.6g). These modified ceratobranchials are heavily impregnated with calcium and persist well in archaeological conditions. Even when the teeth are missing (and they are replaced irregularly throughout life), the bone has a characteristic shape and is frequently identifiable to species.

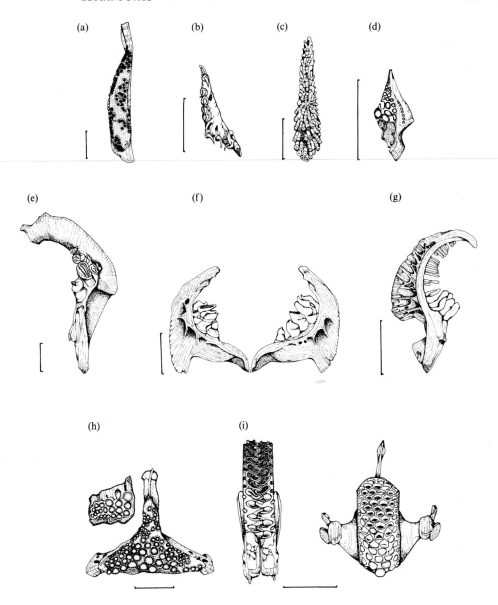

7.6 Pharyngeal bones. With the exception of (f) and (i), only a single lower pharyngeal bone of the pair is illustrated. (a) Cod, *Gadus morhua*. (b) Salmon, *Salmo salar*. (c) Pike, *Esox lucius*. (d) Plaice, *Pleuronectes platessa*. (e) Carp, *Cyprinus carpio*. (f) Roach, *Rutilus rutilus*, both pharyngeals with teeth *in situ*. (g) White sucker, *Catostomus commersoni*. (h) Ballan wrasse, *Labrus bergylta*, lower pharyngeal bone and (left) one of the paired upper pharyngeals. (i) Parrot-fish, *Scarus* sp. (left) fused upper pharyngeal bones, (right) lower bone. (Bar scales 1 cm.)

Cranial bones

The neurocranium provides protection to the brain and the sensory organs and is in effect the skull. A bony fish's skull is composed of a complex of fused and unfused bones, making an extremely complicated structure. In some groups e.g. the order Salmoniformes, some bones of the neurocranium are incompletely formed, remaining in a cartilaginous state and merging together to form a structure in which it is impossible to identify individual elements. (This is one of the reasons why head bones of the family Salmonidae are rarely found in archaeological sites.)

In general therefore the bones of the neurocranium (fig. 7.7) are of relatively little use to the archaeologist, but some do persist in archaeological sites and are distinctive. Most notable of these is the basioccipital (fig. 7.7a), which forms the lower edge in the mid-line of the neurocranium and has an articulating surface for attachment to the first vertebral centrum. Anteriorly, the basioccipital connects to the 'keelbone' of the cranium, the parasphenoid and basisphenoid, which form the base of the cranium and run between and below the eyes as a narrow ridge (fig. 7.7c). The parasphenoid complex is also relatively strong and is usually distinctive at species level.

On the top of the neurocranium lie two large bones which are fairly robust and distinctive. The first is the frontal, which lies above the eyes and brain, forming the roof of the neurocranium. Heavily ridged, and bilaterally symmetrical, it frequently bears a low crest in the mid-line. (In some fishes, e.g. sea-breams (family Sparidae), the frontal bone becomes heavily ossified and swollen in large specimens, producing a massive, bulging bone of puzzling appearance.) The crest on the posterior end of the frontal joins with the frequently high crest of the supraoccipital, which is the second distinctive bone of the neurocranium. The supraoccipital is the most posterior bone on the dorsal surface of the mid-line of the head; it is usually deeply indented to form attachments for the muscles of the trunk (fig. 7.7b).

Bones of the gill covers

The gill covers are seen in most fishes as large bony flaps either side of the rear end of the head; they overlie and protect the delicate tissues of the gills. However, a number of groups have greatly reduced gill openings, e.g. Tetraodontiformes and Anguilliformes (the triggerfishes and others, and the eels) and in these the gill covers are highly modified from the basic form. In most bony fishes the gill covers and other bones concerned with pumping water are identifiable to species or at least species group. They also vary with the major groups of fishes (Hubbs, 1920).

The broad flap of the gill cover (operculum) is composed of four bones. The most posterior in placement is the opercular, which is also usually the largest (figs. 7.9a and 7.9b). Its topmost anterior corner has a moderately conspicuous concave joint socket (where it articulates with the hyomandibu-

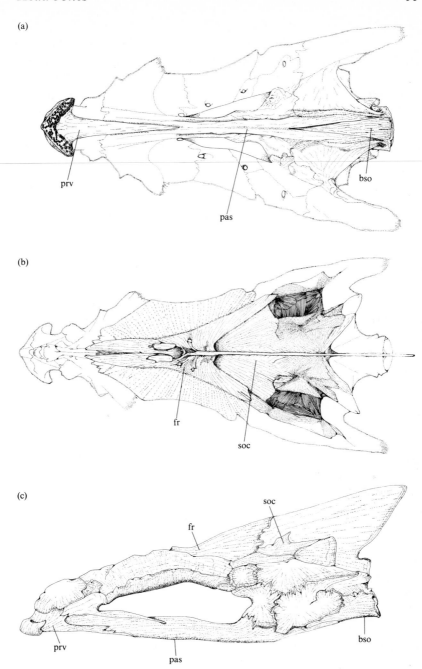

7.7 Cod, *Gadus morhua*, neurocranium. (a) Ventral view shows prevomer (prv), parasphenoid (pas) and basioccipital (bso) highlighted. (b) Dorsal view shows frontal (fr) and supraoccipital (soc) highlighted. (c) Lateral view. (N.B. The margins of neurocranial elements mentioned have complex interdigitating sutures not clear-cut as shown.)

lar) but its anterior edge is hidden beneath the rear edge of the preopercular. The preopercular is frequently heavier and thicker than the opercular, but in a few fishes, for example the siluroid catfishes, it is lacking. In many members of the order Perciformes the preopercular often bears spines or serrations especially on its lower edge; in the tropical Pacific snappers (family Lutjanidae) there is a distinct notch in the front edge of the preopercular which fits around a strong knob on the interopercular. Below the pre-opercular and its upper edge concealed beneath it lies the interopercular, a rather small and usually featureless flattened bony plate. The fourth bone of the opercular series is the subopercular which runs along the lower, rear edge of the opercular; it is usually very thin and relatively featureless.

Anterior to these gill cover bones and partly protected by those that project

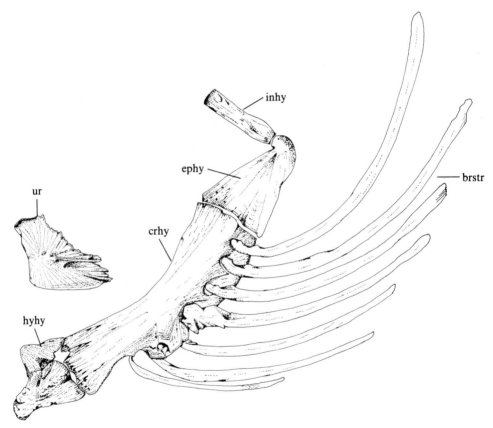

7.8   Cod, *Gadus morhua*. Outer branchial skeleton – left side (gill arches not shown).
Abbreviations

brstr	branchiostegal rays	hyhy	hypohyal
crhy	ceratohyal	inhy	interhyal
ephy	epihyal	ur	urohyal

(a)

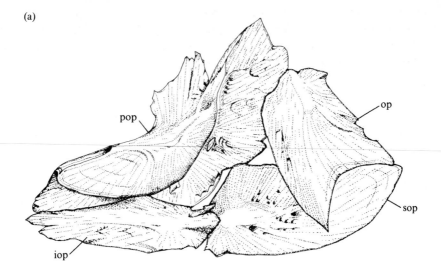

(b)

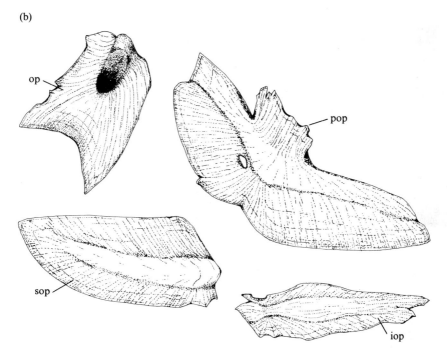

7.9   Cod, *Gadus morhua*. (a) Gill cover bones – left side.
Abbreviations
iop   interopercular   pop   preopercular
op   opercular   sop   subopercular
(b) Opercular bones disarticulated.
Abbreviations as above.

forwards, notably the interopercular, and ventral to the throat of the fish lie a series of bones forming the hyoid arch (fig. 7.8). This arch comprises several rather fragile paired bones, united ventrally by the basihyal, which lies in the mid-line of the throat. Below the basihyal, and also in the mid-line, is a single, more or less triangular, deep bone which lies in the 'throat' of the fish and anteriorly is attached to the hypohyals (see below). This is the urohyal, a bone which is moderately robust and is usually specifically distinct, as has recently been shown from Mediterranean sea-breams (family Sparidae) by Bianchi (1984). A monograph on the urohyal has been prepared covering all systematic groups by Kusaka (1974).

A pair of small hypohyals are joined to the basihyal, one pair on each side, and the much larger elongate ceratohyals are, in turn, joined to them. The third bone in the hyoid arch is the smaller epihyal with the small interhyal on its dorsal surface. The interhyal is connected to the interopercular, thus joining the gill cover series of bones near the base of the skull and giving dorsal rigidity to both structures. The ceratohyal, epihyal and urohyal are the most robust and identifiable of these elements. The ceratohyal is also important in that it is the place of attachment of the slender curved branchiostegal rays which are often found in archaeological sites but are difficult to identify to species on their own. Most fishes have numerous branchiostegal rays which are curved and slender, almost scimitar blade shaped, but eels have strongly curved branchiostegals, and the herring family members (Clupeidae) have rather short flattened branchiostegal rays.

Bones at the junction of head and trunk

Fishes have no neck region and with the exception of the first two or three vertebrae there is very little separating the skeleton of the head from that of the trunk. As if to emphasize this, the shoulder girdle is placed close behind the head and, being caudally attached to the skull, is part of a functional unit with the head. It is appropriate therefore to discuss it here.

Almost all fishes have a pair of pectoral fins which are positioned closely behind the head on each side and are usually rounded in shape. In the lower fishes, e.g. Clupeiformes, Salmoniformes, Cypriniformes and Siluriformes, they are placed low down, close to the belly, but in most other groups they are higher on the sides, even approaching the level of the eyes. It might be parenthetically noted here that there is a similar difference in the position of the pelvic fins: in the groups noted above, the pelvic fins are placed posteriorly on the belly; in most others, especially the Perciformes, they are sited anteriorly and close to the head, and even joined to the pectoral girdle.

The pectoral fins are supported by a pectoral or 'shoulder' girdle (fig. 7.10). The actual fin is supported on a series of small radials which in turn articulate with a scapula (or hypercoracoid) and also the larger coracoid (or hypocoracoid). The scapula and coracoid in turn fasten to the much larger, stronger and distinctive cleithrum, usually a larger curved bone (often the largest single bone in a fish) with a hollow underside (fig. 7.10). On the dorsal surface the cleithrum is firmly linked by ligaments to the smaller, elongate supracleithrum, and this in turn is similarly linked to the distinctively forked posttemporal bone. The posttemporal is fastened firmly to the back of the neurocranium. A long slender postcleithrum is attached internally to the cleithrum and extends ventrally. All these bones are present on both sides of the body. The most readily recognized are the cleithrum, supracleithrum and posttemporal, all of which are strong and are usually identifiable to species.

A series of bones connects the neurocranium and the four principal jaw bones. The largest and most characteristic bone in this series is the hyomandibular. It lies beneath and anterior to the preopercular. The hyomandibular has a very complex appearance consisting of ridges, articulating surfaces and usually at least one elongate hollow process. To its ventral margin is attached

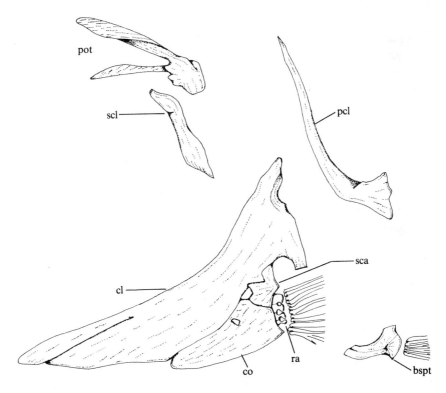

7.10   Pectoral and pelvic skeleton of a gadoid fish.
Abbreviations

bspt	basipterygium	pot	posttemporal
cl	cleithrum	ra	radials
co	coracoid	sca	scapula
pcl	postcleithrum	scl	supracleithrum

the symplectic, typically a roughly triangular flattened bone with few characteristic features.

The hyomandibular and symplectic are attached to the quadrate and metapterygoid. The former articulates with the articular while the metapterygoid is linked anteriorly to the palatine via the entopterygoid. Both the metapterygoid and the entopterygoid are usually fragile, thin, slightly dished bones with few diagnostic features. Lying ventrally and parallel to the entopterygoid is the more robust and highly characteristic ectopterygoid. It should be noted that the nomenclature of the various pterygoid bones is very confusing. The most common synonymy is 'pterygoid' for ectopterygoid and 'mesopterygoid' or 'endopterygoid' for entopterygoid.

Vertebral column

The spine of a fish is composed of a number (compared with the higher vertebrates usually a large number) of segments, the vertebrae. Because fishes have no neck there is very little differentiation between the vertebrae from head to tail, nothing comparable to that in the higher vertebrates. However, there is a difference between each of the vertebrae along the spine even if in places the differences are slight.

Fish vertebrae are almost always amphicoelous, i.e. both articulating surfaces are concave. The only exception to this is the gar-pike family Lepisosteidae (see p. 17), in which the ends of the centra are slightly convex, i.e. curved outwards (fig. 7.11). Some eels are said to have flat-surfaced vertebrae.

The vertebral column is distinguished into three regions by the shape and situation of bony processes on the centra (fig. 7.12). Some authors, e.g. G. Desse (1984), name these employing the nomenclature used for higher vertebrates (cervical, thoracic, post-thoracic or abdominal) but such termin-

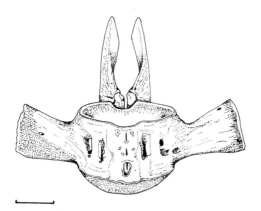

7.11   Longnose gar, *Lepisosteus osseus*, vertebra to show convex anterior articulating surface in this group. Viewed ventrally. (Bar scale 1 cm.)

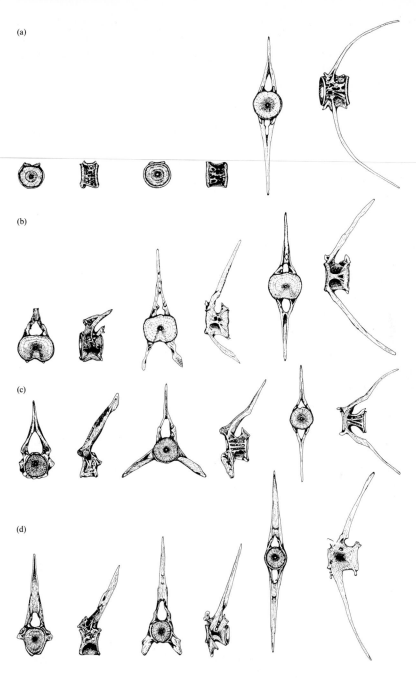

7.12 Variation in teleostean vertebrae both between representatives of four orders (Salmoniformes, Cypriniformes, Gadiformes and Perciformes) and along the vertebral column (from left to right): anterior abdominal, posterior abdominal and caudal vertebrae. (a) Trout, *Salmo trutta*. (b) Carp, *Cyprinus carpio*. (c) Whiting, *Merlangius merlangus*. (d) Sea-bream, *Pagrus pagrus*.

ology is misleading as it implies correlation with the clear-cut divisions of the mammalian vertebral column. The terminology adopted here recognizes three regions only, anterior abdominal (characterized by the lack of rib attachments), abdominal (characterized by the presence of transverse processes to which the ribs are attached, and an open haemal canal), and caudal or tail (in which the haemal canal is closed and forms a haemal spine).

Close behind the head in most fishes the first two centra are strongly compressed and flattened, usually bearing a strong neural spine on their upper surface. These have been called the 'atlas' and 'axis' (although they are not homologous to these vertebrae in mammals, as fishes do not turn their heads in any direction and these terms are best avoid for fishes) and are highly modified for attachment of the anterior ends of the great blocks of swimming muscle that run along the back. These vertebrae are attached by strong ligaments to the posterior surface of the basioccipital. In several groups of fishes, most importantly the Cypriniformes and Siluriformes, the first three vertebrae are modified and fused together and with the base of the cranium. The fusion takes place as the young fish grows and separated vertebrae may be encountered. This fused complex is highly diagnostic for species identification.

In many fishes the anterior abdominal vertebrae suceeding the first two are also compressed but the length of each of the next two or three successive centra increases with their distance from the head. These anterior centra have rounded undersides and the transverse processes (bony struts arising from the centrum) are placed high up on the body of the centrum, often well above the middle of the side. Within one fish the abdominal vertebrae are of more or less uniform length. All have strong double neural spines (neurapophyses) or cavities for their support, which immediately above the centrum make an arch through which the spinal cord passes. Laterally, transverse processes project from each side of the centrum, high up the sides anteriorly, but lower down the body of the centrum further back. In some groups, e.g. pikes (Esocidae), these transverse processes are not always fused to the centrum. These transverse processes, or zygapophyses, form the base for the attachment of the ribs. Ventrally, the centra have a deep hollow in the midline, while further back hollows develop either side of this so that in many species the underside of the abdominal centrum is almost hollow, with two strong bony septa running lengthwise. In members of the cod order Gadiformes, these hollows are relatively large and involve the transverse processes, which are flattened and deeply concave. Into these are fitted extensions of the gas bladder, which is very complex in these fishes (often forming a sound-producing organ). The underside of the abdominal centrum in gadoid fishes is not consistently bilaterally symmetrical. In the ultimate abdominal vertebra the transverse processes are directed strongly downward but are not fused or joined together by a bony connection.

The first caudal vertebra is therefore easily distinguished by the presence of a haemal arch formed either by a bony strut between the ventrally directed transverse processes or by their fusion to form an arch. Through this arch the main axial blood vessels run and, of course, receive protection from the bony ventral walls of the centra. On the dorsal surface of the caudal vertebrae the neural spine is well developed and continues the series of neural spines from the abdominal vertebrae. In general, it is often possible to distinguish the neural spine from the haemal spine in an isolated vertebra because the haemapophyses, on which the haemal spine is based, originate in advance of the vertical from the origin of the neurapophyses which form the base of the neural spine. However, this does not apply to the more posterior caudal vertebrae.

In addition to the neural and haemal spines, which are strongly developed above and below the caudal vertebrae, there are a number of protuberant spines which are more or less well developed according to the group of fishes involved. Virtually all fishes have them but they are most strongly developed in species which are active swimmers. At the front of the centrum on the dorsal surface a pair of prezygapophyses arise and project forwards and upwards. Posteriorly and again on the dorsal surface a pair of zygapophyses project upwards and backwards. The prezygapophyses are joined by strong ligaments to the postzygapophyses on the preceding vertebra. Many fishes also have a pair of zygapophyses on the anterior ventral side of the vertebrae, which join onto similar processes on the rear edge of the vertebra in front. In actively swimming fishes such as mackerel, family Scombridae, these projections form a closely opposed joint (fig. 7.13a), which adds strength to the junction of the two vertebrae and rigidity in the dorso-ventral plane (fishes cannot flex their tails up and down in the manner of whales and dolphins). Their development as major features of the vertebrae seems to reflect a shared life style rather than relationship, for in shads, family Clupeidae, they are also well developed. These are also actively swimming fishes.

This specialization is most pronounced in the tuna or tunnies, family Scombridae, and the billfishes (swordfish, marlin and sailfish), families Xiphiidae and Istiophoridae, which are the most powerful swimmers of all fishes. In these fishes the posterior section of the caudal vertebral column is virtually rigid as a result of the development of massive prezygapophyses above and below the centrum, which lock either side of the neural and haemal spines, which are in turn massively developed (fig. 7.13b). These fishes have a high aspect ratio tail fin of wide spread, which requires a rigid base as the massive body muscles force it from side to side.

In addition to the ligamentary junction between the zygapophyses of the vertebra, the anterior and posterior faces of the centra are opposed to one another and are loosely joined by ligaments along their rims. The space between one centrum and the next is filled by a watery jelly which is incompressible and serves as a fluid ball within the concavities of the ends of the centra. This permits virtually friction-free movement within the limits allowed by the ligaments on the sides of the centra. In fishes (with the exception of the gar pikes *Lepisosteus* spp.) there is no true articulation between one vertebra and the next, such as one sees in mammals and birds.

As has already been noted, fishes generally have more vertebrae than most other vertebrates, snakes excepted. In virtually all bony fishes there is one vertebra for each body segment (monospondyli). (In sharks a number of species have two vertebrae per body segment in the tail [diplospondyli].) Within narrow limits the number of vertebrae is constant throughout life after the larval stage but there is always some variation in the number for each species. Vertebral numbers in fishes have therefore to be expressed as a range e.g. in cod, *Gadus morhua*, there are 49–53 vertebrae (Wheeler, 1969). The number of vertebrae in fishes is affected by, among other factors, the temperature at which the egg develops. Generally speaking, cod hatched in the cold waters of the Arctic will tend to have more vertebrae than those from the warmer southern extremity of the species' range.

As a very broad generalization the more highly placed fishes in the phylogenetic order have fewer vertebrae. There is a tendency to reduction in numbers of vertebrae in the more specialized fishes. Thus, ranges for various groups lie in the approximate regions of Salmoniformes *c.* 50–60, Clupeiformes 45–65, Cypriniformes 25–50, Gadiformes 55–75, Perciformes 23–40, Tetraodontiformes 15–17. This has some application in identification because elongate vertebral centra tend to belong to the 'higher' orders with few vertebrae, and narrow compressed vertebrae are often from 'lower' orders with numerous vertebrae. This is a generality to which there are many exceptions, for example fishes with elongate bodies e.g. the ling, *Molva molva*, have considerably more vertebrae than short-bodies relatives within the same family (Gadidae). A survey of vertebral numbers and variation across a wide range of European marine fishes was attempted by Ford (1937) and more successfully by Clothier (1950) for Californian sea fishes. Another general rule is that the spinal foramen which pierces the centra of some fishes (the remains of the notochord in larval fishes) is large in less highly evolved groups, e.g. Salmoniformes and Clupeiformes, but is absent in most highly specialized groups.

For the archaeologist vertebrae often present a problem. Firstly, they are almost always the most numerous fish remains recovered from sites. Secondly, they are variable within the species depending on their position in the vertebral column. Thirdly, many of their distinctive features relate to often fragile protuberances rising from the centrum, neural and haemal spines, and zygapophyses, which are often damaged in the soil or midden, during recovery, or in sorting. It is therefore more common for the archaeologist to attempt to identify vertebral centra than whole vertebrae. Despite these problems it is possible to identify most vertebral centra to species with the aid of a suitable reference collection. The texture of the bone sometimes proves to be diagnostic to species or at least species-group. Large size is also of occasional assistance. The position of ridges or foramina on the sides of the centrum is often significant, as are the positions of any zygapophyses remaining on the centrum. In practice positive identification increases with the degree of completeness of the vertebra, and is enhanced by an identification strategy of studying first the jaw bones or other bones which are highly characteristic, then turning to vertebrae with the knowledge of the presence of the species already proved to be represented.

Recently Desse and his co-workers have explored the deposition of calcium in the collagen fibrils of vertebrae (G. Desse, 1984; Desse and du Buit, 1971; Desse and Desse, 1976) using radiographs. Their results suggest that it is possible to identify isolated vertebral centra to species (in the presence of a collection of comparative radiographs). In view of the high cost of radiography it is doubtful whether it is a practical means of routine identification. A similar conclusion might be drawn from the study of Meunier (1984), who demonstrated by histological methods the differences between the cellular bone in trout, *Salmo trutta*, vertebrae and the acellular bone in pike, *Esox lucius*, vertebrae. As the two species are in normal circumstances distinguishable by macroscopic inspection, the use of histology is of more academic than practical application.

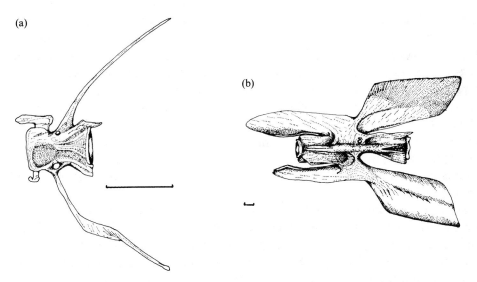

7.13   Vertebrae in active powerful-swimming fishes, showing development of the zygapophyses, which interlock with adjacent vertebral centra to give rigidity to the axial skeleton. (a) Mackerel, *Scomber scombrus*. (b) Marlin, *Makaira* sp., in which the articulation is so close that the tail is rigid. (Bar scales 1 cm.)

Fin skeletons

In most fishes the vertebral column ends at the caudal or tail fin, which is the principal motive power for the swimming fish. Relatively few fishes have no caudal fin and most of these are eels (order Anguilliformes) or eel-like fishes (families Halosauridae, Notacanthidae, Macruoridae) which have adopted a serpentine swimming mode. In sharks the vertebral column continues up the tail fin in a series of ever smaller centra; this gives sharks their characteristic tail shape with the upper lobe longer and better developed than the lower tail fin lobe. This is a heterocercal tail (fig. 7.14a). A few primitive bony fishes (sturgeons, Acipenseridae, gars, Lepisosteidae, and the bowfin, Amiidae) have heteroceral tails, but virtually all others have a tail in which the vertebrae do not noticeably run into the upper lobe. These are homocercal tails (fig. 7.14b).

In the cod family, Gadidae, the vertebrae continue along the body, decreasing in size and with the last centrum modified slightly and rather asymmetrical. The tail fin rays are attached directly to the neural and haemal spines by ligamentary connections. The modified last centrum ends in two small processes to which the lepidotrichia (rays) of the fin are attached.

In virtually all other fishes the skeleton of the homocercal tail is asymmetric, even though externally the fin seems symmetric (fig. 7.14b). In these the last three vertebrae are increasingly modified. The third from last and the penultimate have greatly strengthened neural and particularly haemal spines. The last centrum is turned obliquely dorsal and the neural spine is strengthened and follows this oblique direction. Along its ventral surface a series of broad flattened body plates (the hypurals) are attached; these form the posterior end of the body and to them are attached the lepidotrichia or fin rays. On the dorsal surface of the last vertebra a series of smaller epurals joins the neural arch to form the upper edge of the tail and articulates with the upper tail fin rays. The whole structure is referred to as the urostyle or more loosely as the hypural plate (although only in sticklebacks, family Gasterosteidae, is a single hypural plate present). Because the hypural region is under stress when the fish swims, the bones are strong and well calcified and are often persistent in archaeological material. However, they are not often identifiable to species, although it is relatively easy to recognize the elements including the last vertebrae, which, being single structures in the fish, can permit assessment of minimum numbers of individuals.

The other mid-line or vertical fins comprise one or more dorsal fins on the back and one to two anal fins under the body posterior to the vent. As already noted, the front elements of both dorsal and anal fins may be composed of sharply pointed strong spines. In the dorsal fin series, many fishes of the order Perciformes have a separate spiny fin; such fins are uncommon ventrally, where there are usually three, sometimes two spines (rarely as many as six in the anal fin). The spines and the soft rays form the fins and are joined to one another by the fin membrane. They are supported by means of a simple joint and ligaments to a pterygiophore, a slender, slightly flattened bone which lies in the median septum and is bound by ligaments to the neural spine, if it is a dorsal fin ray or spine, or to the haemal spine in the case of an anal fin ray element (fig. 7.15d). Most fishes with a long dorsal fin have a single flattened pterygiophore per neural spine, and a single fin spine at the distal end of the pterygiophore. A ratio of two or three pterygiophores per neural spine is normal for the dorsal soft rays, which usually equal the pterygiophores in number. In some fishes, e.g. triggerfishes, family Balistidae, there may be four pterygiophores per neural spine posteriorly.

In the anal fin a more or less similar ratio obtains, anteriorly one pterygiophore per haemal spine, posteriorly two or three. However, the first

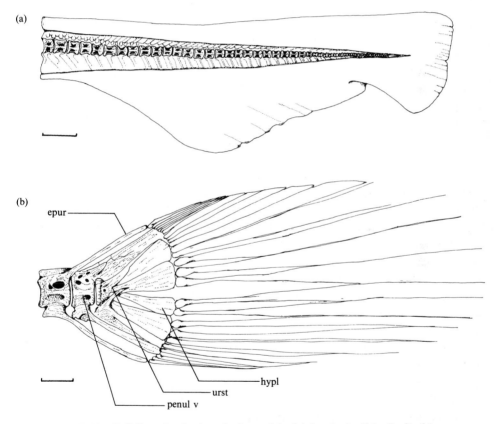

7.14   Tail fins of a shark and a bony fish. (a) Sandy dogfish, *Scyliorhinus canicula*. (b) Grouper, *Epinephelus itajara* (fin rays in outline only). (Bar scale 1 cm.)
Abbreviations

epur	epural	penul v	penultimate vertebra
hypl	hypural	urst	urostyle

anal pterygiophores are frequently fused together and strongly bonded to the first haemal spines. Not infrequently they are massive, either to support strong anterior anal spines, as in the drums, family Sciaenidae, or to provide support to the posterior region of the abdominal cavity in deep-bodied fishes, such as the flatfishes, family Pleuronectidae and others, and John Dory, family Zeidae.

Pterygiophores are occasionally found with an inexplicable finger-nail sized spherical swelling at mid-point. Similar swellings may be found in neural and haemal spines, sometimes both spines belonging to the same vertebra. The cause of the condition is unexplained. It is usually termed hyperosteosis, and at least where it occurs in the first anal pterygiophores they have been called 'Tilly-bones' or 'mouse bones', the latter because of their similarity to a mouse, the fin spine representing the tail. Although bones showing hyperosteosis appear to be pathological, there are some fishes, e.g. the batfishes, *Platax* spp., in which their occurrence is so frequent that it appears to be normal (fig. 7.15b). Some sea-breams, family Sparidae, have the frontal and supraoccipital bones similarly enlarged, and in the haddock, *Melanogrammus aeglefinus*, the cleithrum and posttemporal bones are regularly swollen and massively enlarged. This form of hyperosteosis, if it is comparable to the other, appears to be associated with sexual maturity and normal growth.

Most fishes have two pairs of paired fins, the pectorals, which, because of their close association with the head skeleton, have been discussed earlier, and the pelvics or ventral fins. In the least highly evolved orders, e.g. Clupeiformes, Salmoniformes, the pelvics are placed posteriorly along the belly; in the Perciformes and other more specialized groups the pelvic fins are well forward and are attached to the lower edge of the pectoral girdle (the lower cleithrum). Pelvic fins are relatively simple in form in the Perciformes, typically having a single spine on the outer edge and five branched rays. But there are many variations: the rabbitfishes, family Siganidae, have two spines one on each side of the fin and branched rays between, and blennies, family Blenniidae, have slender two-rayed pelvic fins, for example, and a number of perciform fishes have no pelvic spines. In the less evolved fish orders, herrings (Clupeiformes), salmons (Salmoniformes) and carps (Cypriniformes), there are no spines in the pelvic fins.

Internally the pelvic fins of the teleosts are supported by a pair of elongate, tapering bones, the basipterygia (see figs. 7.1d and 7.10). At its anterior end the basipterygium is bound by ligaments to the cleithrum; at its distal end the fin spine and lepidotrichia articulate directly (fig. 7.1d). The basipterygium is a moderately strong bone with a distinctive shape.

Fin rays and fin spines are in general not easy to identify. When recovered they are usually fragmentary and relatively featureless. However, there are some exceptions. The pectoral and dorsal fin spines of some members of the carp family (Cyprinidae) and many catfishes (notably Clariidae and Mochokidae in northern African sites) are identifiable (fig. 7.15a, b). (These, paradoxically, are not true spines but are thickened lepidotrichia or rays.) The rough-edged pelvic and dorsal spines (fig. 7.15c) of the stickleback, *Gasterosteus aculeatus*, are also highly distinctive and survive in Pleistocene and early Holocene sites in Europe and North America. Massive spines like the first dorsal spine of the triggerfishes, family Balistidae, should also survive, as do the strongly modified fused basipterygia of these fishes (Leach, 1986).

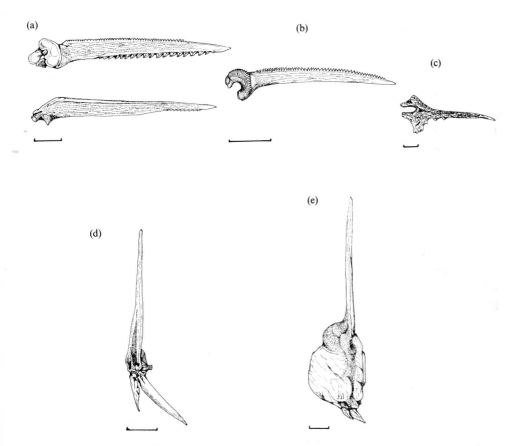

7.15   Fin spines in bony fishes. (a) Nilotic catfish, *Synodontis* sp., pectoral fin spines (two views). (b) Catfish, *Clarias lazera*, pelvic fin spine. (c) Three-spined stickleback, *Gasterosteus aculeatus*, pectoral fin spine. (Bar scale 1 mm.) (d) Sea-bream, *Pagrus pagrus*, first anal fin spines articulating with first inter-haemal bone. (e) Batfish, *Platax* sp., first anal fin spines and interhaemal bone showing hyperosteosis to form the so-called 'Tilly-bone' or 'mouse bone'. (Bar scale 1 cm except where otherwise stated.)

Otoliths

The otoliths or ear-stones develop within the inner ears of fishes, principally bony fishes, for they are not well formed in lampreys or sharks and their relatives. The inner ears of fishes are organs both of hearing and of balance. They are paired, rather delicate structures which lie inside the base of the neuro-cranium towards the back and side, each side. Each inner ear comprises three semicircular canals (the labyrinth), set at right angles to one another (therefore lying in different planes), and joining ventrally in a sac (the utriculus) which has a double-sided pocket (the succulus), from which the second pocket (the lagena) leads. It is these sac-like pockets which contain the otoliths, the sagitta (in the sacculus), the lapillus (in the utriculus) and the asteriscus (in the lagena). In most bony fishes the sagitta is the largest of the otoliths and it is this which is usually intended by references to the 'otolith' in the fisheries literature on ageing and growth. In the carps and suckers (Cypriniformes), the characins (Characiformes) and the catfishes (Siluriformes) the sagitta is comparatively small but long and thin while the asteriscus is large in the first two groups and the lapillus is large in the catfishes. These fishes have an elaborate connecting series of ligaments and small bones from the inner ear which are in close contact with the gas bladder. As a result, they have sensitive hearing.

Otoliths are formed from calcium carbonate deposited from the endo-lymphatic fluid of the labyrinth. In bony fishes the calcium carbonate is in the form of aragonite (as it is in sharks and rays also, but the sturgeons have the unstable vaterite form of calcium carbonate), with organic layers in a regular formation. In common with most of the hard structures of fishes the otoliths increase in size throughout the life of the fish.

It has long been known that fishes from temperate waters reflect the annual change in seasons by differences in growth from one season to another; faster growth occurs in spring and summer than in winter, a change which is clearly related to availability of food and temperature variation. Seasonal changes of this kind are clearly seen in the sagitta as bursts of growth follow the abundance of food, although in mature fishes the metabolic demands on calcium during the breeding season are also reflected in the otoliths by a diminution of growth. With otoliths, however, there does not seem to be the withdrawal of calcium that happens with bones and scales to satisfy the requirements of reproduction, and otoliths continue to grow throughout life even though calcium carbonate deposition is slowed by scarcity of food or reproductive stress seasonally.

The annual and seasonal nature of growth in otoliths has resulted in their becoming a valuable source of information on the growth and thus the age of bony fishes and even the season of capture. In temperate regions seasonal variation in growth of the otolith is very marked. In tropical marine fishes there are no winter checks in the deposition of aragonite in the otolith and

spawning is reflected by several changes in growth during the year (reproduction in many tropical fishes is often intermittent throughout the year). In
both groups there is a sequential periodicity of tissue deposition which is
related to a daily growth period, and a lunar monthly period. Within this
28-day cycle there is a fortnightly pattern which suggests that lunar influence
probably exerted through tidal cycles governs growth. Detailed studies on
otolith growth in both temperate and tropical fishes were made by Pannella
(1971, 1974). Since Pannella's pioneering studies many authors have
explored the phenomenon of daily growth as recorded in otoliths, e.g.
Steffensen (1980) for cod, *Gadus morhua*, Brothers *et al.* (1976) on larval and
adult fishes, and Taubert and Coble (1977) in several freshwater fishes.

The applications of an apparently exact means of establishing season of
capture for archaeological remains will be obvious and are explored in a later
chapter. However, it has to be said that, since otoliths are composed of
calcium carbonate, they do not survive well in archaeological sites unless they
are fortuitously alkaline or neutral in pH.

It is paradoxical that early fossil otoliths are well known to palaeontologists
and many deductions of Oligocene and Miocene ichthyofaunal assemblages
(see, for example, Nolf, 1976) are based on otoliths. This has generated a
wealth of literature concerning recent fish otoliths and comparing them with
fossil otoliths. It has been summarized by Weiler (1968), the literature being
updated from that date by Huyghebaert and Nolf (1979), although many
earlier studies exist.

Most bony fishes have well-developed sagittae, the only major exceptions
being the three ostariophysan orders, Cypriniformes, Characiformes and
Siluriformes, in which the sagitta is small but the asteriscus is large in
Cypriniformes and Characiformes, and the lapillus is the largest in most
Siluriformes. The sagitta of most fishes is oval in shape but more pointed at
one end, concave on the medial side and convex on the lateral (or outer) side.
The two sagitta otoliths lie with the pointed end (the rostrum) towards the
snout of the fish.

The sagitta is conspicuously sculptured along its outer sides. Along the
lateral (convex surface) face is a shallow, often curved, furrow, the sulcus
acusticus, which runs from the rostrum posteriorly nearly to the rear end of
the otolith (fig. 7.16). The degree of sculpturing, the path of the sulcus
acusticus, and most importantly the general shape of the sagitta produce a
feature which is species-specific for identification purposes (fig. 7.17).

Across the range of bony fishes the otoliths are not equally well developed
in all groups, although most have a reasonably large sagitta in relation to their
size. In the salmon and its relatives (order Salmoniformes) and the mackerels
and tunas (family Scombridae) the otoliths are poorly developed and small;
their survival in archaeological contexts would be unlikely. In contrast, the
sagitta in the drums and croakers (family Sciaenidae) is comparatively

(a)   (b)

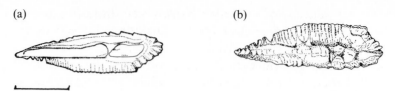

7.16   Sagittal otolith of whiting, *Merlangius merlangus*. (a) Inner surface.
(b) Outer surface. (Bar scale 1 cm.)

7.17   Sagittal otoliths of modern haddock, *Melanogrammus aeglefinus* (top
row), saithe, *Pollachius virens* (middle row), and pollack, *Pollachius pollachius*
(bottom row). Two pairs for each species are shown. Note the variation in form
between medium and large otoliths within the species. (Photographs by
R. Hunter; copyright Department of Biology, University of York.)

massive and so deep that the median surface is partly convex and the sulcus
acusticus is elaborately curved.

A small number of aberrant otoliths occur in most species. They may be
formed from irregular transparent crystals. Furthermore, the two otoliths
from one fish do not always show the same incremental growth rings.

Scales
Most bony fishes have scales covering their bodies in a sheet of overlapping
plates, a substantial part of the lower, more posterior, scale being covered by
the hind part of the scale in front. Their appearance is similar to the tiles or

shingles on a house roof, but they improve on them in function by being
fastened flexibly so that their free edges move as the fish flexes its body in
swimming.

Structurally, there are two types of bony fish scales, ganoid or rhombic
(diamond-shaped) such as are found in a few early fishes, garpikes
(*Lepisosteus*), bichirs (*Polypterus*) and sturgeons (*Acipenser*), and round
scales (or bony-ridge scales) such as are found in most bony fishes.

Ganoid scales are distinguished by having a layer of ganoine covering the
lower layers of cosmine and isopedine. The ganoine is similar to enamel in
many ways and, like enamel, is hard and shiny. These scales are also usually
rhombic or diamond-shaped when viewed singly (fig. 7.18b) and in fishes like
the North American garpikes and the tropical African bichirs give the
appearance of a regularly arranged covering like a coat of mail. Individually,
as in the material recovered from archaeological sites, they can be identified
by the hard shiny ganoine layer, their rhombic shape and (except in the
sturgeons) by the presence of a peg-like process on the dorsal edge, which fits
into the lower side of the scale diagonally above and forward.

In sturgeons these rhomboid scales lie in five regular rows running from
head to tail; they are large, and are often referred to as scutes. Each has a
crest along the mid-line and the surface is roughened, in large specimens with
a honey-comb texture (fig. 7.18a). Only the scutes in the mid-line of the back
are symmetrical. These highly characteristic scales survive well as archaeological material, as they do in Pleistocene deposits.

Round scales, or bony-ridge scales, are found in all those bony fishes which
have scales, even though they are sometimes highly modified in form.
Typically, they are thin and translucent, with the outer surface marked with
low ridges, which can be seen with a lens. The surface of the scale is a mineralized 'bony' or hyalodentine layer, overlying layers of criss-crossing mineralized collagen fibres (isopedine). Growth in these scales takes place both on
the outer surface and from beneath and thus at the edges as well; as most
growth takes place in the covered portion of the scale, the exposed edge is
liable to wear and other damage. The continued growth of fishes through
their lives results in continuing addition to the borders of the scale; the
additions appear as low ridges separated from one another by shallow
depressions, continuous round most of the scale. These are termed circuli or
bony ridges. As the growth of the scales is governed by the calcium
metabolism of the fish, periods of rich feeding (often late spring and summer
in temperate waters) result in fast growth and widely spaced circuli, and lean
seasons result in the circuli being grouped closely together. Spawning also
produces calcium stress and leaves a mark on the scales, in salmonids even
resulting in the exposed edge of the scale receding in size and losing the detail
of surface sculpturing because of the withdrawal of calcium. It follows as a
result that seasonal information can be gleaned from the study of fish scales,

and ageing fishes from scales (especially freshwater species) is a widely practised fishery management procedure. Several stages in the fish's life history
can be read from its scales including spawning marks and annual cycles or
year marks (annuli). Other details of the structure of a scale are that the focus
is more or less central and that in many scales grooves (radii) radiate from the
focus to the margin (primary radii) and these are sometimes intermediate
radii which, however, do not reach as far as the focus (secondary radii).

When a scale is lost by the fish as a result of injury, it is quickly replaced by
a new scale, of the same size as the original, which then continues to grow at
the same rate as all the other scales. Such a replacement scale can be recognized by the featureless appearance of the centre of the scale (which looks
'fuzzy' in enlargement), although the later growth shows normal circuli and
annuli.

There are, however, many variations in shape and structure in fish scales.
Two primary divisions help in recognition. Ctenoid scales have fine teeth in
a band on the exposed edge of the scales. These are detectable on the fish by
the rough, sand-papery feel of the body, if the finger is run from tail to head
of the fish. The second major type are cycloid scales, which have a smooth
posterior margin with circuli clearly visible in the exposed part of the scale.
Broadly speaking ctenoid scales occur only in the higher fishes (e.g.
Beryciformes, Perciformes and Pleuronectiformes), but many of the members of these orders have cycloid scales, and in some species, for example the
European dab, *Limanda limanda*, there are ctenoid scales on the eyed side
and cycloid scales on the blind side of the fish. Cycloid scales are only found
in the lower groups of bony fishes (up to Cyprinodontiformes in chapter 2)
although some, especially some catfishes, have strikingly modified
squamation.

Scales of both types offer the opportunity for identification to family or
even species level but with a few exceptions they are often not easily distinguished one from another within the family. Round scales do not often
survive well in archaeological contexts, except where there are special factors
involved in preservation and particularly in recovery – their fragility means
they require very special handling. In general, ctenoid scales seem to be more
resistant than cycloid scales and they often survive more or less entire.
Cycloid scales, however, frequently suffer loss of the outer margin and tend
to separate into discrete layers. However, with the help of an adequate reference collection, round scales can be identified to species.

Round or bony-ridge scales are often modified to form massive and very
distinctive skin structure which are quite dissimilar to normal scales. Several
families of South American catfishes have the body encased in heavy scaly
plates (families Loricariidae and Callichthyidae) or with bony plates with
spines (fig. 7.18c) on part of the body (family Doradidae). Enlarged scales,
often with spines, are a feature in a number of different groups of fish, for

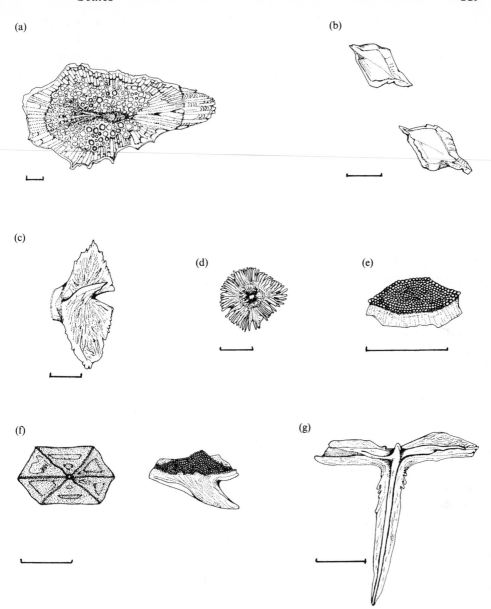

7.18 Modified body scales of bony fishes. (a) Sturgeon, *Acipenser sturio*.
(b) Longnose gar, *Lepisosteus osseus*. (c) South American catfish, *Doras
maculatus*. (d) Turbot, *Scophthalmus maximus*. (Bar scale 5 mm.) (e) Trigger-
fish, *Balistes* sp. (Bar scale 5 mm.) (f) Boxfish, *Ostracion* sp. (left) from side,
(right) from ventro-lateral edge. (g) Porcupinefish, *Chilomycterus* sp. (Bar
scales 1 cm except d and e.)

example many of the jacks and scads (family Carangidae) have thick scutes along the sides of their tails, and some herrings (family Clupeidae) have smaller scutes on the belly; some populations of the three-spined stickleback, *Gasterosteus aculeatus*, have comparatively massive scales on their sides. The turbot, *Scophthalmus maximus*, has distinctive spiky tubercles embedded in the skin (fig. 7.18d). Body armour is also a feature of several groups within the Scorpaeniformes, especially the poachers or pogges (family Agonidae) and sea robins or gurnards (family Triglidae), while many sculpins (family Cottidae) have fine prickles in their skins. Although looking nothing like scales, the sharp blades in the tails of tangs or surgeonfishes (family Acanthuridae) are derived from scales – they are most distinctive where they occur in tropical marine middens.

The most striking modifications of scales occur within the order Tetraodontiformes (fig. 7.18e–g) in which many triggerfishes (family Balistidae) have heavy, almost bony scales which barely overlap at their edges, boxfishes (family Ostraciidae) in which the body is encased in a bony carapace comprising hexagonal plates which fuse together (fig. 7.18f), and the porcupinefishes (family Diodontidae) which have massive spines on their skins arising from double-pronged bases (genus *Diodon*) or three-pronged bases (genus *Chilomycterus*) (fig. 7.18g). The members of this order are all markedly tropical and subtropical marine fishes, but the remains of their specialized scales all offer a promising chance of identification at least to genus level.

Aberrant fish bones

A discussion of fish bones is not complete without mention of the bones which display aberrant growth, signs of trauma or disease. Such bones are commonly found in human and other mammalian bone assemblages but are very rare in collections of fish remains. It is important to stress that little is known about which diseases of fish can be detected from a study of bones, scales or other hard tissues. There is ample evidence that heavy parasite burdens, the physiological stress of spawning, food shortages and low temperature can lead to the formation of false rings in otoliths, scales and vertebrae, but there is no body of data, like that which exists for man and other mammals, which links diseases to features present on fish bones.

The only convincing example of a fish bone displaying a pathological condition known to the junior author is a cod dentary from deposits laid down during the early medieval occupation of Ipswich, Suffolk. This bone possessed a large, randomly shaped cavity on its anterio-lateral aspect. The nature of this cavity was similar to those found in mammalian jaws which are usually interpreted as evidence of jaw abscesses.

Occasionally new modelling of bone on a cleithrum may indicate a healed fracture. Abnormalities in the vertebral column are perhaps the most common. Wheeler (1977) illustrated coalesced vertebrae of cod from Kings Lynn, Norfolk. Large collections of herring and cyprinid vertebrae often contain a few specimens of coalesced centra.

More common, are bones which display a condition often described as 'hyperosteosis' (also discussed on page 112). Fishes which characteristically display this condition are the European haddock, *Melanogrammus aeglefinus*, and the scad, *Trachurus trachurus*. The condition does not seem to be injurious to the fish and so cannot be termed pathological. This marked swelling of selected bones is the normal condition for these species.

Another fairly common aberration, well known to fisheries biologists, may be found in large collections of gadid otoliths. Here occasional specimens are found where part of the otolith is formed from normal opaque calcium carbonate while part has the appearance of a cluster of granulated sugar crystals, presumably calcite. Fishes possessing these aberrant otoliths do not appear to behave different from those with normal otoliths, so again the condition cannot strictly be called pathological.

Although aberrant remains are found in archaeological collections, they are rare and are usually unmistakable as anomalous specimens.

Towards a standard nomenclature for fish remains

Over 100 years ago the great ichthyologist A. C. L. G. Günther (1880) stated 'The bones of the skull of the fish have received so many different interpretations that no two accounts agree in their nomenclature, so that their study is a matter of considerable difficulty to the beginner'. This statement is still largely true today. Confusion exists because most scientists studying fish bones have carried out comparative studies of recent forms or examined fossils in order to understand the problems of homology and evolution of the fish skeleton. Many of these problems have still not been solved and there remain a number of subjective ideas which strongly influence the terminology of different workers. Many zoologists have been aware of the difficulties with the nomenclature of fish skeletal elements and a number have discussed the problems, and given lists of names and synonyms. One of the first to do this was Starks (1901). This work was used by Casteel (1976) and as a result many fish bone workers are familiar with it. However, it suffers from many deficiencies, most of which have emerged as fish osteology has developed over the last few decades. It can no longer be considered a useful starting-point, though as a work of reference its value is assured.

A much-quoted paper in osteological circles is that of Harrington (1955), which discussed the osteocranium of the American cyprinid *Notropis bifrenatus*. Another classic study is that of Topp and Cole (1968) on the sciaenid genus *Sciaenops*. Most recently, Jollie (1986) has produced a primer for the names of bones of the teleost skull and pectoral girdle skeleton. These papers show how fish bone nomenclature has developed in recent decades,

Table 7.1. *List of fish bone names*

Region and element Recommended names	Synonym(s)	Names from Leipksaar (1983) for most entries
NEUROCRANIUM		
Olfactory region		
ethmoid	(= mesethmoid)	ethmoideum [ethmoidea]
nasal		nasale [nasalia]
prefrontal		praefrontale
prevomer	(= vomer)	praevomer [praevomeres]
Orbital region		
frontal		frontale
lacrimal	(preorbital = lachrymal = 1st suborbital)	lacrimale
pterosphenoid	(= alisphenoid)	pterosphenoideum
suborbital	(= infraorbital)	suborbitale
Otic region		
epiotic	(= epioccipital)	epioticum [epiotica]
exoccipital		exoccipitale
opisthotic		opisthoticum
parietal		parietale
posttemporal	(= suprascapula)	posttemporale
prootic	prooticum)	
pterotic	(= squamosal = auto-pterotic + dermopterotic)	
sphenotic	(= autosphenotic)	sphenoticum
supraoccipital		supraoccipitale
Basicranial region		
basioccipital		basioccipitale
basisphenoid		basisphenoideum
parasphenoid		parasphenoideum
BRANCHIOCRANIUM		
Oromandibular region		
angular	(= retroarticular)	angulare [angularia]
articular	(= angular see Harrington, 1955)	articulare
dentary		dentale
ectopterygoid	(= pterygoid)	ectopterygoideum
entopterygoid	(= mesopterygoid = endopterygoid)	entopterygoideum
maxilla	(= maxillary)	maxillare
metapterygoid		metapterygoideum
palatine	(= autopalatine + dermopalatine)	palatinum

Table 7.1 (*cont.*)

Region and element Recommended names	Synonym(s)	Names from Lepiksaar (1983) for most entries
premaxilla	(= premaxillary = intermaxilla)	praemaxillare
quadrate		quadratum

Hyoid region

basihyal	(= glossohyal = entoglossum)	basihyale
branchiostegal		branchiostegale
ceratohyal	(= anterohyal)	keratohyale
epihyal	(= posterohyal)	epihyale
hyomandibular		hyomandibulare
hypohyal		hypohyale
	(upper hypohyal = dorsohyal)	
	(lower hypohyal = ventrohyal)	
interhyal	(= stylohyal)	interhyale
interopercular	(= interopercle = interoperculum)	interoperculare
opercular	(= opercle = operculum)	operculare
preopercular	(= preopercle = preoperculum)	praeoperculare
subopercular	(= subopercle = suboperculum)	suboperculare
sympletic		symplecticum
urohyal		urohyale

Branchial region

basibranchial		basibranchiale
ceratobranchial		keratobranchiale
epibranchial		epibranchiale
gillraker		branchiospina
hypobranchial		hypobranchiale
infrapharyngeal	(= 5th ceratobranchial = lower pharyngeal)	pharyngeum inferior [pharyngea inferiora]
pharyngobranchial		pharyngobranchiale
suprapharyngeal	(= special pharyngo-branchial = upper pharyngeal)	pharyngeum superior

VERTEBRAL COLUMN

abdominal vertebra	(= trunk = precaudal vertebra)	vertebra praecaudalis [vertebrae precaudales]
centrum		centrum [centra]
caudal vertebra	vertebra caudalis	

Table 7.1 (*cont.*)

Region and element Recommended names	Synonym(s)	Names from Lepiksaar (1983) for most entries
rib		costa [costae]
1st vertebra	(= atlas)	vertebra precaudalis 1
intermuscular	(= epicentrals or epineurals)	intermusculare

MEDIAN FINS

acanthotrich	(= fin spine)	acanthotrich [acanthotrichia]
pterygiophore	(= interneural)	pterygiophorus [pterygiophori]
	(= interhaemal)	pterygiophorus
lepidotrich	(= soft fin ray)	lepidotrich

CAUDAL SKELETON

epural		epurale
hypural		hypurale
urostyle	(= fused hypurals)	urostylus

APPENDICULAR SKELETON

radial	(= actinost)	radiale
basipterygium	(= pelvis)	basipterygium
cleithrum	(= clavicle)	cleithrum
coracoid	(= hypocoracoid)	coracoideum
postcleithrum	(= postclavicle)	postcleithrum
scapula	(= hypercoracoid)	scapula
supracleithrum	(= supraclavicle)	supracleithale

OTHERS

otolith		otolith [otolithi]
scale		squama [squamae]
scute		scutum [scuta]
fulcral[1]		fulcrum [fulcra]
1st anal pterygiophore[2]	(= enlarged 1st interhaemal)	os anale

[1] in sturgeons
[2] in flatfishes

Names enclosed in round brackets are synonyms. Some bones in adult fish are formed by the fusion of two separate elements. Some of these are shown in the list of synonyms, the two elements being linked by the symbol +. Plurals for selected Latin names are given in square brackets.

yet the terminology used by many workers examining archaeological material has not developed.

Attempts to clarify fish bone nomenclature for those working with archaeological material have not always succeeded in their aims. For example, Olsen (1968) gives a fine illustration entitled 'Generalized articulated fish skeleton', in which many of the elements which are recognizable in archaeological assemblages are clearly labelled. Yet the text refers to the bones of the opercular series (labelled as opercular, preopercular, subopercular and interopercular) as the operculum, pre-operculum, suboperculum and interoperculum. This lack of consistency in nomenclature is unhelpful. More recently Lepiksaar (1983) has privately circulated a most useful document on fish osteology from which a list of terms can be derived. However, these terms are almost all latinized and therefore are not acceptable to the large number of scientists who use the long-established terms.

Within the archaeozoological community there are two strongly held views on the language for fish bone terms. One group has followed the nomenclature of Lepiksaar; the other strongly resists this terminology, preferring to retain the widely used nomenclature. Because such divergence in nomenclature is not helpful to archaeologists, who are not particularly concerned with the names of elements used by fish anatomists, we tabulate bone names in both usages (table 7.1). This list has been derived mainly from Harder (1975), but it is important to stress that it is intended as a base-line, to which other terms can be added and existing ones altered as necessary. It is obvious, for example, that vertebrae can be divided into more groups than simply abdominal vertebrae and caudal vertebrae. There is no intention to limit or restrict workers from classifying vertebrae or other elements more precisely. However, it is hoped that new terms will be carefully defined and their use fully justified. It might here be noted that users of Lepiksaar's terms add the word 'os' or 'ossa' to the name given here.

No attempt has been made to include all the elements present in all fishes. Instead, the elements listed are those most commonly encountered in assemblages of fish remains recovered from archaeological excavations. Similarly, the list does not present all synonyms. Rather it lists the more common and confusing synonyms relevant to archaeological studies. A number of compromises have been made in drawing up the list in order to accommodate the terms most commonly used by archaeozoologists.

8

APPROACHES TO STUDYING
ARCHAEOLOGICAL ASSEMBLAGES

Introduction

Once fish bones have been obtained from archaeological deposits, it is important to consider both how the material is to be studied and, since not all assemblages warrant very detailed study, in what depth. These judgements will influence the methods used to record the data.

As a result of improved recovery procedures, representative fish bone assemblages are now more commonly retrieved from sites. While it may be academically desirable for each assemblage to be recorded and reported in fine detail, it is impractical to do so given the limitations of funding which beset so much archaeology. Some assemblages will be selected for detailed analysis, others for less detailed work, while others may simply be stored after initial assessment.

In the past the main limiting factor determining whether a fish bone assemblage was studied was the availability of someone, usually a museum employee, to look at the material. Today the key factor is how well the excavator argues the case for carrying out the work, both during the period of planning prior to the excavation and in applying for funds for post-excavation work.

One way of assessing whether material is worthy of detailed study is to address a series of questions. For example: by studying the fish remains, are we likely to learn something new about the people responsible for the assemblage? Have contemporaneous assemblages of fish bones been previously reported for the site or area? Are there likely to be opportunities for obtaining and working on similar material in the future?

Practical constraints will always be important. It is usually necessary to provide funding for someone to do the work (postgraduate research projects have, for example, been used to fund work on fish remains). Access to a suitable reference collection is a prerequisite. Once questions of an academic and practical nature have been resolved, the work can commence.

Having agreed in principle that the work should be undertaken, decisions must be taken concerning the methods of examination and the degree of detail of the final report.

The most basic approach is to simply state that fish remains were present in the deposits. This is acceptable if detailed study of bone assemblages is judged to be inappropriate and under such circumstances reasons should be

126

stated. It is most likely that such records of 'fish' from archaeological sites mean that no-one was available to study the remains more closely.

Lists of the species present at the site are more informative. From these habitat analysis can be undertaken, distribution maps drawn, and inferences made about fishing techniques.

At a slightly more detailed level there are reports which provide species lists for different phases of occupation. Some accounts give numbers of identified fragments per taxon by phase, while a small number of reports (many recent reports follow this pattern) give details of which bones (with their measurements) were present in which layers or phases.

Generally, the earlier the publication date the more scant the report. Today's standards are more exacting than those of the 1930s. However, it is rarely justifiable to publish fish bone assemblages at the level of detail given in some recent work, for example Hallström (1979). An adequate account of the fish fauna can be presented without itemizing the side, position and numbers of branchiostegals for each species recovered.

Many archaeologists, particularly those concerned with publication, question the need to publish all the data concerning a group of fish remains. It is cogently argued that many of the data are of interest to only a very small number of specialists and that the expense of full publication is unacceptably high. As a result, most recent fish bone reports are condensed versions of what could be written (this is also true of other specialist reports forming parts of archaeological publications). Ideally the published report should make it clear where the detailed identifications can be obtained (for example internal laboratory report, microfiche, or computer file). The chief disadvantage of condensing data is that the conclusions cannot always be readily checked.

It is important to keep in mind that the dual objectives of the report are to tell the reader what was found and to interpret the results within the limitations of the data. It is the fish remains that are the subject matter. Thus, identifications must be accurate, details of provenance must be correct and results presented clearly. It is important to enable the reader to distinguish the facts (the remains found) from deductions made from them (what the bones tell us about diet, economy, fishing practices or altered environment). Facts cannot be disputed; inferences can be wrong or open to reinterpretation.

Identification is dependent on the availability of appropriate reference material and experience in comparing archaeological fragments with modern skeletal material. The provenance of the material is the responsibility of the archaeologist but the separation of the facts from reconstruction of fishing techniques or diet is the responsibility of the fish bone worker. To this end it is advisable to adhere to the long-established practice of dividing reports of scientific investigations into five sections: introduction, methods and material, results, discussion, and conclusions.

The introduction should contain details of the site if these are not elsewhere in the published report, its location, geology, history, importance, with reference to relevant work previously carried out at the site and in the region.

The methods and materials section describes how the fish bones were recovered, identified and recorded. If size estimations or seasonal dating are carried out, this section should describe how. It is wise to include some details on the general state of preservation for the assemblage in this section.

The results simply state what was found where – how many bones; how many contexts contained particular taxa; the size of the bones (not the size of the fish); evidence of gnawing, butchery, disease or other damage.

The discussion is the place to compare the assemblage with any relevant published material and with the present-day fish fauna of the area. Here attempts can be made to assess what the bones tell us about diet, fishing methods and other aspects of fish exploitation.

It is clear that there are limitations to the amount of information that can be realistically extracted from assemblages of archaeological fish bones. Many factors will have had an influence on which bones survive in the deposits and which are recovered (see chapter 5 on taphonomy). Discussion of what can be deduced honestly from the examination of assemblages of fish remains forms a major part of this chapter.

The conclusions should draw all the sections together and suggest what further work needs to be carried out in the area.

Hand-collected material

Recent work has clearly demonstrated that hand-collected assemblages of bones are biased in favour of a few species which produce large bones and now much of the archaeological establishment acknowledges the need to sieve for fish bones and other small objects buried on archaeological sites. Soon it will be a thing of the past to receive scruffy boxes containing a small number of hand-collected bones from an excavation. Yet these relatively unpromising groups can provide limited information in the absence of better collected assemblages. Rarely do these assemblages contain remains that tax the osteologist. For medieval sites in Britain, for example, the bulk of the bones are from large marine fish of the family Gadidae, principally cod and ling, with a few bones from other species. Layers laid down in earlier periods may contain a few pike or large salmonid remains. Yet this paltry evidence shows that fish were brought to the site, and even transported considerable distances from the sea. In addition to the very common gadid bones, other species occur, for example, bones of conger eel and dermal structures from sharks and rays are often present.

Occasionally, very rare, even exotic fish will be present in these assemblages. From excavations at Dragonby, Lincolnshire, a curiously toothed spine was found (Jones, 1986b). No fish in the British fauna bears such a structure. However, the bone was clearly identified as the pectoral spine of the Nile catfish *Synodontis*, which has been well illustrated by Driesch (1983). There is no explanation for the natural occurrence of an African catfish spine in Romano-British levels at Dragonby; perhaps a Roman soldier or trader had carried it as a charm or talisman, in a similar way that sharks' teeth are worn today.

A less dramatic example comes from the excavations of Romano-British levels at Bishopstone, Sussex, where Martin Bell (1977) has shown that sea-weed was transported several kilometres from the coast to be used as manure in strip lynchets, simple ancient terraces used in arable agriculture in hilly districts of Britain. The evidence for this activity comes from large numbers of small inedible littoral mollusc and other invertebrate shells (tube worms which are commonly found on seaweeds) recovered from the soil. The invertebrates are thought to have been unintentionally gathered when sea-weed was collected from rocks or from the shore after storms. Amongst the bones to come from this site was a large caudal vertebral centrum of the meagre, *Argyrosomus regius*, a large solitary fish which wanders into the English Channel during the summer months (Jones, 1977). This is the only record of this sciaenid fish in British archaeological deposits.

One group of assemblages which is usually recovered by hand is grave offerings. For example, Ellison *et al.* (1978) examined a variety of miscel-laneous materials collected by Sir Leonard Woolley from tombs excavated at Ur in the early years of the twentieth century. Amongst the desiccated remains were two large fish vertebrae probably from a tunny, *Thunnus* sp., thought to have been food offerings. Tunny must have been transported a distance of some 180 km and it seems likely that the fish had been dried or salted. Both dried and salted fish are known in texts from southern Meso-potamia from the middle of the third millennium, when fish formed an important part of the diet.

These, however, are the exceptions. Most hand-collected fish bone assemblages are dominated by the larger bones (cleithra, dentaries, pre-maxillae and vertebrae) of large fish.

In summary, hand-collected assemblages are usually identified and recorded relatively rapidly, for only a small number of species are usually represented. Remains of rare fish are sometimes recorded. There are rarely enough bones to make worthwhile more than identification of species present and make a few rather tentative observations concerning fishing methods and consumption. For example, it may be safe to determine whether the fish were mainly freshwater or whether they were marine, but it would be unwise to speculate about details of fish processing.

Sieved assemblages

Apart from being a greater challenge and usually more interesting to identify than hand-collected material, assemblages of fish bones recovered by sieving archaeological deposits to 1 or 2 mm deserve more detailed study for several reasons. Because the method of recovery is controlled, the assemblage is more likely to contain the full range of fish present in the deposits than a hand-collected assemblage. In addition, a large number of different kinds of elements and bones of all size classes for the various species are likely to be present. These factors mean that the recovered assemblage is more likely to reflect the fishes brought onto the site in the past, and therefore more faith can be placed in any inferences drawn from data of this quality. Despite all these improvements it may still be difficult to rank species according to their importance as food species. Nevertheless, it is possible to draw inferences from sieved assemblages concerning fishing locations, fish processing, transportation, or fishing techniques.

The mechanics of recording fish bone assemblages

When it has been decided how work on the assemblage should be approached, the mechanics of recording the remains must be finalized. The fine details of each recording system can be developed only by individual workers. However, two aspects demand careful consideration.

First, and most importantly, it is necessary to be consistent in recording. Bones should be named according to a well-known authority and fish names should follow those given in an appropriate recent work. The same procedures must be used throughout identification. For example, it is bad practice to decide halfway through work on an assemblage that abdominal vertebrae should be divided into anterior abdominal and thoracic vertebrae. If a bone is to be measured, a drawing should be used to make sure that the measurement points are the same on each of the measured specimens. Morales and Rosenlund (1979) have produced a booklet which attempts to standardize measurements of fish bones (a second edition is in preparation).

The second aspect to consider is designed to speed up recording and data processing – this is to use codes for as much information as possible. Coding archaeological data is given thorough consideration by Richards and Ryan (1985: 120–33). Prime candidates are the names of bones and species or family identifications. In other words use abbreviations, preferably abbreviations which are mnemonics. The recorded information must be arranged in a system that can be easily sorted (e.g. card index or tape which can be read by computer, or typed directly into a computer disk file). Today, computers are widely available in archaeology and data-base management systems are probably the simplest and most flexible way of storing and processing data. Most data-base management systems are designed to handle both numeric and text variables (i.e. numbers and names/codes) and are particularly efficient for sorting and computing totals. In addition, they have many other useful features. For example, many data-base management systems make it very simple to find inconsistencies in data. It is essential to remember it is time-consuming to learn how to operate the computer and to learn the intricacies of the programs available to it. Hand-written record cards or pre-printed sheets can be the most efficient way of processing small assemblages, even if the totals and percentages have to be individually calculated.

In order to manage the large number of fish bone records from the excavations dealt with by the Environmental Archaeology Unit (EAU) at the University of York, a computer system has been devised. The recording methods make use of a powerful and versatile data-base management system which runs on the university mainframe computer. The fish bone recording system is designed to record a large number of details about the bones as simply and economically as possible.

In the EAU system, several sorts of information are collected for each bone or group or similar bones and this information gathered into a standardized record. Each record is broken into 12 data fields or attributes (fig. 8.1). A large site may produce many thousands of records.

The first three attributes of each record relate to the archaeological provenance of the bone(s); the majority of attributes, however, are characteristics (e.g. name of bone and measurements) of the bone(s). For each record all 12 attributes are filled in. Once a single record has been completed in full, duplicated attributes can be rapidly inserted by instructing the computer to make use of the details contained in the first record.

In the EAU system the first three attributes of each fish bone record are the site code, context number and sample number; these comprise the main data concerning the provenance of the bones. The site code is designated as a text field because most sites are known by a mixture of letters and numbers e.g. NEP67 was the code for material from the 1967 excavations at North Elmham Park, Norfolk. If site codes are composed of numbers, characters such as slashes (an oblique line) or hyphens are often used. For example, in York decimal numbers are used as site codes e.g. 1977.7 is the code for the excavations at 16–22 Coppergate, York carried out in 1977. However, the site code covering all seasons is 1976–81.7. Characters like hyphens are not readily sorted by computers unless they form part of a text field.

Sample and context numbers are often sorted in order to examine remains according to their phase or location and it is important to use context and sample numbers or codes which are easily sorted. Wherever possible numbers (context or sample numbers) should be whole numbers (integers). However, carefully designed coding systems using letters can easily be sorted by computer if they all have the same number of letters. Problems arise when contexts or samples are known by mixtures of numbers and letters.

Other information concerning the date of the deposits could be included if

General Coding Form

NAME		DATE
ADDRESS	PROGRAM TITLE	Page ___ of ___

Column markers: 1 · 10 · 20 · 30 · 40 · 50 · 60 · 70 · 80

```
NEP 67  C          C   42        R       2    |3    |    H
        JK  42         PA  -          |    3  |3    L
            63         PAR -3         |    4  |-2   S
                       VC             |L   5  |3-2  GAD
                       AN             |L   |   |3   L
                       EHY            |L   |   |3   L
        JF  42         P   -          R   2  10·0  S
                       PX  -          |   2  12·4  S
                       P   -          |2  3  13·6  GAD   7·6
                       B   -          L   5  8·5   PG
                       A   -          |   2  -4    HD
                       C   2          4      -2         CR
```

it is available. However, bones are often examined before archaeological phasing is finalized. At York phasing is entered into the data-base independently of fish identifications in a separate file which can be linked to the fish bone data-base via context or sample number.

The next attribute recorded in a fish bone record is the kind of element present. This is coded as three characters or fewer, for example PX = premaxilla, D = dentary, PAR = parasphenoid.

The next field is the number of elements, again a whole number. This is usually 1, but groups of remains of the same kind from a single taxon may be recorded as a single record. Many samples produce large numbers of bones of one species, for example, herring vertebrae. To treat each bone as a separate record would involve a great deal of unnecessary coding and computer storage – thus a group of 42 caudal vertebrae of herring could be coded as 'C' (caudal vertebral centra) '42' as part of a single record.

The side from which the bone is derived is the next item recorded in the EAU system. It is coded as follows: R = right, L = left, − = mid-line, ? = unknown.

A field known as 'group' is recorded for vertebrae only. This is used to distinguish between the different kinds of vertebrae present in a vertebral column. Each species or family has its groups defined independently. As an example, the divisions of gadid vertebrae are explained. Group 1 vertebrae comprise the first vertebra and the following three or four anterior abdominal vertebrae which lack transverse processes. Group 2 vertebrae are the small number of abdominal vertebrae with transverse processes which lie roughly at right angles to the dorso-ventral axis of the bone. Group 3 are the remaining abdominal vertebrae. Group 4 comprise the bulk of the caudal vertebrae. Group 5 are the last ten or so vertebrae, which support the caudal fin.

The condition of the element is assessed in the next field. Condition 1 = complete; 2 = 75–99%; 3 = 50–75%; 4 = 25–50% 5 = less than 25% complete; P = proximal; M = median; D= distal (5D means that less than 25% of the distal portion of the element was present).

The size of the bone(s) is recorded in the next two fields. For some bones, two measurements may be taken from each specimen; thus each specimen must form a unique record. For other elements only one measurement is

8.1   Record sheet used for fish bones at Environmental Archaeology Unit, University of York. Columns indicate (from left to right): site code, context number, sample number, kind of bone element (PA = palatine, PAR = parasphenoid, VC = vertebral central, AN = angular, EHY = epihyal, D = dentary, PX = premaxilla, P = precaudal vertebrae, C = caudal vertebra, B = basioccipital, A = articular), the number of elements, the side from which the bone is derived, group of vertebrae on arbitrary scale 1–5, condition of element, size of the bone, second measurement of size, coded identification, comments. See text for explanation of other codes.

taken, so the two measurement fields contain measurements of two of the elements selected at random. (Care must be taken when processing the data to account for this difference.) It is not always possible to fill these fields with measurements so numeric codes have also been assigned to give an estimate of the size of the bone, for example -2 = small-sized individual; -3 = medium-sized individual; -4 = large individual; -5 = unmeasured. The values -2 to -4 are defined for each species.

The identification is the next field. It is coded as a text field of maximum length five characters. Most identifications are based on a contraction of the scientific name, for example PE-FL = *Perca fluviatilis* L. and GAD = Gadidae. In addition, 'quick' codes have been assigned for species and other taxa which occur commonly, for example H =herring (*Clupea harengus*), C = cod (*Gadus morhua*).

The final field in a record is a comment, usually coded, where additional information, for example evidence of butchery or burning, can be recorded. It is often impossible to give a numeric or definitive text code to every field in a record. Often there will be no special observations. In these cases a hyphen is used to signify a null value for the attribute.

One of the main facilities of a data-base management system is its ability to link different data files together via a common attribute. Thus it has proved possible to build a file of coded fish bone data which can be linked to a 'translation file' which will enable full scientific names (or English names) to be output instead of the coded identifications. Another translation file contains the codes for the elements and their full names. Because these two files are independent of one another and each links to the main data file via different fields, it is possible to use the same abbreviation to mean different things. Thus in the field 'kind of element' the abbreviation 'C' is used for 'caudal vertebral centrum' while in the field identification the same abbreviation is the code for 'cod'.

Rather than attempt to record directly onto a micro- or mainframe computer, 80-column FORTRAN coding sheets have been found to be an efficient means of recording fish identifications (preprinted sheets could also be used). These sheets are filled out at the time of identification and form the primary record for the site. The coded information is typed onto a computer (in the past, punched onto cards) by skilled VDU operators, freeing the identifier from the tedious job of data input.

Other workers have used paper tape onto which coded identifications are punched and later loaded into the computer. Some load all the data into a mainframe statistical package, coding all the data numerically. Some widely available statistical packages (e.g. MINITAB) will accept data with coded alphabetical data.

Many workers who have written computer programs to input and process archaeological data agree that most, if not all, the requirements of archaeoologists can be satisfied by using well-written packages developed for commercial or research purposes. It is most unwise to write programs in a high-level language like PASCAL or FORTRAN when data-base management or statistical packages can perform all necessary procedures. Only when packages have been thoroughly investigated and found wanting should those working on fish remains settle down to write complex computer programs. Our expertise lies in recognizing fish bones and interpreting the results of our labours.

When the data have been systematically and consistently recorded, they are then processed. This can be done with pencil and paper. However, the arrival of computers, and in particular data-base management systems makes coping with large bodies of data far less daunting than it once was. This is not the place to discuss computing in detail; an excellent introduction to the subject has been prepared for this series by Richards and Ryan (1985).

While the use of computers enables vast data sets to be analysed rapidly, removing the need to add long lists of figures and calculate percentages and other basic statistics, it is necessary to invest considerable amounts of money, to purchase the hardware and software, and time to learn to use the system. Many researchers will confess to hours of frustration and wasted time caused by hardware failures, badly written programs and manuals and, inevitably, human error.

Some promising early developments in archaeological computing do not appear to have been enthusiastically pursued. For example, computer-assisted recording of bone measurements was carried out using a pair of vernier calipers fitted with a potentiometer and interfaced to a micro-computer (Hardy, 1982). The system worked reasonably well, but was judged to be too cumbersome for widespread use in one laboratory routinely measuring thousands of bones each year. One important reason why this particular piece of equipment has not been used is a deep-seated (and reasonable) distrust of machinery. Computers do make mistakes; they may be very rare, but computer-generated errors can be very difficult to identify. There are great advantages in keeping a hand-written record (albeit coded) of the bones examined.

Despite a few failures and inefficiencies, computers are beginning to be more widely used for storing and processing archaeological data. The future will doubtless see the development of other applications. In particular, expert systems are being developed to assist with the identification of bird bones and could be applied to fish remains. Similarly, advanced computer graphics may reduce the need for large reference collections.

Examining the fish bone identifications
Once the data have been assembled and ordered, data analysis may begin. At this stage less obvious features of the assemblage will become apparent as the

data are examined systematically. The following section consists of a series of questions which can be asked of archaeological fish assemblages. The questions can be asked at several levels. For example, it is possible to consider the presence and absence of fish taxa. Alternatively, the relative abundance of different fish taxa can be assessed by considering both the numbers of identified fragments and the frequency (number of times a taxon occurs in the sampled contexts). Finally, the element distribution and size range of each taxon can be described and discussed.

Presence or absence of fish taxa

A simple consideration of the range of fish taxa present at a site may be sufficient to reveal the general pattern of fish exploitation. For example, it may become clear whether the fishes were from a locally exploited population or whether transportation of exotic species has occurred.

The kinds of fish do not always remain constant through the occupation of the site. (It is necessary to divide the site into separate phases for this analysis.) Consideration of changes in the taxa present may reflect environmental change or could be attributed to cultural factors, e.g. immigration of different people, economic or political changes.

If species composition is constant in all phases of occupation on a site, we must conclude that fish exploitation and distribution were constant throughout the period of settlement. Many sites show little change in the assemblages of fish during the period of occupation. An exception is the site at 16–22 Coppergate in York (Jones, 1986c). Here the earliest phases of occupation (Roman to early ninth century) produced bones and scales from freshwater and anadromous fishes characteristic of clean, well-oxygenated water. Later these species were replaced by fishes more tolerant of mildly polluted water. At the same time, the concentrations of bones from marine fish showed a dramatic rise.

By contrast, the Alms Lane site in Norwich (Jones and Scott, 1985) produced assemblages of fish bones from a range of species which appeared to have remained constant from the twelfth to the eighteenth centuries, despite marked changes in the nature of the occupation.

The importance of the different taxa recovered from the site

Listing species in order of their abundance according to their numbers or weights of identified fragments, frequency (the number of contexts which contained a particular taxon), minimum numbers of individuals, or estimated body weights, may help to address this difficult question. It should be remembered that the concept of minimum numbers of individuals has been widely discussed and some workers (e.g. O'Connor, 1985) have questioned its relevance when there is no evidence that the material considered was deposited in one episode. Similarly, the assumptions necessary to make meat-weight calculations may not be sufficiently well founded for the results to have any significance, given differences in conformation between individual fishes and cultural influences on the consumption of fish organs.

Element analysis

It is possible to consider which elements are present for each species. The element distribution may provide evidence of butchery or preservation techniques.

A recent example of work using element analysis was presented by Marion Seeman (1986) who discussed work on assemblages of herring remains collected from excavations at a seventeenth-century Dutch whaling station on the west coast of Spitsbergen. Herring cleithra were consistently absent in the assemblages. By referring to contemporaneous illustrations which showed that in the seventeenth century gutted Dutch herring often lacked cleithra, she concluded that the remains found at Spitsbergen were Dutch cured herring.

An example of over-representation of cleithra came to light in excavation at Exeter (Wilkinson, 1979). Here cod cleithra, supracleithra and post-temporals were abundant, while jaw bones were scarce. Wilkinson concluded that the cod were probably brought to the site as stockfish.

The size of fish

Assemblages of pike bones from Mesolithic deposits at Praestelyngen (Denmark) were at one time thought to be from fish which had died naturally and become intermixed with human cultural material. However, Noe-Nygaard (1983) calculated the sizes of fish from measurements of the dentary (lower jaw) and showed that the size class distribution of the archaeological assemblage was quite unlike that found in modern lakes. She concluded that the pike must have been caught by man. Boiko (1964) made both size and age estimations of Russian zander, *Stizostedion lucioperca*, from archaeological and natural deposits in order to evaluate the natural mortality in the species.

Season of capture

Casteel (1976) demonstrated the possibility that fish remains can be used for seasonal dating. Sadly the impression he gave was that such studies can readily be carried out. This is far from the truth. Age estimation is a most complex matter, requiring much careful study of modern material before archaeological data can be accurately used for this purpose. Thus, Noe-Nygaard (1983) examined a sample of 100 modern pike, collected throughout the year, before she analysed the material from Praestelyngen. Several workers have attempted to read incremental growth rings on archaeological specimens and concluded that the results were not sufficiently objective for publication. Scales often fragment along bands of growth and are rarely well enough preserved for ageing.

A recent paper described assemblages of fish bones from Wadi Kubbaniya, an Upper Palaeolithic site in Egypt dated to 20,000 to 12,000 bp (Van Neer, 1986). He examined assemblages from several sites in the Wadi and was able to show seasonal exploitation of different fish populations by considering the sizes of the species present and their ecology and behaviour. Some genera, notably *Lates*, live only in the main channel of the Nile and were not present at those sites on the flood plain. Assemblages composed mainly of large *Clarias* catfish, small *Tilapia*, and eels (*Anguilla*) were interpreted as having been caught early in the flood season. Large *Clarias* move into the Wadi in order to spawn, the *Tilapia* migrate in order to feed and the eels feed on the eggs. By contrast, assemblages dominated by smaller *Clarias* and large *Tilapia* were thought to have been taken from small pools as the water receded towards the main channel. These assemblages contained few eel remains.

The preceding examples, drawn mainly from recent publications, illustrate some of the careful and detailed work which has been undertaken on material collected from archaeological excavations. Doubtless analysis of fish remains will continue to produce exciting and informative results.

9

ESTIMATION OF FISH SIZE

Introduction

Although identifying fish remains is a time-consuming task, the actual recognition of the species present in an assemblage is only the beginning of the study. It is possible also to determine the size of the animals whose bones have been recovered, and to estimate the relative importance of the various species involved and occasionally to make extrapolations concerned with meat weight and method of processing. The interpretation of seasonality of capture and of fishing activity is discussed in later chapters.

The size of a fish may be recorded in several ways in the literature depending on the discipline within ichthyology that requires the data. Lengths may be recorded as standard length (tip of the snout to the end of the hypural plate), fork length (snout tip to the fork of the tail), and total length (snout tip to tail extremity). Weights may be recorded as total weight or gutted weight. The estimation of length and weight cannot be calculated with equal accuracy because bone size has a more direct correlation with fish length than with weight. Clearly, fish of identical length are not all the same weight, as weight fluctuates about a median depending on the condition of the animal and on its reproductive state. Calculations of length are thus more accurate than those of weight, although much information exists in the literature (e.g. Carlander, 1969, 1977), which will allow some extrapolation of length to estimated weight.

Selection of the most appropriate bones

The choice of bones for measurement is determined by the fundamental qualification that the measurements can be reproduced on archaeological material. Fish bones are never so robust and rarely of as consistent thickness as mammalian bones, and therefore do not lend themselves to a system of prescribed measurement based on comparative material. The attempt by Morales and Rosenlund (1979) to provide a standardized system of measuring fish bones from archaeological sites, inspired by comparable texts on mammalian remains, provides a sophisticated analysis for measurements. It is, however, not a practical proposition as some of their suggested measurements lack clearly defined measuring points and many will not be reproducible on archaeological fish bones unless they are in exceptionally good condition. Rather than follow a set of ordained measurements, those working on fish remains should be free to use measuring points which suit the condition of the material available.

The overriding qualifications in selecting bones for size estimation are as follows:

1   they should be possible to identify without doubt;
2   they should be solid structures with clear-cut features which allow accurate and reproducible measurement;
3   the measurement points permit the maximum possible distance.

It is probably desirable to elaborate on these qualifications.

1. Correct identification of both the bone and the species represented is clearly essential if measurements made from the bone are to be extrapolated into estimates of the size of the fish. For example, the use of measurements on the opercular of the European flounder, *Platichthys flesus*, which is difficult to distinguish from that of the related plaice, *Pleuronectes platessa* (a potentially larger species), is suspect, although both the dentary and premaxilla of both would be acceptable as these bones can be certainly distinguished.

2. The location of positive reference points between which to measure is vital. Measurements are usually made between verticals using dial or vernier calipers either visually read and recorded or computer-linked. However, the shape of many fish bones may cause orientation problems and even so obvious a 'long bone' as the maxillary of a cod is difficult to present for measurement of length without any ambiguity of the reference points. While a measuring error may be only a matter of one or two millimetres on the bone, this may result in an error of 10 or more centimetres in length (and a kilogram of weight) if the measurement is related to length and weight of the whole fish. It is therefore essential that measurements are made between points which can be certainly established on the bones. Natural indentations or bosses in the outline of the bone, or foramina, are particularly important measuring sites.

3. When bones are measured to make size estimations, the proposed measurements should be made on points which do not suffer damage in the soil, or during recovery or processing. This is a difficulty in accepting all the methods of Morales and Rosenlund (1979), superficially attractive as their proposals are, for little allowance is made for fragility and damage. In practice, it is commonly found that thin-edged bones and even relatively strong protuberances are too damaged to be used for measuring. For these reasons the measuring points adopted must be a pragmatic decision by the individual worker based on the condition of the material so as to obtain the maximum number of certainly reproducible accurate measurements. Measuring points adopted may therefore vary from site to site even for the same bone and the same species and the decision has to be made so as to maximize the amount

of accurate data to be gained from the material. The only other factor to bear in mind is that the measured feature should be as large as possible so as to minimize proportional error due to damage of the bone or other causes.

Experience has shown that the most useful elements include premaxilla, dentary, articular, quadrate, basioccipital, parasphenoid and abdominal vertebrae. Some robust elements are excluded, for example the maxilla, because of the difficulty of finding well-defined measuring points. Other bones that could occasionally be measured include the opercular, post-temporal, supracleithrum and cleithrum. Many elements occur so rarely in archaeological deposits that there is little point in defining measuring points. Other elements (the nasal, lacrimal, metapterygoid, scapula and the circum-orbitals) are best left unmeasured.

The estimation of size

The quickest and simplest way to estimate the size of fishes is to compare the archaeological specimens with bones from a fish of known size. The archaeo-logical bones can crudely be said to be from fish approximately equal to, or larger or smaller than the size of the bones of a modern comparative speci-men. A refinement is to compare the archaeological bones with those of two or three modern specimens of different sizes. Thus, it is possible to estimate approximately the size of the fish. The value of this approach is its simplicity, speed, and the need for relatively small amounts of modern reference material. The information obtained may not be as accurate as that theoreti-cally possible; in practice it is usually adequate, but if further work is required it will help in developing a strategy for it. Van Neer (1986) used this approach to estimate the sizes of fish from Wadi Kubbaniya, a late Palaeolithic site in Upper Egypt, while Jones (1984b) employed the same approach for examin-ing medieval fish bones from Freswick Castle, Caithness, Scotland.

It is important to remember that the information available from fish remains is limited by the nature of the bones preserved. If the excavated material proves to merit detailed study then more accurate methods can be employed. However, as we have seen in chapter 5, many assemblages rep-resent only a minute fraction of the fishes processed or consumed at a site and it may be reasonable to examine the material relatively rapidly, recording only the kinds of bone, the species of fish and their approximate sizes.

In recent years several studies showing relationships between fish bone size and fish size (usually measured length on comparative material) have been published. These follow two methods: those which simply plot a graph show-ing the relationship between bone size and fish length, and those which use simple regression analysis to describe this relationship.

Examples using the direct relationship include those on cod dentaries and premaxillae studied by Wheeler and Jones (1976) and Wheeler (1977), the lower pharyngeal bone of corkwing wrasse, *Crenilabrus melops* (Wheeler,

1979a), and the opercular bones of the sardine, *Sardina pilchardus*, studied by Wheeler and Locker (1985). Similar measurements and graphs have been used by fishery biologists studying the size of prey of fish-eating predators. For example Mann and Beaumont (1980) estimated the size of fish eaten by pike, *Esox lucius*, by measuring the undigested pharyngeal bones of cyprinid fishes.

Somewhat more elaborate methods can be employed in size estimation and Casteel (1976) compared five alternative schemes. He concluded that the best was the single least squares regression analysis (possibly better described as simple regression using one predictor variable), for it requires only a single regression equation for each bone of each species and it is highly accurate.

Single regression is also recommended, although it may be more accurate to use a weighted regression procedure which takes account of the greater variance in bone size in larger fishes, i.e. the heterotochastic nature of most fish bone measurement/fish length plots when bones from very young (small) and very old (large) fishes are obtained.

Size estimation using a regression equation is most accurate if a large number of comparative specimens is available for study: 30 has been suggested by J. Desse (1984). The comparative fishes should be selected to represent the exploited size range of each species. For some species it may be necessary to measure the bones of more than 30 specimens if there is much variation in bone size.

Desse (1984) has also given a detailed study of the relationship of bone size and fish length in the sea-bream, *Sarpa salpa*, and also (Desse *et al.*, 1987) a similar study of the perch, *Perca fluviatilis* (based on 22 specimens). In both cases clear illustrations are given showing measurement points of several bones and plots showing the linear relationship between bone size and fish length are also presented. However, preparing material on this scale is an enormous task and is probably only justified for the most common bones of the most abundant species represented in archaeological sites (for which, in the absence of experience, an element of prediction has to be employed). The problems of applying sets of measurements of recent comparative material have already been discussed (p. 139). Clearly, the cost effectiveness of such undertakings has to be rigidly scrutinized.

Examples using simple regression analysis include a study of the first vertebra of the herring (Höglund, 1972), pike dentaries by Noe-Nygaard (1983), cod and whiting first vertebra by Enghoff (1983), jaw bones of two species of seabream and a seabass from Jomon shell mounds (Akazawa and Watanabe, 1968), while Casteel (1976) claims to have employed it for the ultimate vertebra of the Sacramento squawfish, *Ptychocheilus grandis*.

Carrying out regression analysis to explore the relationship between bone size and fish length has become easier since the introduction of computer-based statistical packages which make the necessary calculations. This development does not invalidate the simpler technique of plotting the data by hand and fitting a line by eye, although computer-based calculations are likely to be more accurate than reading sizes from a graph. It is important to remember that the limits of accuracy are determined by the nature of the material being studied, that the data are a reflection of accurate measurement, and it is probably wisest not to demand very accurate size estimation techniques for there is always a considerable margin for error inherent in archaeological data.

For most work on ancient fishes it seems that the most practical proposition is for the archaeologist to have access to collections of comparative material which include as many specimens of different sizes as possible so that comparisons can be made directly. It may be desired to undertake the preparation of data by measuring the comparative bones and determining regression equations so that measurement of archaeological specimens and calculation of fish size can proceed with statistically determined confidence. Access to the comparative collections will, however, always be desirable so that unconventional measurements can be made where the condition of the archaeological material requires them. The final decision on methods has to be dictated by cost-effective considerations.

Vertebrae as a guide to fish size

Vertebral centra are usually the most abundant fish remains and their very abundance may impose an obligation to attempt size reconstruction by using them. However, there are inherent difficulties with vertebral centra, sometimes with regard to their identification where several related fishes are represented in the local fauna, and at other times because it is necessary to establish the position of the centrum in the vertebral column, which is frequently difficult. Several of the examples cited above, where vertebrae have been successfully used in size estimation, have relied on the fact that the first vertebra in the column has a distinctive shape and is identifiable. The ultimate and sometimes penultimate vertebrae are also of potential use for size estimation, the former having been used by Casteel (1976) for the Sacramento squawfish, and both by Wheeler (unpublished) for tuna remains from the Franchthi excavations. The disadvantage of using these vertebrae is that they are small in comparison with those from the main vertebral column.

Where the vertebral centrum is preserved in a more or less complete state with neural spines and zygopophyses or haemal spines intact, identification of the species and the position of the centrum in the column are more certain. Measurement of the diameter of the centrum can then be used to estimate the size of the fish. However, the anterior and posterior edges of vertebrae are commonly abraded and measurement of their diameter may be difficult. Even the relatively massive vertebral centra of blue-fin tuna, *Thunnus thynnus*, often have the edges so abraded that this measurement becomes

Table 9.1. *Correlation between otolith length, and length and weight of whiting,* Merlangius merlangus

OL (mm)	FL (mm)	CL	FW (g)	CL
4.0	66.9	±7.5	1.7	±0.3
8.0	145.7	±5.1	19.8	±1.6
12.0	224.5	±3.8	82.9	±4.8
16.0	303.3	±4.5	229.2	±17.2
20.0	382.1	±6.8	504.4	±50.7
24.0	460.9	±9.4	961.0	±119.6

OL otolith length; FL fork length; FW fish weight; CL confidence limit. (Adapted from Härkönen, 1986, with permission)

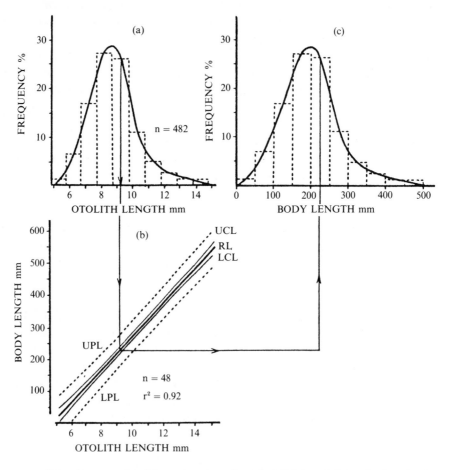

9.1 An example of the estimation of original fish length from the length of otoliths in cod, *Gadus morhua*. (Reproduced from Härkönen [1986] with permission of the publisher.)

inaccurate, and in practice it is possibly more effective to measure the length of the centrum, as an accurate measurement in this dimension can more often be attained than that of diameter.

Otoliths as a guide to fish size
In species where the otoliths are of a relatively large size they can be employed for size estimation even though there are only two large otoliths (most often the sagitta) per fish (see p. 114). However, in some groups, e.g. the families Salmonidae and Scombridae, which contain several important food fishes, the otoliths are relatively small (otolith length to fork length between 1:80 and 1:120, and 1:68 to 1:93 respectively) (Härkönen, 1986).

It is possible that in recent fishes otolith weight may be a better guide to the length of the fish than otolith length (Blacker, 1974) but the change in weight of otoliths in archaeological sites has not been investivated. Bearing in mind their composition (see chapter 7) the weight of an otolith may be more a reflection of taphonomic factors than its true original weight.

The relationship between the width of otoliths and the body length of cod was discussed by Blacker (1974), who also cited work on north-west Atlantic haddock, *Melanogrammus aeglefinus*, by Templeman and Squires (1956). One of the results of this study was to establish that older but slow-growing fishes had longer and heavier otoliths than fast-growing fishes of the same species. As Blacker summarized it, 'fish with the slowest growth rate have the largest otoliths' and he then pointed out that this was reflected in differences between the sexes, because males mature earlier than females and their growth rate slows down earlier in life.

Such refinements are perhaps irrelevant to the archaeologist but they serve to alert one to the fact that calculations of this kind are not absolute. At best, where material allows, they are a guide to the possibility otoliths offer.

The field of fisheries contains many examples where otoliths have been studied in relation to the size of food fishes. Archaeologists will find this literature a useful guide to the potential of these remains, but must extrapolate from recent to ancient otoliths with caution. An example of the relation between otolith and body length in cod is given in figure 9.1. A recent excellent guide to otoliths of virtually all the species important as food fishes (and many small species of importance as prey to fish-eating birds and mammals) in northern Europe's coastal and freshwaters has been published by Härkönen (1986). In addition to illustrations of the otoliths he has given tables of correlation between otolith length and fish length and otolith length and fish weight (see table 9.1).

Scales as a guide to fish length
Like the elements of the bony skeleton and otoliths, a fish's scales continue to increase in size (but not in number) throughout its life. Scales therefore

have the capacity to yield information on the size of the fish from which they came. Casteel (1976) has addressed this topic exhaustively, as well as the possibility of using fish scales to establish seasonality of capture, but his examples are based largely on theoretical considerations and fail when rigorously tested against archaeological material. Only scales of a moderately large size relative to the fish are likely to be useful for size estimation. Species which have up to 50 scales in the longitudinal series (i.e. along the length of the fish) are potentially useful; those which have more than this (such as the orders Gadiformes and Pleuronectiformes, and most of the family Salmonidae) have relatively small scales.

Measurement of the length of large scales (or the diameter measured from the focus near the centre to the posterior edge of the scale) should bear a linear relationship to the length of the fish. Such measurements made on scales from fishes of known length might provide a means of estimating the length of ancient fishes from preserved scales. However, scales are extremely fragile and very few scales recovered from archaeological sites are complete (they tend to separate into growth layers both vertically and concentrically). It is only in the most exceptional cases that recovered scales will be in a condition which allows measurement.

Fish biologists employ the circuli or growth rings on scales (see chapter 7) to make estimates of the age of fishes. Methods of back calculation are widely used to establish the growth of the fish over a period of time by measuring the winter growth zones (when the circuli are clustered together during the period of slow growth). Simply counting the number of circuli (as attempted by Casteel, 1976) as a means of estimating size of the fish is not accurate, as the number of circuli is dependent solely on growth and this is affected by availability of food, the effects of parasitic infestation and also by disease. Moreover in large, mature fishes a certain amount of scale tissue may be resorbed during gonad development or abraded during spawning. Fish scales, although superficially attractive as a means to establish length, are not reliable, firstly because they are rarely preserved whole in archaeology and secondly because their interpretation is subject to many qualifications.

Extrapolation of length from estimation of age

As indicated above, fisheries literature contains many examples of the use of the hard parts of fishes (bones, otoliths and scales) for the estimation of the age of a fish. The assessment of age from scales of recent fishes is most widely practised because scales can be taken from a live fish without major injury and the fish is released to the population (this is particularly the case in ecological studies and fisheries work on freshwater species; most marine fish are killed in capture).

The general literature on fisheries gives an overview of fish growth and techniques for establishing the age of fishes. Particularly good examples exist in Bagenal (1974) and general discussions in Lagler *et al.* (1962, and later editions), Moyle and Cech (1982), Weatherley and Gill (1987) and Summer-felt and Hall (1987). Essentially the determination of age depends on the identification of annual (or seasonal) growth zones in hard parts of the body. Various parts have been employed: opercular bones for pike (Frost and Kipling, 1959), vertebrae in blue shark (Stevens, 1975) and tuna (Hui-Chong *et al.*, 1965), pectoral fin rays in *Coregonus* (Mills and Beamish, 1980) and in sturgeon (Berg, 1962: 71), otoliths and scales for many species.

When the age of a fish has been established, it is possible to estimate its size by referring to the many studies of living fishes in the literature. These are too numerous to list but a search of the literature should reveal some data on age and size relationship for most species of commercial or sporting interest in cool-temperate seas and freshwaters and for some species in the tropics.

However, attempting to estimate the fish's age from archaeological material and thence to calculate fish length, will never produce more than a rough approximation with possibly so large a margin of error that it would rarely be acceptable. The reasons for this are both archaeological and zoological. Archaeological remains of fishes are so rarely recovered in good enough condition for accurate age determinations that only exceptional sites can provide suitable material. However, studies of the relationship of growth and age in fishes have shown that, while age is relatively simple to establish, growth is highly variable and depends on the availability of food, both to the population and to the individual fish, the intensity of competition for food within the species population, the physical environment, and the effects of parasites and diseases. As a result many studies of fish length related to age are applicable to specific populations, geographical areas and ecological conditions, and are valid only within these limits, but when extended to encompass the whole species range the variation may be so large that the value of the information is minimal. Reconstructing fish length or weight from the estimated age of archaeological material might be worth undertaking in exceptional circumstances but would not be productive as a general practice.

Length/weight relationship and yield of flesh

Although the length of a fish is easier to obtain than its weight and is inherently less affected by extraneous factors such as seasonal changes in gonad weight, fullness of gut with food, starvation, or parasite load, there is a considerable amount of data in the fisheries literature on weight of some species for given length. As growth represents an increase in three dimensions while length measurements are in one dimension only, the increase in the former is approximately to the power of 3. An example showing five common European marine food fishes is given in table 9.2.

Inspection of this table shows that weight increases roughly to the cube

Table 9.2. *Length/weight relationship for five European marine food fishes*

Total length (cm)	Average gutted weight (kg)				
	Plaice	Cod	Haddock	Whiting	Hake
20	0.08	0.07	0.07	0.07	—
30	0.23	0.20	0.20	0.18	0.16
40	0.59	0.54	0.50	0.48	0.39
50	1.14	1.09	1.02	0.93	0.77
60	1.95	1.88	1.77	—	1.14
70	—	3.00	2.77	—	2.04
80	—	4.45	4.13	—	3.09
90	—	6.36	—	—	4.45
100	—	8.67	—	—	6.13

Adapted from Blacker, 1979

power of the length at least in 'round fishes' (e.g. cod) as opposed to flatfishes (e.g. plaice). This stands as a general relationship for all similarly shaped fishes.

The relation between length and weight can be expressed as follows: $W = a \cdot L^n$ (where a is a constant and the exponent n fluctuates between 2.4 and 4, but is usually 3, and thus the cube). Individual fish or populations of the same species can be compared by establishing the constant a, which can also be represented as the condition factor K in the formula $K = W/L^3$.

The simple expression of weight, however, is not a useful guide to the weight of protein available from a fish. It may represent the total weight (table 9.1), or, as in the case cited above (table 9.2), be gutted weight. Neither is the same as flesh weight. A rule of thumb used by British fishmongers is that roughly half of the weight of gutted round fish and large flatfishes is lost in filleting. Thus, if 100 kg of gutted fish are landed, only 50 kg will be saleable as fillets. This, of course, ignores the dietary importance of such organs as the liver, swimbladder and gonads, and other parts (such as jaw muscles) which are usually discarded by contemporary fishmongers. The use of these parts is governed by social and cultural factors and extrapolation from modern practice to ancient use may not be wholly valid. Moreover, the yield of total protein from fish would certainly increase under the influence of hunger.

10

ESTIMATION OF MINIMUM NUMBERS OF INDIVIDUALS

Introduction

The estimation of the minimum number of individuals represented in an archaeological assemblage appears to be one of the parameters which is expected of the osteoarchaeologist, although its value seems questionable. The method normally used to obtain this information is to count the frequency of occurrence of some single skeletal or other hard structure in the assemblage and compare it with the known frequency of occurrence of the individual animal, at the same time making correction for differences in size. The issue has become clouded with controversy as to its value, and several mathematical methods have been suggested to remove the elements of chance that are ever present. Most of the discussion has related to workers with mammalian remains but the general principles are directly relevant to fish remains and readers are recommended to consult the publications of White (1953), Cornwall (1968), Krantz (1968), Daly (1969), Chaplin (1971), Grayson (1973), Lie (1980) and Fieller and Turner (1982). All of these publications cite the work of others who have addressed the subject. Casteel (1976) discussed the possibility of using the proposed methods for fish remains, and Nichol and Wild (1984) have pointed out the difficulties, using examples from their work on fishes from New Zealand sites.

Single and paired skeletal elements

Potentially the most critical skeletal structures to use in the estimation of minimum numbers are bones from the mid-line of the body of which only one is present in each fish. Such bones as the prevomer, basioccipital, supraoccipital, basisphenoid and parasphenoid occur as single bones in the neurocranium, but only the first two have clearly defined features which permit certain identification (most of the time) and are stout enough to survive as recognizable bones. The dorsal or anal fin spine of some fishes, for example the carp, also occurs singly in each specimen, as does the distinctive anal pterygiophore of pleuronectid flatfishes, such as the plaice and flounder. Bones, or other remains, which occur as pairs in each individual fish are potentially as useful, and of these the premaxillaries, maxillaries, dentaries and sagittal otoliths are especially significant in that they are usually unequivocably identifiable and all, except the otoliths, survive well in most archaeological deposits. Being paired structures is an advantage as they are all quickly differentiated into left or right elements, which doubles the chances of survival, recovery and recognition.

A crude estimation of minimum numbers of individuals represented by the identified material can therefore be made by counting the number of single bones (e.g. prevomer), or by sorting the paired bones in a sequence of left and right and later by visual estimate or measurement for size. Left and right examples of the same bone which are identical in size have to be assumed to be a pair from the same fish specimen, but unmatched bones can all be counted as representing single individuals. The maximum number of matched and unmatched elements present represents the minimum number of individuals in the material.

While several mathematical methods have been suggested (see Nichol and Wild, 1984, for a review relating to fish and mammalian remains) to eliminate errors or to enhance the data, there seems to be little point in attempting to elaborate the information, for reasons which will be advanced later. If the material from a single horizon yields a minimum number of individuals on the basis of counted single features, or paired features maximized as shown above, then the only statement that can be made safely is that the surviving remains represent n individuals at least, but n is likely to bear no relationship to the number of individual fish which were brought to the site and which formed that horizon.

Only in very special circumstances where the fish remains are in a sealed horizon can minimum numbers be more meaningful. Thus, the remains of sardines, *Sardina pilchardus*, from amphorae recovered from a Roman wreck in Sicily, were subject to minimum number estimates by counting dentary and opercular bones and sorting left from right by Wheeler and Locker (1985 and in press). A similar mass of material, possibly in a container or dumped in a confined space and then protected by the collapse of a nearby Roman wall at Chapel Street, Chichester, Sussex, was studied by Locker (pers. comm.). It comprised vertebral centra and auditory capsules (otic bullae) of another clupeid, the sprat, *Sprattus sprattus*. The latter numbered 2,010 and represented at least 1,005 individual fish.

Minimum numbers estimated from other remains

As vertebrae are the most common remains of fishes to be found in archaeo-logical assemblages, it may be felt that some attempt should be made to use them for estimation of minimum numbers. They must, however, be centra which can be identified for certain. If distinctive centra such as the first abdominal, the first caudal, or the penultimate caudal centra are present then a statement can be made that, based on these elements, and taking size of individual fish represented, a minimum number of fish is represented by these remains.

Simply counting the number of vertebrae will not give a meaningful result because of the large number of centra each fish possesses (e.g. Salmoniformes *c.* 50–60, Clupeiformes 45–65, Gadiformes 55–75 – see chapter 7). Where abdominal centra can be clearly identified as such, their employment somewhat narrows down the numbers involved, but even then the results are unlikely to be convincing.

Scales may be equally numerous in archaeological material but, as has already been discussed, are so rarely preserved or recovered entire that their use for the establishment of minimum numbers is never justified or if it is possible then it can only be in quite exceptional circumstances.

Neither vertebrae nor scales have therefore any use in the estimation of the number of fishes represented in a single horizon. This contrasts starkly with the statements of Casteel (1976) that 'Fish vertebrae, in particular the vertebral centra, have been shown to be valuable sources of information . . . concerning . . . estimation of the minimum number of individuals in an assemblage' (p. 92) and 'fish scales . . . may be used to examine the question of the minimum number of individuals represented in an assemblage' (p. 71). The examples used to reach these conclusions were drawn from vertebrae and scales of a small number of comparative preparations (three skeletons for vertebrae, and 12 scales from two fish, all of known length) and are quite unconvincing.

The problem with fish remains for estimation of numbers

The relative abundance of the remains of a species of fish in an archaeological assemblage is inherently more difficult to assess than that of mammals, because of the greater number of elements in a fish skeleton and because they are less robust than the comparable bones of animals.

The taphonomic aspects of fish bone survival have been discussed in chapter 5, but it is relevant to mention briefly here the major factors. Fish bones are vulnerable to digestion (Jones, 1984a), to damage by trampling underfoot (Jones and Bullock, in preparation), and by cooking (Colley, in press). As a consequence there is less chance of fish bones being deposited, or surviving if deposited, at archaeological sites than bones of other classes of vertebrates.

The effects of decay of bones in relation to estimates of minimum numbers have been addressed by Nichol and Wild (1984). Using data from assemblages of bones of the sea-bream (known as 'snapper' in New Zealand – identified as *Chrysophrys auratus* Forster, although this name is dubious) from nine coastal middens, they found that, of five paired head bones, the premaxillae were the most common class in each assemblage. However, they had earlier established that there was a considerable loss of even premaxillae, many of the surviving bones were damaged, and most of the surviving left and right bones lacked the corresponding bone from the other side. They also drew attention to the presence of a layer of ash at one of their sites, below which survival of fish bones (as well as leaves and fish scales) was better than in layers above. They concluded that an unknown quantity of bone is destroyed by acids in rainwater, particularly carbonic acid, and that material in the upper layers of a site may protect that in lower layers, thus giving differential survival inverse to the chronological expectation.

These taphonomic factors, in addition to the factors involving physical damage outlined above, skew any numerical assessment of minimum numbers of individuals so markedly that their presentation becomes meaningless except in unusual circumstances.

Other objective assessments of numbers

Because so many archaeological assemblages are obviously dominated by one species, or a very small number of species, with groups of fishes which are rather less important or which occur rarely, the archaeologist must make some attempt to describe these frequencies of occurrence objectively. Several measures are possible but each has strengths or weaknesses.

The simplest method is to count the number of identifiable fragments for each species (or other taxonomic grouping) in the assemblage. This approach is biased in favour of species which possess large numbers of robust and easily recognized bones.

Some workers record the weight of identified bone for each taxon. This method might be acceptable for the bones of large mammals which have relatively consistently sized bones at maturity, according to species. However, fishes have enormous size ranges and, because they are obtained from wild populations, there is relatively little consistency in size of captured fish, and their bones range from minimal density (e.g. salmon and trout, angler fishes, and all the cartilaginous fishes) to relatively solid bone (e.g. cods, seabreams, sea perches, etc.). Weight of bone is thus not comparable for different species. Moreover the weight of bones is biased in favour of species which have large and solid bones, and is impractical unless the remains are scrupulously cleaned.

A relatively recent approach in archaeological work, but one used for many years by zoologists studying otter spraints and other bone-rich faeces (for example, Erlinge, 1968) is to assess the frequency with which a species occurs in remains. The adoption of this technique has been suggested by O'Connor (1985) and is particularly appropriate when there is little chance that all the remains of fishes brought onto the site are preserved in a deposit. Frequency can be calculated for material collected by hand or for sieved material. It requires counting the number of times a species occurs in the contexts or in samples excavated. Thus, a single cod bone from a sample or context will count as 1, but 100 cod bones from a single context will also count as 1. If 100 contexts of a site yield fish bone and cod proves to be present in 90 of them, then cod can be said to be present in 90% of the contexts. It is unimportant whether cod is represented in those contexts by a single bone or whether it is represented by a vast mass of material, because the single bone is still evidence for the occurrence of cod in that sample and thus its use at this level of occupation. Similarly, if plaice is present in 15 of the 100 contexts, its frequency of occurrence is 15%. The fact that three of the 15 contexts yielded many hundreds of plaice bones is irrelevant in this kind of quantification. Some zoologists consider relative frequency to be a better estimate of abundance because the figure given is the percentage of the total number of species recorded, rather than the number of samples containing the various species. Watson (1978) discusses this approach in detail.

Another strategy that might be useful could be adopted from the points method of estimating relative abundance of food in the gut of fishes (Hynes, 1950). In this method the bones in a context or sample are sorted and identified as far as possible. A subjective assessment is then made of the number of individuals of each species represented using all the available evidence (i.e. differences in size of bones, numbers of bones, presence of single bones, or the sum of matched and unmatched paired bones). Then, using an arbitrary scale of 20 (or 50, or 100), points are allocated to each species in accordance with the estimate of the number of species present. This would then indicate the relative importance of each species in a context. Essentially it depends on subjective estimates which are converted to apparently objective numerical assessments, which are more attractive than totally subjective descriptors.

Whichever method of quantification is adopted, it must always be remembered that the end result is an assessment based on a flawed sample in almost every case. It can never be an accurate picture of fish abundance and it is not justifiable to extrapolate from such data to the amount of protein represented by the bones (cf. Shawcross, 1968).

11

ESTIMATION OF SEASON OF CAPTURE

Introduction

The possible use of fish remains as a means of throwing light on seasonality of occupation of early sites or seasonal exploitation of food resources has been discussed by several authors. For example, Casteel (1976) gave several references to this use and propounded some mainly hypothetical examples, while authors such as Mellars and Wilkinson (1980) actually employed archaeological remains to establish seasonality of capture for fish at Mesolithic sites on Oronsay (Inner Hebrides). There is no doubt that, with careful observation and interpretation, the remains from occasional sites have the potential to be used for evidence of seasonality of capture. However, such data cannot be obtained from all archaeological remains, for reasons which will become apparent.

Seasonal growth

As discussed earlier, fishes have the capacity to grow virtually throughout their lives although with senescence or under adverse environmental conditions, or in cases of heavy parasitization or disease, growth can become very slow or even cease altogether. In the wild, fish probably rarely experience this, although it has been observed in long-lived captive fishes in pools and aquaria. In virtually all fishes growth proceeds in bursts, depending on physiological changes induced by alterations in the environment. In temperate and near-polar waters the growth cycle is seasonal and is controlled by day-length and the consequent warming of water, which causes food to become more abundant and which in turn results in an increase in growth. However, in some fishes, e.g. populations of whitefish, *Coregonus clupeaformis*, growth may be closely correlated with increased day-length (with a time lapse of about a month) and only weakly correlated with temperature (Ricker, 1979). Other studies have indicated that increases in growth are in fact a daily phenomenon, and daily growth bands have been detected in otoliths in a number of species (see Barkman and Bangtson, 1987 for references). Most of these studies have been made on young fishes and, while they are important to fisheries studies of growth and survival of juveniles, their interest for archaeologists is rather academic.

In tropical waters growth zones are also related to environmental factors but are less clearly associated with seasonal changes. Pannella (1974) showed

154

that in Puerto Rican waters growth patterns in the otoliths of marine fishes reflect the lunar cycle, and bimonthly (14 days) or monthly (28 days) changes in growth can be detected. In mature fishes this could reflect the influence of lunar periodicity on gonad maturation but it is also detectable in immature fish.

Regular cycles of growth are, however, detectable in tropical marine fishes, where they are probably related to reproductive activities rather than seasonal environmental change. In tropical freshwater fishes growth cycles are also related to reproductive activity but this, in turn, is often associated with seasonal rainfall, as Fagade (1974) demonstrated for brackish-water populations of the cichlid fish *Sarotherodon melanotheron* in a Lagos lagoon.

Spawning seasons also appear to be closely related to rainy periods, especially in flood plains (Lowe-McConnell, 1975), and these regular cycles will be as well represented in the growth of fishes as the 'physiological winter' to which Lowe-McConnell aptly likens the dry season.

Seasonal growth can be detected on several hard parts of the fish by the marks registering periods when the daily growth increments are closer together (i.e. at times when growth is slow) than when the marks are more widely spaced (i.e. when conditions are optimal and growth is rapid). Such growth zones can be detected on parts of the skeleton and other hard structures, but for practical reasons the most frequently utilized structures are vertebrae, opercular bones, scales and otoliths, in increasing order of importance.

Examination of the scales of a fish from temperate waters will show a series of more or less concentric rings around the nucleus. These are close-set during periods of slow growth (usually winter time) and widen during spring and summer. It is thus possible to make a subjective assessment of the season at which the scale was removed from the fish. Scales have the advantage of being flattened, which allows examination under magnification with only minimal preparation (cleaning, and pressing flat between two sheets of glass). If they are thin and translucent, fresh or modern otoliths can be viewed in the same way (either by reflected or by transmitted light) but they are often distinctly three-dimensional and too thick for direct viewing, in which case they have to be sectioned. Sections can be made simply by snapping the otolith across its width and 'reading' the broken end for growth zones, or by more elaborate techniques such as thin sections. Large numbers are processed for fisheries' purposes by setting them in resin in lines then cutting and polishing the resin blocks so that precise cross-sections of the otolith are presented for examination and interpretation. A useful review of the processes involved in age determination from otoliths was presented by Williams and Bedford (1974).

Fisheries management and investigations into age and growth of fishes involve the examination of large numbers of scales, otoliths, opercular bones and other parts of the skeleton (as appropriate to the species involved). To achieve accuracy fishery scientists frequently examine thousands of specimens and have long experience in interpretation; archaeologists should not expect simply to examine one or two scales or otoliths and establish seasonality of capture on this basis.

Factors affecting growth

In addition to the environmental factors which affect the growth of fish by producing changes in the physiology of fishes, other circumstances affect growth. As mentioned above, perturbations in growth rate can be caused by a number of endogenous and exogenous factors.

The most marked of these is the effect of reproduction. The demands made on the metabolism of a mature fish by the increase in gonad size as spawning approaches (mainly in calcium metabolism) causes an interruption in the regular cycle of growth. This is reflected most clearly on the scales, but in some species may be detected in growth zones in other hard structures. It is particularly apparent in the Atlantic salmon, *Salmo salar*. In large, mature fish calcium metabolism is strongly affected to the extent of withdrawal of much calcium from the bony skeleton during gonad maturation following migration from the sea to the riverine spawning ground, during which time the fish does not feed. The scales of salmon which have spawned show considerable regression and even loss of material at the margin, leaving a clear spawning mark (which may obscure some of the growth circuli). Similar, but less extreme, loss of scale tissue following spawning can be seen in other salmonid fishes, and in some unrelated fishes. Pacific salmon, *Oncorhynchus* spp., suffer such physiological stress as a result of migration into fresh water and spawning that they die. Their scales at spawning show considerable degeneration.

Spawning marks on the scales of some species therefore offer strong indicators of seasonality of capture in recent fishes. It is possible that exceptionally well-preserved scales from archaeological sites might be interpreted for seasonality provided that the spawning season for ancient fishes can be assumed to be the same as that for comparative material.

Growth can also be affected by the effect of 'stunting' in a population of fishes. Most observations of stunting have been made in freshwater fishes, many (if not all) of which have been affected by human interference. As a result, it is not certain that the causes of stunting would operate in a wholly natural environment although they are of major importance in some freshwater fisheries. Stunting is essentially a result of there being insufficient food to support the population of fish in the water. The imbalance between food and fish may be caused by low productivity, due to the acidity of the water, or to an excess of fish as a result of the absence of predators or the high fecundity of the fish. The perch, *Perca fluviatilis*, is well known for its tendency to form stunted populations in lakes. Unlike other species it is to some extent self-regulatory, as a successful year-class will dominate a lake, preying on the smaller fishes of later year-classes for several years until it dies out, whereupon it will be succeeded by another strong year-class.

Loss of condition can also be caused by disease and by heavy parasitic infestation. Both can negatively affect the growth of fish, causing perturbation to the regular increase in size of the fish and its scales or otoliths. Although these factors have been recognized in studies on living fishes, they have not been observed in archaeological fish remains (and are unlikely to be so). They are mentioned here so that archaeologists will be aware of the complexity of factors affecting fish growth and interpretation of seasonality.

Relating data from study of recent fishes to archaeological material
Discussion of the growth processes of fish, especially its seasonal variation, suggests that it offers good possibility for use in interpreting seasonality of capture for archaeologists. However, in spite of several attempts, few workers have successfully exploited the potential of this encoded information. The reasons for this failure are several, but the most common is that growth zones obvious in modern material are rarely preserved with sufficient clarity in archaeological remains. Indeed, the area of greatest significance for these studies, the edges of scales and thin bones, such as the opercular, is the most vulnerable to damage in archaeological material. A second reason for the paucity of convincing studies in this field is that a great deal of experience is necessary before it is possible to assess growth zones accurately and consistently. While it is simple to illustrate growth lines or rings in a text book, ichthyologists who examine large amounts of modern material are acutely aware of the difficulty of making accurate judgements as well as of recognizing anomalous specimens. For example, a fish usually has two identical sagittal otoliths, but specimens have been found in which one otolith will give an age clearly different from the other (Reinsch, 1976). Spawning marks can also lead to confusion in scale rings.

Unfortunately the confident assertion of Casteel (1976) that seasonality could be established from archaeological remains (which was not supported by evidence of practical experience) has led some archaeologists into making bold statements regarding seasonal exploitation of fishes. For example, the claim of Henderson (1986: 68) that the season of capture of the fish represented in a medieval rubbish dump at Eyemouth, Scotland, 'can be determined by studying the width of the last annual ring on the faces on the vertebrae' seems to betray ignorance of the subtle nature of fish growth, as no ring is 'annual' in formation. The sweeping conclusions drawn from this statement are unsupported by any confirmatory evidence. Such claims are best ignored.

However, some researchers have produced strikingly informative results from their material. Noe-Nygaard's (1983) study of pike from Mesolithic sites in Denmark showed that large numbers were killed in May and the majority between May and August. She arrived at this conclusion by examining seasonal growth zones on vertebrae, supplemented by observation of the cleithrum and basihyal. Her scholarly study was aided by the excellent preservation of the material in lake sediment, and by comparison with the bones of 100 modern pike. Only in studies utilizing material of this number of specimens from environments similar to those of the ancient material can convincing results on seasonality be achieved.

Otoliths from saithe, *Pollachius virens*, were used in an impressive study of season of capture for Mesolithic shell-midden sites on Oronsay (Inner Hebrides), Scotland, by Mellars and Wilkinson (1980). Basing their study on the length of the otolith, they showed firstly a bi-modal distribution which correlated with the exploitation of two year-classes (fig. 11.1). Secondly, they demonstrated a distinct seasonality in size distribution within the year-classes

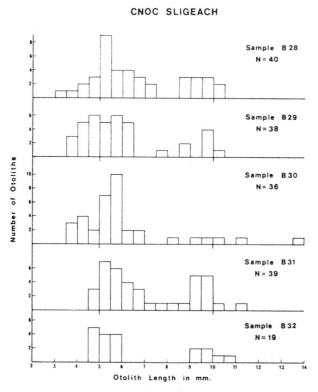

11.1   Length distribution of sagittal otoliths of saithe, *Pollachius virens*, from five samples at Cnoc Sligeach, Oronsay. All samples show two year-classes; sample B30 has a single otolith, possibly of a third year-class. (From Mellars and Wilkinson, 1980.)

and between different shell-middens, concluding that from the Cnoc Sligeach midden the fish were caught between the end of June and mid- or late August while from the nearby Cnoc Coig midden the fish appeared to have been captured between early September and late November or early December. The Oronsay material was exceptionally well preserved – unusually so for otoliths – and was present in large numbers (more than 1,300 otoliths from these two middens). Interpretation of the material was only possible with a large volume of comparative specimens (more than 300 otoliths from recent fishes).

These two examples show most graphically that seasonality of capture can be deduced from fish remains. Both, however, make the same points about the specifications of material to be analysed. The remains have to be present in large numbers, they have to be exceptionally well preserved, and their study will only be possible if a large set of comparative material in which seasonal data is encoded is available. Bold statements that 'annual rings' are visible are even less convincing in the absence of such detailed study.

Assessment of seasonality from ecological information

The establishment of seasonality of capture from the study of growth rings on skeletal remains or scales, or analysis of otoliths has the clear attraction of providing objective data and is to be preferred when the material is adequate and well preserved. However, seasonality can be inferred from a knowledge of the ecology of modern fishes, especially from migration, and although this is highly subjective it can offer some guide to season of capture. Thus a knowledge of the distribution of modern saithe in Scottish waters might have led to the presumption that the fishery at Oronsay was prosecuted mainly during the warmer months of the year. Juvenile saithe are common close inshore in low-shore rock pools with dense algae and in kelp beds during their first year. During their second and third years they live close to the shore. All three year-groups move offshore in the winter when the weather deteriorates and live in schools in slightly deeper water. It could therefore be argued that the remains of large numbers of small fishes would probably indicate a fishery during the warm season, when the fish were inshore and more easily available to a low-technology Mesolithic culture. Such *a priori* reasoning is clearly less convincing than the objective and scholarly methods adopted by Mellars and Wilkinson (1980). However, in some cases it is the best that can be done with the material.

Migratory fishes also show seasonal behaviour which it can be inferred make them more accessible at some time in the year than in others. Migration of herring in the North Sea even as late as the 1930s resulted in seasonal exploitation and an associated migration of fishermen and processors along the east coast of the United Kingdom and of boats from Denmark, Germany and Holland. So rooted was the seasonal nature of the herring fishing in the culture of East Anglia that it had a recognized season from 29 September to 11 November, and the Herring Free Fair was held at Great Yarmouth between these dates from 1270 until the eighteenth century (Hodgson, 1957). Archaeological remains of herring in this area might therefore be expected to have been captured during this period. Conversely, if it could be proved by objective methods that they were not autumn-caught fish, then the possibility of imported preserved fishes might be considered.

Cod, *Gadus morhua*, also make local migrations, for example moving southwards into the eastern English Channel during the winter months. This might be significant in the context of the interpretation of fish remains in southern England (although as this species is known to have been widely traded it would not be a significant deduction). Local knowledge of the behaviour of fish species might help the archaeologist make judgements on seasonal availability anywhere in the world.

Migrations of tuna, *Thunnus thynnus*, in the Mediterranean are well known for their strongly seasonal nature (Tortonese, 1975), which at times brings them close inshore, where they are vulnerable to relatively simple fishing techniques. Even in the twentieth century this species (and the swordfish *Xiphias gladius*) are regularly captured by interruption of the migration by nets leading to enclosures in which these often massive fishes are harpooned. Although the materials used have changed and the scale probably increased, the fishing technology is relatively simple and relies on seasonal migration. Large aggregations of tuna bones, as at Franchthi, Pelepponesus (Wheeler, unpublished) might well be a result of seasonal fishing, the interpretation of which would be aided by local modern knowledge of their migrations.

The seasonal migration of fishes in coastal waters has led to many local fisheries which were recorded in historical times and were no doubt well established in prehistory. The capelin, *Mallotus villosus*, widely distributed in northern polar seas, spawns in the early Arctic summer actually on the shore and in shallow water in dramatic numbers. The fish can be captured in large quantities at this season and Jangaard (1974) published a photograph dating from 1885 of east Greenlanders from Angmagssalik district with traditional dipnets.

Like the capelin, the migration of anadromous members of the salmon family is associated with the reproductive cycle of the species. A detailed and wide-ranging discussion of the significance of anadromous fishes has been presented by Schalk (1977). Atlantic salmon, *Salmo salar*, enter rivers from the sea at all times of the year and migrate upstream at different speeds depending on river flow and water temperature, but all arrive at the spawning beds between November and February (Mills, 1971). Here they are highly vulnerable as they are in shallow water and usually preoccupied with spawning. However, the salmon migration in individual rivers is far more localized temporally than this winter period and fish are concentrated in pools below the spawning grounds where again they can be captured without much effort.

The several species of Pacific salmon (*Oncorhynchus* spp.) spawn in different parts of the rivers of the northern Pacific basin, but migrations take place in relatively short periods of time. For example, Schalk (1977) cites the run of pink salmon, *O. gorbuscha*, in a small stream in southeastern Alaska, where 80% of the total run of fish passed between 14 and 26 days, and in some years 40% of the run passed in three days. Such intensive seasonal migrations would offer unrivalled opportunities for capture to aboriginal communities (indeed, the economic structure of many such communities in the northern Pacific basin was dependent on the migration of salmon). Fish bone assemblages from such areas, which contain species known to migrate seasonally, could often be interpreted for seasonality with this in mind.

Even fishes which make local spawning migrations within river systems do so at certain times of the year and their presence in archaeological remains can be an indication of seasonality of capture. An example that can be cited is Follett's (1967) account of the remains of the cyprinid fish, the cui-ui, *Chasmistes cujus*, in Lovelock Cave, Nevada, in which he suggests that these fish were caught when they were most vulnerable during their springtime spawning migration in the nearby lower Truckee River. This again exemplifies that access to detailed local knowledge of the ecology of the fishes allows reasonable assumptions to be made as to seasonality of capture.

To summarize, seasonality of capture can sometimes be postulated with accuracy where appropriate material (mainly otoliths and some critical bones) is preserved in good condition. Such events are unusual in archaeological fish material, and their interpretation require large comparative collections. In other cases subjective assessments as to seasonality of capture can be made with a knowledge of the seasonal availability of modern fishes. Such assessments can never be absolute and can be treated only as indications of seasonality.

12

INTERPRETATION OF
FISHING ACTIVITY

Introduction

The excavation and identification of fish remains are clearly not final objectives. Correct identification is merely one step towards analysis of the material, aimed at the assessment of the cultural and economic development of the community occupying the site. Analysis has to bring together a knowledge of the biology, distribution and habits of the fish species identified, in addition to making judgements as to the possibility of environmental change between 'then' and 'now'. Only with such analysis can answers to the important questions such as where the fish were caught, how they were caught and whether the presence of certain species suggests seasonality of occupation, be advanced. With such knowledge it is possible to postulate the technology required to catch these fishes. Taken with evidence from other faunal remains, as well as artefacts, the interpretation of fish remains will add to the overall image of the cultural and economic background. However, it must once again be emphasized that no interpretation of fishing activity and certainly no calculation of protein intake from fishes can be attempted (by an archaeologist of whole mind) unless the identification of the remains is accurate (for a discussion of one example of misinterpretation see Wheeler, 1978a).

There is one assumption central to the interpretation of all ancient biological remains. It is that the ecology of plants and animals has not altered appreciably in the last 20,000 years. In fact, there is little evidence to suggest that the aspects of fish behaviour observed today were substantially different in the past, although there is evidence that geographical distribution differs slightly as a result of changes in climate, and modern spatial distribution may be different because of intense fishing pressure. Thus it is possible to apply data from modern studies to ancient assemblages of fish remains and by so doing infer a great deal about past fishing activity.

Drawing inferences is a different process from describing what was found. Given careful methods and adequate reference material it is possible to give an objective and accurate picture of what was found. Inferring fishing methods is a different kind of analysis; it is based upon a great number of assumptions and often draws on evidence from historical and ethnographic sources.

162

Faunistic interpretation
The compilation of a list of fish species represented by the remains in any excavation, with some qualification as to the most important (or frequently occurring) species, produces a set of data which will form the basis for interpretation. At its most simple, examination of the list of most abundant species can reveal whether the fishes exploited were freshwater or marine taxa, or a little less certainly estuarine or brackish-water species. For an inland site in England for example the identification of carp, tench, some other cyprinids, and perch and pike would indicate that a freshwater lake might have been the source of the fishes exploited. If eel, salmonid and shad were also represented in addition to the above species, then it would be sufficient evidence to postulate that the habitat being exploited was a river, or possibly a river and a still water together. If, however, there were a significant number of marine fishes represented (e.g. cod, ling or hake) then clearly the inhabitants of the site had also been supported by a trade in fish from the coast (which may imply salted or smoked fish) and reasonably efficient transport and communications. An instructive demonstration of such an analysis has been given by Brinkhuizen (1979a) in which he tabulates fishes identified from 15 sites in the Netherlands from the Neolithic to the medieval periods. This shows a positive emphasis on freshwater species in the five sites dated from 3,500 to 2,000 years BC but the latest site contains marine species. This suggests that the development of coastal fisheries occurred in the late Neolithic. It must also be borne in mind that, because of changes in land/sea levels in the Netherlands during the Atlantic period, the present sites that are accessible now are those which were far inland when they were occupied. Interpretation of fish remains, particularly if they can be integrated with similar information from invertebrates, such as molluscs, will produce important evidence for the source of food for the community inhabiting the site. Knowledge of the species present, and the habits of these fishes can be used to hypothesize the means by which they were captured, a topic which will be explored later.

Interpretation of the fish remains may also be assisted by an approximate estimation of the size of the specimens represented. Thus, saithe or coalfish, *Pollachius virens* (known on the Atlantic coast of North America as the pollock), are common in shore pools and close inshore during their first two years and can be caught in large numbers on a hook and line fished from a long rod. Such fishing was important in areas such as the northern islands of Scotland, where land-based food resources were minimal (Fenton, 1973), and presumed the use of minimal technology. Probably this technique or a similar one was employed to capture the large numbers of young saithe represented in the shell middens from Mesolithic sites on the island of Oronsay in the Inner Hebrides (Mellars and Payne, 1971; later studied by Mellars and

Wilkinson, 1980). However, had the saithe remains been from mature fish then it would be necessary to postulate a different capture strategy involving fishing in deeper water.

A knowledge of the size of fishes represented in a site could also be of importance if the fishes are migratory. For example, the European eel, *Anguilla anguilla*, breeds in mid-Atlantic, its juveniles ascend rivers in Europe from February to June (the month depends on how distant the river is from the breeding area) as elvers at 10–12 cm length, spend variable periods (from five to 20 years) in fresh water then migrate as maturing adults in the autumn down river to the sea. Eel bones are commonly identified in inland sites in England, especially those close to rivers. The presence of the bones of eels of varying sizes would suggest that the fishery was conducted in a river or lagoon, probably throughout the year but at least by generalized fishing methods (baited lines, leisters and possibly also traps), but a heavy preponderance of large eels would suggest a fishery using traps to catch maturing eels on their seaward migration and thus also suggest seasonality for capture from September to early November when the migration is at its height.

The presence of large numbers of eel bones in medieval Oldenburg in Schleswig-Holstein (FRG) was explained by Prummel (1986) as due to the neighbouring presence of a large freshwater lake which would have been inhabited by large (mostly female) eels. This constrasts with the brackish fjord on which nearby Viking Haithabu was sited, from which relatively few eel bones were reported. Prummel's explanation seems soundly based and might have been extended by reference to the ease with which migrating eels can be caught in very simple traps.

In can be noted parenthetically here that this freshwater eel has considerable populations on the sea coast, as well as in lower estuaries. The presence of *Anguilla* bones in a coastal site does not necessarily imply the transport of eels from inland fresh water.

These examples are all drawn from European sites or are postulated from hypothetical European situations. They are only possible because knowledge of the fishes of this region is detailed. Comparable examples could be expected in other areas where comprehensive accounts of the fish fauna exist, but in large parts of the world where the fauna is both richer and the fishes comparatively less well-known the archaeologist will find difficulty in extrapolating meaningfully from lists of species identified.

The knowledge of the distribution of fishes which ichthyologists have built up is an important resource for the archaeologist. At the very minimum it provides information as to which species might be expected to occur in a site and which of those tentatively identified require confirmation because they are rarely found in the area today. However, there are qualifications to be made to the use of present-day data concerning distribution, abundance and size that make the interpretation of archaeological information of interest to the zoologist.

The presence of considerable numbers of the pharyngeal bones of the corkwing wrasse, *Crenilabrus melops*, in the Neolithic tomb at Quanterness, Orkney Islands, was postulated by Wheeler (1977) to be evidence for a greater abundance of this species during the occupation of the site than at present (for it is now not very common in the Orkneys). As this species is Atlanto-Mediterranean in its distribution, reaching the northern limits of its regular distribution in the Orkneys and the Atlantic coast of Sweden, Wheeler suggested that it could be seen as an indication of a warmer climate during the use of the tomb.

A comparable example was provided by Necrasov and Haimovici (1959), who found the sea-bream, *Sparus aurata*, to be well represented in a Neolithic site near Techirghiol on the Romanian Black Sea coast. Although this species, the glithead bream, is common today in the Mediterranean, it is rare in the Black Sea. They postulate from this evidence (confirmed by pollen analysis) that the climate there was warmer during the occupation of the site. They also suggest that the lake at Techirghiol may then have been saline and provided a suitable habitat for this species, which favours water of low salinity.

Another fascinating example of archaeological fish remains revealing previously unsuspected information on the original distribution of a fish has been provided by Lernau (1986–7). The Israeli scholar reported the occurrence of Nile perch, *Lates* cf. *niloticus*, remains in five dated archaeological excavations extending from the Late Bronze Age to the Islamic period. The Nile perch is widely distributed in tropical Africa, including the River Nile, but it does not occur today in Israel. Its occurrence in these sites in Israel can only be explained by postulating trade with Egypt over a very long period, or by recognizing that *Lates* was originally a member of the fauna of present-day Israel. As there is a strong element of the Nilotic fauna present today in Israel, and other representatives are known to have been present but to have become extinct, it seems that the Nile perch must have been present in sufficient numbers to have been exploited for food over a considerable period of time.

There is some evidence that the present distribution of fishes may be affected by human activity so that there have been significant changes in availability. The most obvious of these, overfishing, is a result of highly developed technology and unrestricted catches, which eventually reaches a level at which catches can no longer be sustained. However, there are more subtle changes resulting from overfishing in that, once numbers have been reduced, the range of the species contracts. Examples are not difficult to find: the halibut, *Hippoglossus hippoglossus*, was present in numbers in shallow inshore waters of 9–18 m in the Gulf of Maine in the mid-nineteenth century.

Today after years of heavy exploitation it is caught only in deep water and offshore (Bigelow and Schroeder, 1953). A comparable example concerns the hake, *Merluccius merluccius*, which today is caught in deep water around 165–550 m (90–300 fathoms) in the eastern Atlantic by commercial trawlers (Wheeler, 1969). However, west-coast fishermen have told one of us (A.W.) that in the immediately post-war period of 1947–50 good-sized hake were caught in 10–20 m and well within the headlands of the coastal bays. For archaeologists, the significance of these examples is that in conditions of heavy exploitation the range of a fish species may diminish. In both cases, the presence of halibut or hake bones may not be evidence for high technology offshore fishing; both species could be caught close inshore where exploitation was at a uniformly low level.

The recognition of fish remains in certain sites and circumstances can have considerable interest for the zoologist. Thus, Miller (1955) reported the remains of the Colorado squawfish, *Ptychocheilus lucius*, from sites occupied in the eighteenth century AD by Sobaipuri Indians of southern Arizona and inferred from this that the San Pedro River was then and later a much larger and more stable stream than it was in later historical times. Gehlback and Miller (1961) also found the remains of the longnose gar, *Lepisosteus osseus*, and the blue sucker, *Cycleptus elongatus*, from sites in northern New Mexico, species which are no longer found in the Colorado River and the upper Rio Grande basin respectively. They concluded that the gars were secured for food from the Rio Grande basin and imported to the site, and the blue sucker was probably evidence that the upper Rio Grande was a clearer, larger and more stable stream during the period of occupation and was a suitable habitat for this relatively large fish. All three examples produced information on the hydrography of these regions and new light on the distribution of fishes in the area.

The carp, *Cyprinus carpio*, is now widespread by introduction in many parts of the world from its original range of the Danube basin, southern and eastern Europe and northern Asia. Considerable interest centres on the date of its first introduction to western Europe; Brinkhuizen's (1979a) report of carp remains from medieval Leeuwarden is the earliest hard evidence for its introduction.

Brinkhuizen (1979b) has also drawn attention to the discovery of the bones of the European catfish or wels, *Siluris glanis*, in seven sites in the Netherlands dating from between ± 3450 BC to ± 1150 AD. Before his report was published, it had been assumed by ichthyologists that this species was an introduction from the Danube basin. The species has subsequently been introduced and cultured by fishery interests in the Netherlands, but with this evidence from archaeozoology it can now be seen as an indigenous fish.

Some finds of fish remains from archaeological sites relate not to local fish fauna but to distant ones, because the excavated remains are of fishes imported considerable distances. Here, however, careful consideration of the species composition of archaeological assemblages can indicate the source or sources of the fishes. Lernau (1986) examined fish remains from two late Roman fortified sites (castella) in southern Israel. Both sites were located in arid areas with a very restricted indigenous fish population. However, bones of the African catfish, *Clarias gariepinus*, and other freshwater species, showed that fish were imported, presumably from the Jordan. Remains of the marine species white grouper, *Epinephelus aeneus*, and two sparids showed that fishes from the Mediterranean were imported, while bones of *Lethrinus* sp. and parrotfishes, *Scarus* sp., indicated that fishes from more eastern waters, probably from the Gulf of Eilat or the Red Sea, were brought to the sites. In this case careful faunistic analysis, considering principally biogeographical data, have helped to identify sources of fish and suggested trade routes.

Elaboration of fishing techniques

Not only does an analysis of the species present in a site provide information of the location and nature of past fish populations, but it also permits inferences about the methods used in their capture. Man has developed a plethora of techniques to exploit the range of fishes in each locality. An excellent study by Stewart (1977) demonstrates the range of fishing techniques used by Indians of the Pacific northwest coast of America. Such a detailed study shows the diversity of techniques devised by a human group and is an object lesson in the care which must be taken in interpreting fishing practices.

There is a range of additional sources of information on past fishing techniques, some of which may give a fuller picture of fishing methods than extrapolation from fish remains. Some methods of fishing leave little or no direct evidence in the archaeological record. Brinkhuizen (1983) discussed early fishing gear and traditional fishing methods in northwestern Europe. He summarized the variety of fishing techniques and pointed out that some do not require specialized fishing gear. Fish can be caught by hand, by 'tickling' them or swiftly snatching them from the water. Alternatively, fish can be caught by striking them with a stick or cudgel. During the autumn boys used stones mounted on sticks to stun fishes swimming just below the ice (Sirelius, 1934). Another technique is to stir up mud in small pools, bringing the fish to the surface where they can be caught. Poisoning is a well-known technique used in many parts of the world. Many plants contain substances (frequently alkaloids) which are toxic to vertebrate animals and have been adapted as fish poisons. Their development and use have probably evolved independently on many occasions in different continents and are part of the 'herbalist' knowledge of many cultures. Their use has been documented recently by Gunda (1984) for the Carpathian area and the Balkan peninsula, although he also includes a general review of piscicides. Another general review by Heizer (1953) concentrated on the aboriginal use of plants for killing fishes. Many plants well-known as garden or native species in Europe have piscicidal properties including *Cyclamen* spp., *Verbascum* spp., mulleins, *Daphne* spp., and *Euphorbia* spp., spurges, while plants such as *Datura* (the thorn apple), which have considerable important in the pharmaceutical industry, are also toxic to fishes. Derris or rotenone, which is derived from the roots of the South American plants of the genus *Derris*, and cubé, *Lonchocarpus nicou*, widely used by natives there to catch fishes, have proved so efficient as piscicides that they are in widespread use as a means of eradicating unwanted fishes by fisheries managers in Europe and North America (although their unauthorized use in fresh water is illegal).

Among other unusual techniques is the use of trained cormorants, *Phalacrocorax* spp., loosely tethered in a boat, each with a ring placed round its throat to prevent it from swallowing the prey. They were traditionally, and are still, used to catch fish in Japan (Kani, 1984). Kings James I and Charles I of England and Louis XIII of France also employed cormorants for catching fishes (Zeuner, 1963). In the West Indies remoras (suckerfishes), *Echeneis naucrates*, were kept in captivity and released on a line used to pull them in once they had attached themselves to desirable prey, usually turtles and fishes (Wing and Reitz, 1982). These authors point out that although remains of remoras were found at one of the sites studied there is little chance of recognizing this fishing technique in an archaeological assemblage of fish remains.

Although there are a host of less common methods used to catch fish (see Brandt, 1984, for more examples), it is clear that the following methods were the most widespread prior to industrialization: spear, harpoon, leister and rakes; nets of a multitude of different forms; traps, often associated with weirs or fences; and hooks, gorges and lures. The reason for the diversity of methods is that each technique has been evolved to capture particular targets, and no single fishing method is efficient for all kinds of fishes. For example, floating nets are the best way to catch shoaling pelagic fishes. Prior to the development of deep-water trawls, hooks were the most economic way of catching large bottom-feeding species, while traps set in rivers are effective in catching both anadromous and catadromous species. Fishing methods are usually targeted to catch a particular species or range of species of a limited size range. Thus, by considering the species composition and size of fishes represented in archaeological assemblages it may be possible to suggest which fishing technique was used in the past.

Most commentators agree that a wide range of techniques was developed, probably in the late Pleistocene, although dating these developments is difficult. Clearly human groups widely separated in time and space have invented identical fishing gear. Clark (1948, 1952), writing of prehistoric Europe, attempted to show a gradual development in fishing technology through time and Cutting (1955) reinforced this evolutionary notion by suggesting that techniques for preserving fishes developed gradually over the last 10,000 years or so. However, Radcliffe (1921) suggested that the spear, harpoon, hook and net were all technologies available to early societies. There seems to be no reason to expect fishing technology to have evolved stage by stage; a culture capable of crafting a fish hook was equally capable of making a fish spear, and vice versa. Indeed, a harpoon or spear would be a better investment of time and material as it could be used as a multi-purpose implement.

Given the diversity of fishing techniques available to past human populations, it is not surprising that the study of fish remains from archaeological sites rarely gives definite evidence of fishing techniques. However, by drawing on evidence from a range of disciplines, for example, archaeology, anthropology, ethnography and history, it is possible to infer a great deal about past fishing methods. For an excellent example of such a multi-disciplinary approach see Reinman (1967).

The most clear-cut evidence of techniques is that of finds of equipment which can only have been used in fishing. In exceptional circumstances such gear is found associated with fish remains. Fishing spears, harpoons and projectile points are often seen in museums, and Fenton (n.d.) has studied Scottish salmon spears in detail. The famous British Mesolithic site at Star Carr produced many barbed points which could have been used for fishing, perhaps for salmonid fishes such as arctic charr *Salvelinus* (Brinkhuizen, 1983), although the absence of fish bones from this site has frequently been mentioned and discussed (Wheeler, 1978b). Wooden objects made from hazel, *Corylus avellana*, found at the Danish Mesolithic site of Tybrind Vig are thought to be leister prongs (see illustrations by Trolle-Lassen, 1984). Many sites have yielded barbed points which may have been used to catch fishes (Clark, 1948, 1952) and other animals, although their presence does not prove that they were used for fishing, only that they were available for that purpose. However, discoveries in lakes dated to the Mesolithic period in the Baltic region provide incontrovertible evidence of the use of barbed points for fishing. The remains of pike with barbed points *in situ* was illustrated and discussed by Clark (1948, 1952) who hypothesized that the fish had been harpooned, but escaped and swam away to die later, probably from the injury inflicted.

Nets are made in an immense variety of shapes and sizes and are used to catch fishes (and other animals) in innumerable ways: dip nets can be hand-held; gill nets can be set and hauled by one man using a boat; seine nets require a small team to haul; trawls may require winches. Fishes from whitebait to 2-metre long halibut are caught in nets.

Finds of ancient nets are rare, but at the Key Marco, Florida, pre-Columbian fragments of nets were found associated with wooden floats and perforated shell weights (Cushing, 1896). Two kinds of net were identified, a coarse one thought to have been used as a gill net and a finer one interpreted as a dip net. Brinkhuizen (1983) gives examples of archaeological finds of ancient nets from Mesolithic Finland and Sweden, and Neolithic examples from several Scandinavian sites.

Often objects are assigned the term 'net-sinker' or 'line-sinker' without any clear evidence that they were used for either of those purposes and caution must be used before accepting the interpretation of artefacts in museum collections of archaeological finds. Ethnographic collections are more likely to be reliably named and many collections contain stones, some pierced, others grooved, which were definitely used in fishing. Generally, weights for sinking nets are usually rather small, unlike line sinkers, which often weigh 1 kg or more.

A convincing collection of lead net weights was recovered by field walking, with the help of a metal detector and limited excavations at Oldstead Grange, North Yorkshire. This site is adjacent to medieval fish ponds constructed for Cistercian monks of Byland Abbey by AD 1250. The monks employed labourers who dammed a valley with a substantial earth bank to form the pond. The dam was provided with an overflow channel to keep the water level constant and may have also had a complex wooden pipe which could be unplugged to drain the entire 20 hectares of pond. Excavations at the edge of the pond revealed a small stone-built structure with a large hearth. This has been interpreted as a fishermen's hut and smoke house. Included in the collection of metal artefacts from the site and its vicinity was an accurately trimmed weight weighing almost exactly 7 lb (3.17 kg), which was probably used for weighing the catches from the ponds (Kemp, 1984). While some historians have suggested that medieval monastic ponds may have produced a surplus of fish which could be sold, it is likely that the demand for fish within the monastery and the relatively low yield of monastic ponds meant that the majority of fish was consumed by the inhabitants of the monastery.

Hurum (1976) gives a catholic view of the development of fish hooks and gorges from the Palaeolithic to recent times. Wooden gorges, made of yew, *Taxus*, were found in excavations of medieval deposits at Elisenhof, West Germany, and have recently been described by Heinrich (1986). It has been pointed out that these objects may have served a number of functions. For example, they may have been used to catch birds, been used as awls or prickers, or even been used for personal ornamentation. Tribesmen in various parts of the world today use sharpened sticks for nose infibulators; such artefacts closely resemble gorges.

Other examples of ancient fishing gear are to be found in antiquarian and archaeological literature all over the world. Hooks are recovered during archaeological excavations and occasionally even traces of line may be attached. Trolle-Lassen (1984) illustrates a hook with a fragment of line, probably animal sinew, from Mesolithic Tybrind Vig, Denmark. A large collection of early medieval fish hooks was published by Rogerson (1976) for a site at Great Yarmouth, UK, and Leach (1979) states that the Washpool Site, New Zealand, produced rotating and jabbing hooks made from shell and bone in addition to other fishing gear. Consideration of the size of fish hooks may suggest what kinds of fishes were caught.

Traps, usually constructed of wickerwork woven around upright stakes or heaped boulders, depend upon tidal excursion and were used by many human groups in the recent and distant past, for example Indians of North Florida and the Antilles (Wing and Reitz, 1982) and a number of tribes in South Africa (Avery, 1975). Fish traps or pots are sometimes associated with weirs to catch fishes. Alternatively traps, usually of wicker, can be used independently of weirs. Brinkhuizen (1983) has discussed archaeological finds of fish weirs and traps in mainland Europe in considerable detail, while Losco-Bradley and Salisbury (1979) have described an ancient fish weir from Nottinghamshire, England. Fish traps are especially effective for catching migratory fishes, mainly in rivers. Trapping is today the most frequently used method of catching fishes in waters where hooks or nets may become entangled. Traps are used in rivers, estuaries, on tidal foreshores and on reefs. Trapping is one of the most cost-effective fishing techniques, as the trap needs no attention once set and is usually fairly simple to construct.

A second source of information on fishing is epigraphic evidence on stone and wooden carvings, in mosaics and in other kinds of illustration. Ancient rock carvings occasionally show fishermen. A well-known example is given on the cover of Höglund's (1972) paper on the Bohuslän herring fishery. Kreuzer (1984) discussed the significance of fish in the religion and myths of ancient Mesopotamia and Egypt and drew on low reliefs and paintings showing fishes and objects in the form of fishes to illustrate his argument. At the small English church at Gosforth in Cumbria, a famous carved stone is claimed to represent Thor fishing. This object is interesting as it clearly shows that line fishing from a boat was practised in Britain before the Norman Conquest of 1066 AD. Roman mosaics and tombstones show both angling and net fishing. Medieval documents illustrate various methods of catching, preparing and eating fishes. For example, the Queen Mary Psalter (British Library, Royal MS 2B VII) shows three fishermen in a boat, disentangling fishes from a net.

Further information on fishing may be gleaned from anthropological and ethnographic literature, of which the works of Brandt (1984) and that edited by Gunda (1984) give general accounts. Fenton (1978) details many aspects of everyday life, including fishing, of the inhabitants of Orkney and Shetland, and fishing techniques used by the indigenous population of the north-western coast of North America is given by Stewart (1977).

Historical records are increasingly being used by archaeologists and others as a source of information on aspects of life in the past. Hitherto, documentary references to fishes, fishing and fisheries have been little researched; however, a number of recent publications show that interest in this area of scholarship is growing. Documentary evidence, be it pictorial or written, can be immensely rewarding. Radtke (1977) has contributed a valuable account of early fishing in the Haitabu area of West Germany. A combination of careful field work and scrupulous historical research has enabled McDonnell (1981) to trace the development of fish ponds in Yorkshire, UK from AD 1066 to 1300. In this detailed and most informative study disparate documentary sources are used to elucidate details of the stocking and techniques used in the management of several ponds, particularly those at Byland Abbey, North Yorkshire. A similar study by Roberts (1986), based on information in the pipe rolls of the bishops of Winchester, southern England, provided information on the use of fishes cultivated in ponds between AD 1150 and 1400. Most notably it showed the considerable distances over which live fish were carried at that period. Information in a sixteenth-century journal recording the management of fish cultivated in ponds was used by Hickling (1971) to illustrate the development of fish culture in England.

The cultivation of fishes has been practised for many centuries particularly in Asia and on medieval European royal and monastic estates. Within the last century it has become widespread in Europe, North America and elsewhere. Traditionally cultivation is based on breeding from wild-captured stock fish, or growing on naturally produced fry in enclosed waters. Only in the case of the carp, and in the twentieth century certain salmonids, has cultivation been intensive and selective, leading to changes in body form (and, with carp, coloration). These fishes have shown an enhanced growth rate, notably an increase in the ratio of body depth to length, thus producing heavier fish. However, these methods are not related to skeletal development. It has not been established that it is possible to distinguish wild from cultivated fishes on the evidence of bones. The culture of fishes has not resulted in the same scale of morphological changes as those brought about by the cultivation of mammals, birds or plants.

A detailed and fascinating study of historical references to the pike, *Esox lucius*, is given by Hoffmann (1987). Hoffmann quotes writers from the Roman Ausonius to the Swiss physician Konrad Gessner (1515–1565), one of the founders of modern ichthyology. In this study we see the pike first portrayed as a voracious predator representative of nature hostile to humankind; later, by the thirteenth century, it is protected by royal ordinances. From careful and critical consideration of ancient documents it is sometimes possible to gain insights into aspects of fisheries and fishes which may not be clear from other sources. Hoffmann (1985) has also recently reviewed the evidence for sport fishing in medieval Europe and concludes that the pursuit of fishes as a recreational pastime was well known in France and Germany in the thirteenth century, in England by the fifteenth and in Spain by the early sixteenth. He points out that the origins of sport fishing in Europe must precede these centuries.

Recent years have seen an increased interest in the relationship between documentary and archaeological data. Rosenlund (1984) compared the documentary evidence for fishes brought to a Cistercian monastery at Øm, Jutland, with the bones recovered during extensive excavations spanning the period 1912 to 1978. He concluded that, while the written sources provide a picture of fishing and consumption of fish in the Øm monastery, the picture is far from complete. The excavated bone material adds much new information about the range of species consumed at the site.

One further source of information which is increasingly used in interpreting archaeological assemblages is evidence from modern experiments and surveys of fish populations. Gifford and Behrensmeyer (1978) studied a camp site made during a foraging expedition by a group belonging to the Dassaneth in Kenya. The site was occupied by eight men for four days, during which 14 catfishes and two Nile perch, *Lates niloticus*, were eaten, in addition to crocodiles, terrapins and scavenged zebra meat. When the site was abandoned, bone was scattered around it but concentrated round the hearth. The site was left for a year and the position of the bones replotted. Most of the large bones had disappeared, and only small bones and fragments which had been trampled below the surface survived. These were thought to have been protected from rain and scavenging by their size and burial.

Enghoff (1986) experimented with wicker traps near the classic site at Ertebølle to see what kinds of fishes can be caught using traditional traps. She then compared her catch with the remains from archaeological excavations and found the range and sizes of fishes she caught to be very similar to those represented in ancient deposits. A second piece of work on Mesolithic fish bones from Denmark was carried out by Noe-Nygaard (1983). Here the population structure of fishes from a poisoned lake was compared with archaeological finds to determine whether the ancient remains were a natural death assemblage or one accumulated by humans. She concluded that the age structure of the archaeological assemblage differed from that of a modern lake.

Perhaps the most interesting source of information on ancient fishing is that which can be gleaned by careful scrutiny from archaeological assemblages of fish remains. The following examples are taken somewhat haphazardly, mainly from recent literature, in order to illustrate how this can be done.

Wing and Reitz (1982) suggested that multipronged spears, tridents, harpoons and arrows (sometimes trident) were used to best advantage in ancient West Indian fishing where large fish, cetaceans, manatee or turtles are concentrated in shallow water. Large fishes which swim in such waters include rainbow parrotfishes, *Scarus gaucamaia*. They maintained that fishes which congregate at narrow passes, such as drums (Sciaenidae) and snooks, *Centropomus* sp., would be relatively simple prey for an experienced harpooner.

By determining the size of the pike from Praestelygen, Denmark, Noe-Nygaard (1983) was able to suggest that the fishes (which were mainly 30–70 cm total length) were probably caught using spears. This fishing method 'strongly biases the catch in favour of the larger fishes, as they are easier to hit' (1983: 130). She went on to suggest that the fishes might have been caught at their spawning grounds at low water near the margin of the lake. To account for the absence of very large pike Noe-Nygaard suggested that behavioural differences between very large and 30–70 cm pike made the largest specimens less vulnerable to human predation. However, because the largest pike are females, which are accompanied by several smaller mature males when spawning, there is some difficulty in reconciling this deduction with the behaviour of the species. Thus the expected size distribution would be a few large fish with larger numbers of medium-sized fishes but very few small fishes – the distribution Noe-Nygaard presents (p. 131, fig. 4).

Many species of fishes can most efficiently be caught using nets. Nets are particularly useful for surface-swimming, shoaling fishes and in many reports authors suggest which kind of net-fishing techniques may have been used to catch the range of fishes present on the site.

An elegant piece of work describing the remains of fishes from several sites in western New South Wales, Australia, was carried out by Balme (1983). By carefully measuring the otoliths of ancient golden perch, *Macquaria ambigua*, from four sites Balme was able to produce total length frequency distributions of the fishes represented in the excavated material. By considering the theoretical length frequency distributions for fishes caught using various kinds of fishing gear, Balme suggested that gill nets were used at two of the sites.

In a survey of traditional fishing in the West Indies, Wing and Reitz (1982) suggested that mullets, *Mugil* spp., and jacks, *Caranx* sp., were fishes likely to have been caught using nets. They maintained that the inshore–estuarine habitat and its resources were particularly suitable for intensive exploitation by nets.

The vast numbers of herring, *Clupea harengus*, remains recovered from so many eastern English medieval towns, e.g. Great Yarmouth (Wheeler and Jones, 1976), Norwich (Jones, 1983b; Jones and Scott, 1985) are most likely to have been caught by using floating nets.

Many reports on fish remains give convincing reasons for suggesting the use of hooks in the past. Leach (1979), when considering anthropological, artefactual and faunal evidence from the Washpool Site, New Zealand, concluded that the Maori possessed the advanced fishing technology which is familiar in Polynesia. This relied on long lines and baited hooks. Wing and Reitz (1982) suggested that hooks could be used to catch common carnivorous fishes such as sea catfishes (Ariidae) of the inshore–estuarine habitats in the West Indies. Hooks are the most likely means employed by past human groups to catch large gadid fishes in the North Sea and Atlantic Ocean. Some authors have suggested that cut marks on the dentary bones of cod, usually close to the symphysis, were made when fishermen attempted to remove a swallowed hook (Colley, 1984b; Henderson, 1986).

The faunas from many sites clearly indicate the use of traps, because the aperture of their entrance select fishes by size. Large fish are too large to enter, while very small fishes are able to escape. Thus, a well-defined size range of fishes is trapped. A sample of dentaries of the stoplight parrotfish, *Sparisoma viride*, from the Mill Reef site, Antigua, had an average height of 16.2 mm (range 11.7–22.8 mm). These bones are estimated to have come from fishes about 240 mm long (range 180–340 mm) (Wing and Reitz, 1982). This species attains at least 520 mm, showing that the fishes present at Mill Reef were young ones. The same sample also contained a group of green parrotfishes, *Scarus vetula*, which were all from individuals of the same size class.

Discussing fish remains from Ertebølle, Denmark, Enghoff (1986) argued that the range of species and the small size of the fishes suggests that fishing took place with traps in shallow water. Although traps were not found at the site, careful examination of flint flakes showed patterns of damage consistent with having been used to split osiers, the raw material for making traps.

This chapter has endeavoured to show how the study of fish remains and associated material can provide evidence for understanding past fisheries. While it is important to point out that historical sources and ethnoarchaeological studies may help to interpret archaeological assemblages, caution must be exercised in applying these data to those from archaeological sites. The use of analogy in archaeology has been widely discussed in the theoretical literature and Hodder (1982) has dealt with the topic in an accessible manner. He pointed out that the use of analogy from anthropological studies to interpret archaeological evidence can be justified only if a large number of similarities can be seen in the cultures being compared. For example, if anthropological and archaeological evidence are both from the same geographical and climatic zone, and if the cultures share similar technological knowledge or social organization, then analogies may be valid. Yet even if there are good grounds for using the analogy, he states: 'The use of analogy does not lead to the final solution, a definite interpretation. Assumptions, logic and conclusions may be wrong' (Hodder, 1982: 211).

There has been no attempt in this chapter to review all studies of fish remains in archaeology which have shed light on ancient fishing techniques. Rather it is hoped that the examples cited can be used as signposts, aids for future students of archaeology and palaeoecology, to show the potential of fish remains in helping to understand past fishing activity and to highlight the limitations associated with their study.

It is advisable to make a contour sketch or take a colour photograph of the fish before preparation commences as well as to measure it. The following measurements are recommended: total length, fork length, standard length, body depty and head length (see fig. 13.1). The total and gutted weights of the fish should also be recorded. It should be noted that specimens kept in a deep-freeze for periods longer than two to three weeks dehydrate and their weights and lengths decrease. Dehydration can shrink a large fish by several centimetres. Thus, the fresher the fish the better.

Scale samples should be taken from different parts of the body and placed in plastic boxes, glass vials, or small paper envelopes; alternatively, they can be mounted between two microscope slides.

Once the preliminary data and scales have been collected the fish can be prepared for the reference collection.

Dried fish should be soaked in warm water before boiling. Whole fish can be prepared by gentle simmering for between five and 10 minutes until the skin, musculature and connective tissue are loosened from the bones. The fish is carefully removed from the water, placed on its side on a dissection board and allowed to cool.

It is important to keep the bones of each side of the body separate. The following notes apply to one side of the fish. In order to avoid later confusion the following scheme is recommended:

1. Remove the nasal(?s) from the region of the external nostrils.

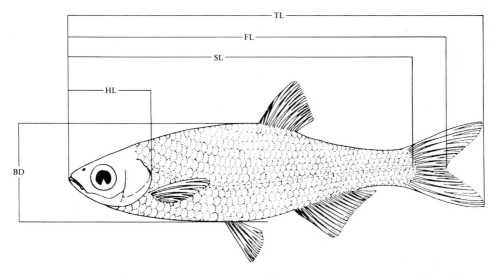

13.1   Recommended measurements made on a fish before preparation of the skeleton: TL = total length, FL = fork length, SL = standard length, HL = head length, BD = body depth. (From Wheeler, 1969.)

2. Remove the eyeball in order to gain access to the circumorbitals. These are thin, scale-like bones provided with muciferous canals, which surround the orbit superficially.

In some fish the lens of the eyeball may be resistant and occasionally persist in archaeological deposits; it is wise to clean and preserve lenses, though it is unlikely that species determinations of ancient material will ever be possible.

3. Once the circumorbitals have been removed, the infraorbitals can be located. There are usually five or six infraorbitals which form the infraorbital arch. The arch can be lifted, separated anteriorly from the ectethmoid and posteriorly from the sphenotic. Alternatively they can be picked out individually. It is extremely difficult to identify infraorbitals so they should be placed in strict order as they are removed. If a supraorbital is present it will be found attached to the upper edge of the orbit.

4. The 'scale bone' is next removed. This may be the extrascapular, tabular or supratemporal bone. The 'scale bone' is a superficially situated bone with a muciferous canal – part of the lateral line system. It is located in the temporal region above the opercular and between the posttemporal, pterotic and epiotic. It closely resembles the infraorbitals.

5. The bones forming the opercular series are the next removed. These consist of the opercular, the preopercular, the interopercular and the subopercular bones. At its anterior part, the preopercular is attached to the hyomandibular by a ligament. Its inferior part is attached to the hind part of the quadrate. This connection can be broken by gently bending the preopercular forwards. Then it can be picked out with the interopercular.

The opercular is articulated to a knob-like formation on the dorsal hind part of the hyomandibular. It is easily detached and the opercular and subopercular can be removed.

6. Bones of the secondary upper jaw are then removed. These consist of the premaxilla, the maxilla and in some species one or two supramaxillae. The premaxilla must be disengaged at the symphysis from its counterpart on the other side. The maxilla, which articulates with the premaxilla anteriorly, can be easily removed. The supramaxilla/e (when present) are removed next.

7. Once the opercular series and the upper jaw have been removed, a series of bones known as the palatoquadratum (consisting of the palatine, ectopterygoid, entopterygoid, metapterygoid, quadrate, hyomandibular and the symplectic) is revealed. To remove these, the palatine is detached from the ectethmoidal part of the neurocranium and the hyomandibular articulation with the sphenotic and pterotic is broken. The whole complex, together with the articular, angular and dentary, can then be lifted, once the two dentaries are separated at the symphysis.

The lower jaw (dentary, articular and angular) can be detached from its articulation with the quadrate. The dentary and articular are separated by pulling them apart along the longitudinal axis of the fish.

8. The paired bones of the hyoid arch (excluding the hyomandibular and the symplectic) and the branchiostegal rays are next removed. The hyoid bones comprise the interhyal, the epihyal, the ceratohyal and two hypohyals. The number of branchiostegal rays varies in different fishes. There are three per side for the Cyprinidae, six or seven per side for the Acanthopterygians, eight per side for *Clupea*, ten per side for the Salmonidae and 34 per side for *Tarpon*.
These bones should be separated from the basihyal.

9. The urohyal (an unpaired element) can be removed next, once the musculature of the throat has been dissected. The urohyal is found ventro-medially beneath the branchial apparatus.

10. The skeletal elements of the shoulder girdle and of the pectoral fin are removed next. The shoulder girdle is composed of the following bones: the posttemporal, usually a forked bone attached to the cranial roof; the supracleithrum, usually a robust straight bone which connects the posterior part of the posttemporal and the cleithrum; the postcleithrum (this element may be absent or there may be up to three on each side); the cleithrum; the scapula; and the mesocoracoid (for example in the clupeids, salmonids, cyprinids and silurids). The pectoral fin comprises the radials (small bones which allow the fin rays to articulate), and the fin rays (these may be spinous – acanthotrichia – or they may be soft flexible rays – the lepidotrichia).
The processes of the posttemporal are freed from their connections with the hind part of the neurocranium. They usually join the epiotic and opisthotic bones. The posttemporal is removed, preferably with the supracleithrum. It is best to feel behind the cleithrum for any postcleithra. If present, the postcleithra, cleithrum and the entire pectoral fin are detached from the body with their associated musculature. Once removed, the musculature is cleaned from the bones.

11. The elements of the pelvic fin are removed next. These are the basipterygium and the fin rays. The basipterygium, together with the rest of the pelvic fin, is taken from the body of the fish with any surrounding muscles. The bony parts are then freed from skin, muscles and other soft tissue.

12. The branchial apparatus (basket) is removed next. This is composed of a large number of elements: the glossohyal (basihyal, entoglossum); the basibranchials; the hypobranchials; the ceratobranchials; the epibranchials; the pharyngobranchials; the upper and lower pharyngeals; and the gillrakers. In some large fish, for example the gadids, the principal bones of the branchial

arches may bear small toothed plates which are found in the tissue adhering to the main bones.

Because the branchial apparatus has a rather complicated structure, it is best freed from the floor of the neurocranium. Remains of the pharyngeal wall, muscles and other soft tissues are also carefully removed while the connections between the various elements of the branchial apparatus are kept intact. The gill filaments should be removed from the aboral side of each branchial arch. Gillrakers should be collected. The branchial apparatus can either be dehydrated by soaking in 80% ethanol for one to two weeks and then dried, or the various elements can be picked out from the soft tissue, cleaned and dried.

13. The neurocranium. It is desirable to have two neurocrania of each species in the collection. One should be kept entire, the other broken into its constituent elements.

The neurocranium should be removed from the vertebral column at its occipital contact with the first vertebra (sometimes erroneously referred to as the 'atlas' vertebra). It is often necessary to use a scalpel or sharp knife to sever the basioccipital from the first vertebra. The neurocranium can then be freed by bending and gently pulling it away from the vertebral column. The soft tissue on the outer surface of the neurocranium can then be washed from the bone. The brain can be flushed out of the cerebral cavity into a sieve by a jet of water, in order to collect the otoliths. Alternatively, otoliths can be collected by shaking the washed neurocranium. All otoliths should be retained, although the larger ones (usually the sagitta, but in the cyprinids the asteriscus and the lapillus) are those most often found in archaeological material.

14. The vertebral column, the ribs (costae), the intermuscular bones and the elements which support the unpaired fins.

Each side of the body should be treated separately.

The skin and the side muscles of the trunk should be removed but the radial muscles of the median fins are kept to one side.

The ribs should be carefully freed from musculature preserving their order in the fish. Where they are present, some intermuscular bones (epicentrals and epineurals) should be collected and preserved.

The elements of the dorsal and anal fins next receive attention. It is best to remove the whole fin with its musculature and then the hard parts separated from the musculature, preserving their natural sequence. It is helpful to retain some fins of the more common fishes as whole preparations, cleaning off the skin and the majority of the soft tissue, but allowing the fin to dry entire.

The two halves of denticulated spinous lepidotrichia (for example in

Barbus and *Cyprinus*) are best separated, for they occur in archaeological deposits in this state.

Because pterygiophores are usually surrounded by fat, it is best to store them in 50% ethanol for some weeks before final cleaning.

The caudal fin. The lepidotrichia are first removed from the caudal end of the vertebral column. The epurals, the hypurals and the urostyle of the ultimate vertebra remain and are removed next.

Once the fins have been removed from one side of the fish, the vertebral column, together with the remaining ribs, can be freed from the musculature. The vertebral column can now be washed clean of any muscle fragments, parts of kidney etc., and dried. It is advisable to keep the order of the vertebrae for one specimen of each species. This can be done by breaking the column into four or five zones: the first few vertebrae (anterior abdominal); the main abdominal vertebrae; the transitional zone between the abdominal and caudal region; the main part of the caudal region; and the last few caudal vertebrae together with the penultimate and ultimate vertebrae. Alternatively the vertebrae can be picked out one by one and preserved in sequence.

In some groups of fishes, for example herrings, salmons and pikes, the neural arches of the anterior abdominal vertebrae, and the neural and haemal arches of the posterior caudal vertebrae, fall out of their sockets in the vertebral centrum. This is also true for the neural arch of the first vertebra in many species and for the modified anterior vertebrae of the Weberian apparatus in the cyprinids.

In cyprinids, clupeids, salmonids and pikes, the parapophyses are loosely located in pits on the side of the vertebral centrum and their sequence can be lost if great care is not taken.

Once all the skeletal elements have been recovered they should be soaked for two to six days in an aqueous solution of enzyme-based laundry powder diluted following manufacturers' instructions ('Biotex' and 'Bold' are two commonly available brands). Thereafter, they can be washed and dried.

A rapid way to prepare a fish skeleton is to weigh, measure and gut the fish and place it in a linen or nylon-mesh bag with a plastic label bearing its skeleton number. In order to keep the vertebrae in their natural sequence, a nickel alloy or other suitable wire can be passed through the spinal foramen (salmonids, *Esox*) or through the neural arches (cyprinids, gadids and most other families). The bag containing the fish is placed in a tank of enzyme solution until digestion is complete. Alternatively the fish can be cooked for 10–15 minutes and left in enzyme-based laundry powder solution for one to two weeks at room temperature. The bag of fish is then washed in clean running water and the bones picked out and dried. (This technique is best carried out in a fume cupboard for it is extremely malodorous.)

Storage of fish reference collections

Once the bones have been prepared they need to be stored in such a manner that they can be readily used for identification. The choice of containers used to store fish bones will be influenced by the size of the specimens. Ideally boxes should be transparent plastic or have a glass top. Very large specimens are best stored in stout cardboard or wooden boxes. Stationery cabinets with shallow drawers (⅝ths of an inch – roughly 16 mm depth) have been found to be most convenient containers for small and medium-sized plastic boxes containing the comparative anatomical collection. Deeper drawers (2 inches – roughly 5 cm depth) are necessary for the larger elements of big fish, for example dentaries and cleithra of large cod, and for storing bags or boxes of vertebral centra.

The prepared specimens can be arranged in several ways with the objective of speeding up identification of archaeological specimens. Two types of collection are necessary: a comparative anatomical collection and a taxonomic collection.

In a comparative anatomical collection the various skeletal elements (dentaries, cleithra etc.) from different species are stored in taxonomic order side by side. This arrangement is necessary because it is often possible to identify the element of the archaeological specimen, but it is inefficient to search through boxes containing all the elements of each fish. With a comparative anatomical collection all specimens of a particular element can be rapidly scanned.

A comparative anatomical collection can be built up gradually by placing elements in small plastic boxes and arranging elements from different fish in the same drawer or other suitable container. It is not necessary to treat each bone separately; some, for example vertebrae, intermuscular bones, branchiostegal and fin rays, can be grouped. As a general rule, it is best to box individually those bones that can readily be assigned to species (or other taxonomic level).

In the taxonomic collection the specimens are arranged in a recognized systematic sequence with all elements of a single specimen kept together, either in a box, in bags within a box, or attached to stiff card using plastic adhesive material such as 'Blutak'. Specimens arranged in this manner are particularly useful when large assemblages of archaeological material are being examined, especially those which contain abundant remains of a few fairly closely related taxa. For example, the large gadids, cod, saithe, pollack, haddock and ling may all be caught from the northern North Sea using hand lines. To have specimens of these fish arranged on labelled card sheets (all elements labelled) greatly speeds up the identification process. The taxonomic collection can also be used to check for variability within the species, and to look for age-related changes to the morphology of the particular element if there are several specimens of each species. Such a collection is of particular value when, as is often the case, one or a few species dominate archaeological assemblages.

The simplest and quickest way to store fish, particularly those specimens prepared by enzyme digestion, is to place all bones, scales and other hard parts in a clear plastic box or glass-topped cardboard box (wooden boxes may be necessary for the largest specimens).

Any discussion of reference collections would be incomplete without mention of the techniques used to examine fish (and other vertebrate) skeletons within the musculature of the animal. These staining techniques are used on fish up to 30 cm length, though most specimens are less than 15 cm total length. Alizarin red is the main stain used as it is taken up by the calcium in bone, but Dingerkus and Uhler (1977) reported a more elaborate technique using alcian blue. A modification of this method is extensively used in the Fish Section of the British Museum (Natural History). This technique produces fish with clear flesh, deep blue cartilage and dark red bones. It is particularly useful for investigating the relationships of bones within the fish, and may be of great assistance in teaching basic fish osteology. For identifying archaeological samples it is of more limited value.

FUTURE DIRECTIONS FOR RESEARCH

No subject worthy of scholarship remains static; new ideas and techniques bring new approaches and insights. It is already apparent that the study of fish remains from archaeological sites is a rapidly developing field and it is likely to continue to contribute a great deal to our understanding of the complex relationship between mankind and the remainder of the natural world. In this concluding section an attempt is made to suggest areas of research which need attention and the directions along which the subject may develop in the near future.

It is clear to anyone who has searched the osteological literature that detailed, bone-by-bone studies are not available for many species of fish, in either the classic works of pioneer scholars or more recent publications. Most of the published osteological studies of fishes were undertaken in order to contribute to fish taxonomy and the understanding of phylogenetic relationships of groups of fishes.

Few anatomists have studied fish bones in order to show differences in the form of the same element from several closely related species. A notable exception is Williamson's (1902) study of the cranial osteology of the cod, saithe and lythe (pollack). Studies undertaken to highlight characteristic features of the various elements in modern specimens of closely related species are urgently needed.

In many regions of the world the fish fauna is not well known. Comparative anatomical studies of fishes are required for many groups and it would seem appropriate that ichthyologists be encouraged to include detailed osteological descriptions showing the shape and distinctive features of each element to complement morphological, ecological and behavioural studies. Izquierdo (1988) has recently examined the lower jaw bones of virtually all the economically important species in the Iberian fauna. This study would have been much more useful had it included notes, photographs or drawings showing diagnostic parts of bones which are likely to be preserved in archaeological sites.

Not only are jaw bones and other readily recognized elements in need of systematic scrutiny in order to aid identification, but apparently insignificant small bones, scutes, scales and teeth require study. Recently, Enghoff (1986) drew attention to the many small scutes at the base of the fins in the European

flounder, *Platichthys flesus*. Since that time these scutes have been recognized in finely sieved samples from a number of sites. This example amply
illustrates the adage 'You only find what you are looking for'. There is still
much to be learnt about the osteology of fishes and it is only by patient and
systematic work, of a kind pioneered in the last century, that the range of
recognizable remains will be increased and the standards of identification be
improved.

Improving the level of identification is perhaps the most important area for
future work, but another trend, which is already emerging, is examining
assemblages of bones for evidence of their taphonomic history. By closely
studying remains, perhaps using the scanning electron microscope, for signs
of cut marks, damage from scavengers, evidence of post-burial changes e.g.
fungal hyphal penetration, much new information will emerge. Equally
important is the need to carry out more experiments investigating how bones
survive and the conditions leading to their destruction. For example, little is
known of the mechanical properties, strength and resistance of fish bone.
Histological studies of bone collagen by Richter (1986) have shown alterations caused by heat, while Meunier and Castenet (1982) explored the three-
dimensional organization of collagen in teleost scales using the scanning
electron microscope. There is thus great potential for detecting alteration to
bone if appropriate techniques, e.g. scanning and transmission electron
microscopy and thin section microscopy, are used. Such studies will make it
possible to piece together a more detailed picture of the processes which had
lead to the excavated assemblage.

One area of research which already commands great interest is the study of
incremental growth marks to determine a fish's age and approximate point of
death in the growth cycle. By using techniques such as scanning electron
microscopy, polished thin sections, and microradiography of bone samples,
combined with studies of tetracycline-injected specimens of modern fishes,
the potential and limitations of incremental growth-mark analysis will
become clear.

Archaeology provides data, albeit often poor-quality data, on the populations of fishes exploited by human groups in the past. These data are in
many ways similar to those examined by ecologists studying species associ-
ations and community structures. Muniz *et al.* (forthcoming) have recently
used Shannon's index of diversity to compare fish assemblages from Danish
and Iberian sites. It is not surprising to learn that the Danish Mesolithic
assemblages were less diverse than those from prehistoric and Roman sites
on the Iberian peninsula. However, this work is symptomatic of a more
mathematical approach to archaeological fish bone studies and mirrors the
mathematical and statistical leaning of other branches of archaeology
(Grayson, 1984). It is possible that diversity analysis of archaeological fish

assemblages following procedures currently used in the analysis of modern communities will make apparent patterns which might allow the recognition of distinct assemblages associated with different cultures.

Indirect evidence of the exploitation of fishes has been reported by chemists studying fatty acids present within sherds of pottery (Patrick *et al.*, 1985) and sediments (Mogan *et al.*, 1984). Although it is so far only possible to suggest that a vessel was used to cook or store fish or fish products – and there are a large number of uncertainties connected with the interpretation of such analyses – it is likely that the future will see more of these studies. It seems probable that other biochemical analyses will be applied to archaeological fish remains. The analysis of amino-acid composition of archaeological fish eye lenses could confirm species identification and may determine the racial origin of herring or other species.

While curiosity continues to be a major impetus behind archaeological research, we can expect to see an increase in the number of fish bone workers prepared to experiment with reproductions of traditional fishing gear to understand more fully the technology of ancient fishing.

Finally, there are likely to be major developments in computer systems. Perhaps the most useful would be the establishment of a data bank of standard bone measurements. Such a database, perhaps overseen by the International Council for Archaeozoology, could be linked to researchers' recording systems to reconstruct the total length and estimate the weight of fishes automatically, within known confidence limits. Doubtless computer systems will improve to produce tables and histograms giving summaries of the bones identified and detailing the individual fishes thereby represented. Such a system could also be designed to carry out community analysis.

There is considerable potential for the application of three-dimensional imaging to fish bones using computer graphics routines. Using scaling procedures, and techniques developed for 'expert systems', computers might be valuable tools to assist with identification and size estimation of bones.

Many of these developments are already in their embryonic stages, and many more will doubtless be made as long as archaeologists carry out their fieldwork in a responsible and thorough manner. Careful fieldwork will ensure that the numbers of fish bones recovered during excavation will increase, making it necessary to train researchers prepared to bridge the disciplines of biology and archaeology. It is hoped that this book will help students see both the potential and challenge of studying fish remains and will enable some to become actively engaged in this fascinating and rewarding area of research.

REFERENCES

Akazawa, T. and Watanabe, H. 1968. Restoration of body size of Jomon shellmound fish (preliminary report). *Proceedings of the VIIIth International Congress of Anthropological and Ethnological Sciences* 3: 193–7.

Anderson Smith, W. 1883. Curing and preserving fish at home and abroad, in Herbert, D. (ed.), *Fish and fisheries: a selection from the prize essays of the International Fisheries Exhibition, Edinburgh, 1882*, pp. 93–104. William Blackwood and Sons, Edinburgh.

Avery, G. 1975. Discussion on the age and use of tidal fish-traps (visvywers). *South African Archaeological Bulletin* 30: 105–13.

Badham, C. D. 1854. *Prose Haleutics or ancient and modern fish tattle*. John W. Parker, London.

Bagenal, T. B. (ed.) 1974. *The ageing of fish*. Unwin Brothers Ltd, Old Woking.

Balme, J. 1983. Prehistoric fishing in the lower Darling, western New South Wales, in Grigson, C. and Clutton-Brock, J. (eds.), *Animals and archaeology. 2. Shell middens, fishes and birds*, pp. 19–32. British Archaeological Reports International Series, No. 183, Oxford.

Barker, G. 1975. To sieve or not to sieve. *Antiquity* 49: 61–3.

Barkman, R. C. and Bangtson, D. A. 1987. The record of daily growth in otoliths of Atlantic silversides, *Menidia menidia*, from field and laboratory. *Journal of Fish Biology* 31: 683–95.

Bateman, N. and Locker, A. 1982. The sauce of the Thames. *The London Archaeologist* 4 (8): 204–7.

Batey, C. E., Morris, C. D. and Jones, A. K. G. 1982. Freswick Links, Caithness, progress report on survey and excavations, 1981, in Harding, A. F. and Haselgrove, C. C. (eds.), Archaeological reports for 1981, pp. 54–8. *University of Durham and University of Newcastle upon Tyne Archaeological Reports*, 5. Durham.

Bell, M. 1977. Excavation at Bishopstone, Sussex. *Sussex Archaeological Collections* 115: 1–299.

Berg, L. S. 1962. *Freshwater fishes of the U.S.S.R. and adjacent countries* 4th edn (English translation), vol. 1, I.P.S.T., Jerusalem.

Bianchi, G. 1984. Study of the morphology of five Mediterranean and Atlantic sparid fishes with a reinstatement of the genus *Pagrus* Cuvier, 1817, *Cybium* 8: 31–56.

Bigelow, H. B. and Schroeder, W. C. 1953. *Fishes of the Gulf of Maine*. Fishery Bulletin of the Fish and Wildlife Service, Vol. 53, Washington.

Binford, L. 1981. *Bones: ancient men and modern myths*. Academic Press, London.

Blacker, R. W. 1974. Recent advances in otolith studies, in Jones, F. R. H. (ed.), *Sea fisheries research*, pp. 67–90. Elek Science, London.

Blanc, M., Bănărescu, P., Gaudet, J.-L., and Hureau, J.-C. 1971. *European inland water fish: a multilingual catalogue*. Fishing News Books Ltd., London.

Bodner, C. C. and Rowlett, R. M. 1980. Separation of bone, charcoal and seeds by chemical flotation. *American Antiquity* 45 (1): 110–16.

Boiko, E. G. 1964. Evaluating natural mortality in Azov zander (*Stizostedion lucioperca*).

189

Fisheries Research Board of Canada Translation Series, 541. (Original title, K. otsenke estestvennoi smertnosti azovskogo sudaka.) From *Trudy Vsesoiuznogo Nauchno-issledovatelskogo Instituta Morskogo Rybnogo Khoziaistva i Okeanografii, (VNIRO)* 50: 143–61.

Brain, C. K. 1967. Hottentot food remains and their bearing on the interpretation of fossil bone assemblages. *Scientific Papers of the Namib Desert Research Station* 32: 1–11.

1969. The contribution of Namib Desert Hottentots to an understanding of australopithecine bone accumulations. *Scientific Papers of the Namib Desert Research Station* 39: 13–22.

1981. *The hunters or the hunted? An introduction to African cave taphonomy*. University of Chicago Press, Chicago.

Brandt, A. von. 1984. *Fish catching methods of the world* (3rd edn). Fishing News Books, Farnham, England.

Brinkhuizen, D. C. 1979a. Preliminary notes on fish remains from archaeological sites in the Netherlands. *Palaeohistoria* 21: 83–90.

1979b. On the finds of European catfish (*Siluris glanis* L.) in the Netherlands, in Kubasiewicz, M. (ed.), *Archaeo-zoology I. Proceedings of the IIIrd International Archaeozoological Conference held 23–26th April 1978*, pp. 256–61. Szczecin.

1983. Some notes on recent and pre- and protohistoric fishing gear from northwestern Europe. *Palaeohistoria* 25: 7–53.

Brothers, E. B., Mathews, C. B. and Lasker, R. 1976. Daily growth increments in otoliths from larval and adult fishes. *Fishery Bulletin of the National Oceanic and Atmospheric Administration* 74: 1–9.

Burgess, G. H. O., Cutting, C. L., Lovern, J. A. and Waterman, J. J. (eds.), 1965. *Fish handling and processing*. Her Majesty's Stationery Office, Edinburgh.

Carlander, K. D. 1969. *Handbook of freshwater fishery biology*, 1. Iowa State University Press, Ames, Iowa.

1977. *Handbook of freshwater fishery biology*, 2. Iowa State University Press, Ames, Iowa.

Casteel, R. W. 1976. *Fish remains in archaeology and paleoenvironmental studies*. Academic Press, London.

Chaplin, R. E. 1971. *The study of animal bones from archaeological sites*. Seminar Press, London.

Chasler, C. R. 1972. An investigation into some mechanical and physical properties of cellular and acellular bone in teleost fish. Unpublished B.Sc. dissertation, University of York, York, England.

Cherry, J. F., Gamble, C. and Shennan, S. (eds), *Sampling in contemporary British archaeology*. British Archaeological Reports, No. 50, Oxford.

Clark, J. G. D. 1948. The development of fishing in prehistoric Europe. *Antiquaries Journal* 28: 45–85.

1952. *Prehistoric Europe: the economic basis*. Methuen, London.

1980. *Mesolithic prelude, the Palaeolithic–Neolithic transition in Old World prehistory*. Edinburgh University Press, Edinburgh.

Clason, A. T. 1986. Fish and archaeology, in Brinkhuizen, D. C. and Clason, A. T. (eds.), *Fish and archaeology*, pp. 1–8. British Archaeological Reports International Series, No. 294, Oxford.

Clason, A. T. and Prummel, W. 1977. Collecting, sieving and archaeozoological research. *Journal of Archaeological Science* 4: 171–5.

Clothier, C. R. 1950. A key to some Southern Californian fishes based on vertebral characters. *Fish Bulletin. State of California, Fish & Game Commission*, No. 79: 1–83.

Coles, J. 1971. The early settlement of Scotland: excavations at Morton, Fife. *Proceedings of the Prehistoric Society* 37: 284–366.

Collette, B. B. and Nauen, C. E. 1983. FAO species catalogue, Vol. 2. Scombrids of the world. An annotated and illustrated catalogue of tunas, mackerels, bonitos and related species known to date. *FAO Fisheries Synopsis* 125 (2): 1–137.

Colley, S. M. 1984a. The role of fish bone studies in economic archaeology, with special reference to the Orkney Isles. Unpublished Ph.D. thesis, University of Southampton, England.

1984b. Some methodological problems in the interpretation of fish remains from archaeological sites in Orkney, in Desse-Berset, N. (ed.), 2nd fish osteoarchaeology meeting, CNRS. Centre de recherches archéologiques. *Notes et Monographies Techniques* 16: 117–31.

in press. Cooking fish on a fire: an experiment in differential burning. British Archaeological Reports International Series, Oxford.

Cornwall, I. W. 1968. *Prehistoric animals and their hunters*. Faber and Faber, London.

Couch, J. 1865. *A history of the fishes of the British Islands*. Groombridge, London.

Cruse, R. J. and Harrison, A. C. 1983. Excavation at Hill Road, Wouldham. *Archaeologia Cantiana* 99: 81–108.

Cushing, F. H. 1896. Explorations of ancient key dwellers remains on the Gulf Coast of Florida. *Proceedings of the American Philosophical Society* 35 (153): 329–433.

Cutting, C. L. 1955. *Fish saving: a history of fish processing from ancient to modern times*. Leonard Hill, London.

Daly, P. 1969. Approaches to faunal analysis in archaeology. *American Antiquity* 34: 146–53.

Desse, G. 1984. Nouvelle contribution à la diagnose des pièces rachidiennes des poissons, in Desse-Berset, N. (ed.), 2nd fish osteoarchaeology meeting, CNRS. Centre de recherches archéologiques. *Notes et Monographies Techniques* 16: 25–39.

Desse, G. and Desse, J. 1976. *Diagnostic des pièces rachidennes des Téléostéens et des Chondrichthyens. III: Téléostéens d'eau douce*. L'Expansion Scientifique Française, Paris.

1983. L'identification des vertèbres de poissons; applications au matériel issu de sites archéologiques et paléontologiques. *Archives des Sciences* 36 (2): 291–6.

Desse, G. and de Buit, M.-H. 1971. *Diagnostic des pièces rachidennes des Téléostéens et des Chondrichthyens. II: Chondrichthyens*. L'Expansion Scientifique Française, Paris.

Desse, J. 1984. Propositions pour une réalisation collective d'un corpus: fiches d'identification et d'exploitation métrique du squelette des poissons, in Desse-Berset, N. (ed.), 2nd fish osteoarchaeology meeting, CNRS. Centre de recherches archéologiques. *Notes et Monographies Techniques* 16: 67–86.

Desse, J., Desse-Berset, N. and Rocheteau, M. 1987. Contribution a l'osteometrie de la perche (*Perca fluviatilis* Linné, 1758). *Fiches d'osteologie animale pour l'archéologie Series A: Poissons* No. 1. Centre de Recherches Archéologiques du CNRS.

Dingerkus, G. and Uhler, L. D. 1977. Enzyme clearing of alcian blue stained small vertebrates for demonstration of cartilage. *Stain Technology* 54 (4): 229–32.

Donaldson, A. M., Jones, A. K. G. and Rackham, D. J. 1980. Barnard Castle, Co. Durham. A dinner in the Great Hall: report on the contents of a fifteenth-century drain. *Journal of the British Archaeological Association* 133: 74–96.

Driesch, A. von den. 1983. Some archaeological remarks on fishes in ancient Egypt, in Grigson, C. and Clutton-Brock, J. (eds.), *Animals and archaeology. 2. Shell middens, fishes and birds*, pp. 87–110. British Archaeological Reports International Series, No. 183, Oxford.

Ellison, R., Renfrew, J., Brothwell, D. and Seeley, N. 1978. Some food offerings from Ur, excavated by Sir Leonard Woolley and previously unpublished. *Journal of Archaeological Science* 5: 167–77.

Enghoff, I. B. 1983. Size distribution of cod (*Gadus morhua* L.) from a Mesolithic settlement at Vedbaek, North Zealand, Denmark. *Videnskabelige Meddelelser fra dansk naturhistorisk Forening* 144: 83–97.

    1986. Freshwater fishing from a sea-coast settlement – the Ertebølle *locus classicus* revisited. *Journal of Danish Archaeology* 5: 62–76.

Erlinge, S. 1968. Food studies on captive otter *Lutra lutra* L. *Oikos* 19 (2): 259–70.

Fagade, S. O. 1974. Age determination in *Tilapia melanotheron* (Rüppell) in the Lagos Lagoon, Nigeria, with a discussion of the environmental and physiological basis of growth markings in the tropics, in Bagenal, T. B. (ed.), *The ageing of fish*, pp. 71–7. Unwin Brothers Ltd, Old Woking.

Fenton, A. 1973. Craig-fishing in the Northern Isles of Scotland and notes on the poke-net. *Scottish Studies* 17: 71–80.

    1978. *The Northern Isles: Orkney and Shetland*. John Donald, Edinburgh.

    n.d. *Scottish salmon fishing spears*. National Museum of Antiquities of Scotland Edinburgh.

Fieller, N. R. J. and Turner, A. 1982. Number estimation in vertebrate samples. *Journal of Archaeological Science* 9: 49–62.

Flower, B. and Rosenbaum, E. 1958. *The Roman cookery book: a critical translation of the art of cooking by Apicius*. Harrap, London.

Follett, W. I. 1967. Fish remains from coprolites and midden deposits at Lovelock Cave, Churchill County, Nevada. *University of California Archaeolaogical Survey Reports* 70: 94–115.

Ford, E. 1937. Vertebral variation in teleostean fishes. *Journal of the Marine Biologica Association of the United Kingdom* 22: 1–60.

Frost, W. E. and Kipling, C. 1959. The determination of age and growth of pike (*Esox lucius* from scales and opercular bones. *Journal du Conseil Permanent International pou l'Exploration de la Mer* 24: 314–41.

Garrick, J. A. F. 1982. Sharks of the genus *Carcharhinus*. *NOAA Technical Report NMF Circular* 445: 1–194.

Gehlbach, F. R. and Miller, R. R. 1961. Fishes from archaeological sites in northern New Mexico. *Southwestern Naturalist* 6 (1): 2–8.

Gifford, D. P. and Behrensmeyer, A. K. 1978. Observed depositional events at a modern human occupation site in Kenya. *Quaternary Research* 8: 245–66.

Goodlad, A. 1971. *Shetland fishing saga*. The Shetland Times, Lerwick, Shetland.

Goodrich, E. S. 1930. *Studies on the structure and development of vertebrates*. Macmillan, London.

Grayson, D. K. 1973. On the methodology of faunal analysis. *American Antiquity* 39: 432–9.

    1984. *Quantitative zooarchaeology*. Academic Press, Orlando, Florida.

Gregory, W. K. 1933. Fish skulls: a study of the evolution of natural mechanisms. *Transactions of the American Philosophical Society* 23 (2): 75–481.

Guerreschi, A. 1973. A mechanical sieve for archaeological excavations. *Antiquity* 47: 234–5.

Gunda, B. (ed.) 1984. *The fishing culture of the world: studies in ethnology, cultural ecology and folklore*. Akadémiai Kiadó, Budapest.

Gunda, B. 1984. Fish poisoning in the Carpathian area and in the Balkan Peninsula, in Gunda, B. (ed.), *The fishing culture of the world: studies in ethnology, cultural ecology and folklore*, pp. 181–222. Akadémiai Kiadó, Budapest.

Günther, A. C. L. G. 1880. *An introduction to the study of fishes*. Black, Edinburgh.

Hallström, A. 1979. Die Fischknocken, in Boessneck, J., Driesch, A. von den and

Sternberger, L. (eds.), *Eketorp – Befestigung und Siedlung auf Öland (Schweden). Die Fauna*, pp. 422–92. Almquist and Wikseil International, Stockholm, Sweden.

Harcourt, R. A. 1969. Animal remains, in Rahtz, P. A., Excavations at King John's Hunting Lodge, Writtle, Essex, 1955–7. *Society for Medieval Archaeology Monograph* 3: 113–14.

Harder, W. 1975. *Anatomy of fishes*. E. Schweizerbart'sche Verlagsbuchhandlung, Stuttgart.

Hardy, E. 1982. A microcomputer-based system of recording bones from archaeological sites, in Aspinall, A. and Warren, S. E. (eds.), *Proceedings of the Micro-Computer Jamboree. University of Bradford, 3rd April 1982*, pp. 11–17. University of Bradford, Bradford.

Härkönen, T. 1986. *Guide to the otoliths of the bony fishes of the northeast Atlantic*. Danbui ApS, Denmark.

Harrington, R. W. 1955. The osteocranium of the American cyprinid fish *Notropis bifrenatus*, with an annotated synonymy of teleost skull bones. *Copeia* 1955, pp. 267–90.

Hart, J. L. 1973. Pacific fishes of Canada. *Bulletin of the Fisheries Research Board of Canada*, No. 180: 1–740.

Heinrich, D. 1986. Fishing and the consumption of cod (*Gadus morhua* L. 1758) in the Middle Ages, in Brinkhuizen, D. C. and Clason, A. T. (eds.), *Fish and archaeology*, pp. 42–52. British Archaeological Reports International Series, No. 294. Oxford.

Heizer, R. F. 1953. Aboriginal fish poisons. Anthropological Papers, No. 38. *Bulletin of the Bureau of American Ethnology*, 151: 225–83.

Henderson, D. 1986. The fish remains, in Dixon, P. Excavations in the fishing town of Eyemouth 1982–1984, pp. 65–74. *Border Burghs Archaeology Project Monograph Series*, 1.

Herrmann, B. 1985. Parasitologisch-Epidemiologische Auswertungen mittelalterlicher Kloaken. *Zeitschrift für Archäologie des Mittelalters* 13: 131–61.

Hickling, C. F. 1971. Prior More's fishponds. *Medieval Archaeology* 15: 118–23.

Hodder, I. 1982. *The present past: an introduction to anthropology for archaeologists*. Batsford, London.

Hodgson, W. C. 1957. *The herring and its fishery*. Routledge & Kegan Paul, London.

Hoffmann, R. C. 1985. Fishing for sport in medieval Europe: new evidence. *Speculum* 60 (4): 877–902.

1987. The protohistory of pike in western culture, in Crossman, E. J. and Casselman, J. M. *An annotated bibliography of the pike, Esox lucius (Osteichthyes, Salmoniformes)*, pp. vii–xvii. Royal Ontario Museum, Toronto.

Höglund, H. 1972. On the Bohuslän herring during the great herring fishery period in the eighteenth century. *Reports for the Institute of Marine Research, Lysekil, Series Biology*, No. 20: 1–86.

Holden, M. J. and Meadows, P. S. 1962. The structure of the spine of the spur dogfish (*Squalus acanthias* L.) and its use for age determination. *Journal of the Marine Biological Association of the United Kingdom* 42: 179–97.

Hubbs, C. L. 1920. A comparative study of the bones forming the opercular series of fishes. *Journal of Morphology* 33 (1919): 61–71.

Hui-Chong, T., Nose, Y. and Hiyama, Y. 1965. Age determination and growth of yellowfin tuna *Thunnus albacares* Bonnaterre by vertebrae. *Bulletin of the Japanese Society of Scientific Fisheries* 31: 414–21.

Hurum, H. J. 1976. *A history of the fish hook, and the story of Mustad, the hook maker*. Adam and Charles Black, London.

Huyghebaert, B. and Nolf, D. 1979. An annotated bibliography of palaeontological and systematic papers on fish-otoliths published since 1968. *Mededelingen van de Werkgroep voor Tertiaire en Kwartaire Geologie* 16: 139–70.

Hynes, H. B. N. 1950. The food of freshwater sticklebacks (*Gasterosteus aculeatus* and

Pygosteus pungitius), with a review of methods used in studies of the food of fishes. *Journal of Animal Ecology* 19: 36–58.

Izquierdo, E. R. 1988. *Contribución al Atlas Osteológico de los Teleósteos Ibéricos. I Dentario y Articular*. Colección de Estudios. Ediciones de la Universidad Autonóma de Madrid, Spain.

Jangaard, P. M. 1974. The Capelin (*Mallotus villosus*), biology, distribution, exploitation, utilization, and composition. *Bulletin of the Fisheries Research Board of Canada* 186: 1–70.

Jarman, H. N., Legge, A. J. and Charles, J. A. 1972. Retrieval of plant remains from archaeological sites by froth flotation, in Higgs, E. S. (ed.), *Papers in economic prehistory*, pp. 39–48. Cambridge University Press, Cambridge.

Jensen, A. C. 1972. *The cod*. Thomas Y. Crowell, New York.

Jollie, M. 1986. A primer of bone names for the understanding of actinopterygian head and pectoral girdle skeletons. *Canadian Journal of Zoology* 64: 365–79.

Jones, A. K. G. 1976. The fish remains, in Black, G. Excavations in the sub-vault of the Misericorde of Westminster Abbey, pp. 170–6. *Transactions of the London and Middlesex Archaeological Society* 27: 135–78.

  1977. The fish bones, in Bell, M. Excavation at Bishopstone, Sussex, pp. 284–5. *Sussex Archaeological Collections* 115: 1–299.

  1978. Fish remains, in Bird, J., Graham, A. J., Sheldon, H. and Townend, P. (eds.), Southwark excavations 1972–1974, *passim*, esp. pp. 171–2, 220, 414–18 and 601. Parts I and II *Southwark and Lambeth Archaeological Excavation Committee. Joint Publication*, No. 1, London and Middlesex Archaeological Society and Surrey Archaeological Society, London.

  1983a. A comparison of two on-site methods of wet-sieving large archaeological soil samples. *Science and Archaeology* 25: 9–12.

  1983b. Fish remains, in Ayers, B. and Murphy, P. A waterfront excavation at Whitefriars Street car park, Norwich, 1979, pp. 32–4 and fiche B5. *East Anglian Archaeology* 17: 1–104.

  1984a. Some effects of the mammalian digestive system on fish bones, in Desse-Berset, N. (ed.), 2nd fish osteoarchaeology meeting, CNRS. Centre de recherches archéologiques. *Notes et Monographies Techniques* 16: 61–5.

  1984b. Fish, in Batey, C. E., Morris, C. D. and Rackham, D. J. (eds.), Freswick Castle, Caithness: report on excavations carried out in 1979, p. 111, microfiche III–IV. *Glasgow Archaeological Journal* 2: 83–218.

  1985. Fish remains from excavations at 1–5 Aldwark, York. *Ancient Monuments Laboratory Report*, 4598.

  1986a. Fish bone survival in the digestive systems of the pig, dog and man: some experiments, in Brinkhuizen, D. C. and Clason, A. T. (eds.), *Fish and archaeology*, pp. 53–61. British Archaeological Reports International Series, No. 294, Oxford.

  1986b. Fish bones from Dragonby, Lincolnshire. *Ancient Monuments Laboratory Report*.

  1986c. Provisional remarks on fish remains from Anglo-Scandinavian deposits at 16–22 Coppergate, York, in Creswell, R. and Bailey, S. (eds.), *Proceedings of the Institute of Fisheries Management 16th Annual Study Course*, pp. 192–9. Institute of Fisheries Management.

  (forthcoming) Studies on the mechanical properties of fish bones.

Jones, A. K. G., Jones, J. J. M. and Spriggs, J. A. 1980. Marker trail. *Rescue News* 11: 6–7.

  1986. Results of a second marker trail. *Circaea* 4: 69–70.

Jones, A. K. G. and Scott, S. A. 1985. The fish bones, in Atkin, M., Carter, A. and Evans, D. H. Excavations in Norwich 1971–1978 part II. *East Anglian Archaeology* 26: 223–8.

Kani, H. 1984. Fishing with cormorant in Japan, in Gunda, B. (ed.), *The fishing culture of the world: studies in ethnology, cultural ecology and folklore*, pp. 569–83. Amadémiai Kiadó, Budapest.

Kemp, R. 1984. A fishkeeper's store at Byland Abbey. *Ryedale Historian* 12: 44–51.

Kenward, H. K., Hall, A. R. and Jones, A. K. G. 1980. A tested set of techniques for the extraction of animal and plant macrofossils from waterlogged archaeological deposits. *Science and Archaeology* 22: 3–15.

Krantz, G. S. 1968. A new method of counting mammal bones. *American Journal of Archaeology* 72: 286–8.

Kreuzer, R. 1984. Fish in religion and myths of ancient Mesopotamia and Egypt, in Gunda, B. (ed.), *The fishing culture of the world: studies in ethnology, cultural ecology and folklore*, pp. 593–618. Akadémiai Kiadó, Budapest.

Kusaka, T. 1974. *The urohyal of fishes*. University of Tokyo Press, Tokyo.

Lagler, K. F., Bardach, J. E. and Miller, R. R. 1962. *Ichthyology*. John Wiley & Sons, Inc., New York and London.

Lartet, É. A. I. H. and Christy, H. 1875. *Reliquiae Aquitanicae; being contributions to the archaeology and palaeontology of Périgord and the adjoining provinces of southern France . . . 1865–75*. London.

Leach, B. F. 1979. Fish and crayfish from the Washpool Midden site, New Zealand, their use in determining season of occupation and prehistoric fishing methods. *Journal of Archaeological Science* 6: 109–26.

  1986. A method for the analysis of Pacific Island fishbone assemblages and an associated database management system. *Journal of Archaeological Science* 13: 147–59.

Lepiksaar, J. 1983. *Osteologia. I. Pisces*. Privately distributed, Göteborg.

Lepiksaar, J. and Heinrich, D. 1977. Untersuchungen an Fischresten aus der frühmittelalterlichen Siedlung Haithabu. *Berichte über die Ausgrabungen in Haithabu* 10.

Lernau, H. 1986. Fish bones excavated in two late Roman Byzantine Castella in southern Israel, in Brinkhuizen, D. C. and Clason, A. T. (eds.), *Fish and archaeology*, pp. 85–102. British Archaeological Reports International Series, No. 294, Oxford.

  1986–7. Subfossil remains of Nile perch (*Lates* cf. *niloticus*): first evidence from ancient Israel. *Israel Journal of Zoology* 34 (1986/87): 225–36.

Levitan, B. 1982. *Excavations at West Hill Uley: the sieving and sampling programme*. Western Archaeological Trust, Gloucester.

Lie, R. W. 1980. Minimum number of individuals from osteological samples. *Norwegian Archaeological Review* 13: 24–30.

Losco-Bradley, P. M. and Salisbury, C. R. 1979. A mediaeval fish weir at Colwick, Nottinghamshire. *Transactions of the Thoroton Society of Nottinghamshire* 83: 15–22.

Lowe-McConnell, R. H. 1975. *Fish communities in tropical freshwaters*. Longman, London.

Macleod, R. D. 1956. *Key to the names of British fishes, mammals, amphibians and reptiles*. Sir Isaac Pitman & Sons Ltd, London.

Mann, R. H. K. and Beaumont, W. R. C. 1980. The collection, identification and reconstruction of lengths of fish prey from their remains in pike stomachs. *Fisheries Management* 11 (4): 169–72.

Mantle, S., Ramsey, R., Maynard, D. and Williams, G. 1984. Wet sieving at Llawhaden, Dyfed. *Circaea* 2 (3): 141–3.

McDonnell, J. 1981. Inland fisheries in medieval Yorkshire. *Borthwick Papers* 60: 1–42.

Meehan, B. 1983. A matter of choice? Some thoughts on shell-gathering strategies in Northern Australia, in Grigson, C. and Clutton-Brock, J. (eds.), *Animals and archaeology. 2. Shell middens, fishes and birds*, pp. 3–17. British Archaeological Reports International Series, No. 183, Oxford.

Mellars, P. and Payne, S. 1971. Excavation of two Mesolithic shell middens on the island of Oronsay (Inner Hebrides). *Nature, London* 231: 397–8.

Mellars, P. A. and Wilkinson, M. R. 1980. Fish otoliths as indicators of seasonality in prehistoric shell middens: the evidence from Oronsay (Inner Hebrides). *Proceedings of the Prehistoric Society* 46: 19–44.

Meunier, F. J. 1984. Sur la détermination histologique de vertèbres de poissons trouvées dans les sites archéologiques, in Desse-Berset, N. (ed.), 2nd fish osteoarchaeology meeting, CNRS. Centre de recherches archéologiques. *Notes et Monographies Techniques* 16: 15–23.

Meunier, F. J. and Castanet, J. 1982. Organisation spatiale des fibres de collagène de la plaque basale des écailles des Téléostéens. *Zoologica Scripta* 11 (2): 141–53.

Miller, R. R. 1955. Fish remains from archaeological sites in the lower Colorado River basin. *Papers of the Michigan Academy of Science, Arts and Letters* 40 (1954): 125–36.

Mills, D. M. 1971. *Salmon and trout: a resource, its ecology, conservation and management.* Oliver & Boyd, Edinburgh.

Mills, K. H. and Beamish, R. J. 1980. Comparison of fin-ray and scale age determinations for lake whitefish (*Coregonus clupeaformis*) and their implications for estimations of growth and annual survival. *Canadian Journal of Fisheries and Aquatic Sciences* 37: 534–44.

Mogan, E. D., Titus, L., Small, R. J. and Edwards, C. 1984. Gas chromographic analysis of fatty material from a Thule midden. *Archaeometry* 26 (1): 43–8.

Morales, A. and Rosenlund, K. 1979. *Fish bone measurements: an attempt to standardize the measuring of fish bones from archaeological sites.* Steenstrupia, Copenhagen.

Moyle, P. B. and Cech, J. J. 1982. *Fishes: an introduction to ichthyology.* Prentice-Hall Inc., New Jeresey.

Mueller, J. W. 1975. *Sampling in archaeology.* University of Arizona Press, Tucson.

Muniz, A. M., Lopez-Gordo, L. J., Izquierdo, E. R. and Rosenlund, K. forthcoming. Spanish and Danish ichthyoarchaeological assemblages: patterns of diversity and abundance in a palaeocultural perspective. Paper presented at the 4th meeting of the International Council of Archaeozoology Fish Remains Working Group, September 1987, University of York.

Murphy, P. 1983. Studies on the environment and economy of a Bronze Age fen-edge site at West Row, Mildenhall, Suffolk, a preliminary report. *Circaea* 1 (2): 49–57.

Necrasov, O. and Haimovici, S. 1959. Sur la présence de la dorade (*Aurata aurata* L.) dans les eaux du littoral Roumain de la mer Noire, pendant la néolithique. *Sesiume Stiitifice a Statiunii Zoologice Marine 'Prof. Ioan Borcea' de la Agigea* (1956), pp. 563–6, pl. 1.

Nelson, J. S. 1984. *Fishes of the world* (2nd edn). John Wiley & Sons, New York.

Nichol, R. K. and Wild, C. J. 1984. 'Numbers of individuals' in faunal analysis: the decay of fish bone in archaeological sites. *Journal of Archaeological Science* 11: 35–51.

Noe-Nygaard, N. 1971. Spur Dog spines from prehistoric and early historic Denmark. *Bulletin of the Geological Society of Denmark* 21: 18–33.

1983. The importance of aquatic resources to Mesolithic man at inland sites in Denmark, in Grigson, C. and Clutton-Brock, J. (eds.), *Animals and archaeology. 2. Shell middens, fishes and birds*, pp. 125–42. British Archaeological Reports International Series, No. 183, Oxford.

Nolf, D. 1976. Les otolithes des Téléostéens de l'Oligo-Miocene Belge. *Annales de la Société Royale Zoologique de Belgique* 106 (fasc. 1): 3–119.

Norsander, G. 1984. Fishfood among Swedish countrypeople, in Gunda, B. (ed.), *The fishing culture of the world: studies in ethnology, cultural ecology and folklore*, pp. 359–79. Akadémiai Kaidó, Budapest.

O'Connor, T. P. 1983. Aspects of site environment and economy at Caerleon Fortress Baths, Gwent, in Proudfoot, B. (ed.), *Site, environment and economy*, pp. 105–13. Symposium of the Association for Environmental Archaeology, No. 3. British Archaeological Reports International Series, No. 173. Oxford.

1985. On quantifying vertebrates – some sceptical observations. *Circaea* 3: 27–30.

Olsen, H. 1967. Fisk. Varanger-Funnene IV Osteologisk materiale innledning – fisk–fugl. *Tromsø Museums Skrifter* 7 (4): 19–78.

Olsen, S. J. 1968. Fish, amphibian and reptile remains from archaeological sites. Part I. Southeastern and southwestern United States. *Papers of the Peabody Museum of Archaeology and Ethnology, Harvard University* 56 (2).

Panella, G. 1971. Fish otoliths: daily growth layers and periodical patterns. *Science, N.Y.* 173: 1124–7.

1974. Otolith growth patterns: an aid in age determination in temperate and tropical fishes, in Bagenal, T. B. (ed.), *The ageing of fish*, pp. 28–39. Unwin Brothers Ltd, Old Woking.

Patrick, M., Koning, A. J. de, and Smith, A. B. 1985. Gas liquid chromatographic analysis of fatty acids in food residues from ceramics found in the southwestern Cape, South Africa. *Archaeometry* 27 (2): 231–6.

Payne, S. 1972. Partial recovery and sample bias. The results of some sieving experiments, in Higgs, E. (ed.), *Papers in economic prehistory*, pp. 49–63. Cambridge University Press, Cambridge.

Payne, S. and Munson, P. J. 1985. Ruby and how many squirrels? The destruction of bones by dogs, in Fieller, N. R. J., Gilbertson, D. D. and Ralph, N. G. A. (eds.), *Palaeobiological investigations: research design, methods and data analysis*, pp. 31–48. Symposia of the Association for Environmental Archaeology, No. 5B. British Archaeological Reports International Series, No. 266. Oxford.

Ponisch, M. and Tarradell, M. 1965. Garum et industries antiques de salaison dans la Méditerranée occidentale. *Université de Bordeaux et Casa de Velasquez, Bibliotheque École Hautes Études Hispaniques* 36: 93–119.

Prummel, W. 1986. The presence of bones of eel, *Anguilla anguilla*, in relation to taphonomic processes, cultural factors and the abundance of eel, in Brinkhuizen, D. C. and Clason, A. T. (eds.), *Fish and archaeology*, pp. 114–22. British Archaeological Reports International Series, No. 294, Oxford.

Radcliffe, W. 1921. *Fishing from the earliest times*. John Murray, London.

Radtke, C. 1977. Bemerkungen zum mittelalterlichen Fischfang mit Heringszäunen in der Schlei, in Lepiksaar, J. and Heinrich, D. Untersuchungen an Fischresten aus der frühmittelalterlichen Siedlung Haithabu, pp. 123–40. *Berichte über die Ausgrabungen in Haithabu* 10.

Reinman, F. M. 1967. Fishing, an aspect of Oceanic economy: an archaeological approach. *Fieldiana, Anthropology* 56: 95–208.

Reinsch, H. H. 1976. *Köhler und Steinköhler Pollachius virens and P. pollachius*. A. Ziemsen Verlag, Wittenberg.

Richards, J. D. and Ryan, N. S. 1985. *Data processing in archaeology*. Cambridge University Press, Cambridge.

Richter, J. 1986. Experimental study of heat induced morphological changes in fish bone collagen. *Journal of Archaeological Science* 13: 477–81.

Ricker, W. E. 1979. Growth rates and models, in Hoar, W. S., Randall, D. J. and Brett, J. R. (eds.), *Fish physiology*, vol. 8, pp. 677–743. Academic Press, New York.

Roberts, E. 1986. The Bishop of Winchester's fishponds in Hampshire, 1150–1400: their development, function and management. *Proceedings of the Hampshire Field Club and Archaeological Society* 42: 125–38.

Rogerson, A. 1976. Excavations on Fuller's Hill, Great Yarmouth. *East Anglian Archaeology* 2: 131–245.

Rosenlund, K. 1984. The fish-bone material from a medieval Danish monastery and an 18th century mission station in Greenland – an investigation of materials with a known key, in Desse-Berset, N. (ed.), 2nd fish osteoarchaeology meeting, CNRS. Centre de recherches archéologiques. *Notes et Monographes Techniques* 16: 145–53.

Ross, J., Jr. 1883. Curing and preserving fish in Scotland and its Islands, in Herbert, D. (ed.), *Fish and fisheries: a selection from the prize essays of the International Fisheries Exhibition, Edinburgh, 1882*, pp. 106–29. William Blackwood and Sons, Edinburgh.

Samuel, A. M. 1918. *The herring; its effect on the history of Britain*. John Murray, London.

Sauvage, H. E. 1870. Essai sur la pêche pendant l'époque du renne. *Mém. Soc. Acad. Boulogne-sur-Mer* (1870–72) 4: 267–6.

Schalk, R. F. 1977. The structure of an anadromous fish resource, in Binford, L. (ed.), *For theory building in archaeology*, pp. 207–49. Academic Press, London.

Seeman, M. 1986. Fish remains from Smeerenburg, a 17th century Dutch whaling station on the west coast of Spitsbergen, in Brinkhuizen, D. C. and Clason, A. T. (eds.), *Fish and archaeology*, pp. 129–39. British Archaeological Reports International Series, No. 294, Oxford.

Shawcross, W. 1968. An investigation of prehistoric diet and economy on a coastal site at Galatea Bay, New Zealand. *Proceedings of the Prehistoric Society*, n.s. 33: 107–31.

Sirelius, U. T. 1934. *Die Volkskultur Finnlands I. Jagd und Fischerei*. Berlin.

Smith, N. J. H. 1981. *Man, fishes and the Amazon*. Columbia University Press, New York.

Spencer, P. J. 1979. Fish that men gnawed upon. *Interim* 6 (1): 9–11.

Starks, E. C. 1901. Synonymy of the fish skeleton. *Washington Academy of Sciences* 3: 507–39.

Steenstrup, J. J. 1862. *Et Blik paa Natur- og Oldforskningens Forstudier til Besvarelsen af Spörgsmaalet om Menneskeslaegtens tidligste Optraeden i Europa*. Inbydelsesskrift til Kjøbenhavns Universitets Aarsfest til erindring om Kirkens Reformation, Kjøbenhavn.

Steffensen, E. 1980. Daily growth increments observed in otoliths from juvenile East Baltic cod. *Dana* 1: 29–37.

Stevens, J. D. 1975. Vertebral rings as a means of age determination in the blue shark (*Prionace glauca* L.). *Journal of the Marine Biological Association of the United Kingdom* 55: 657–65.

Stewart, H. 1977. *Indian fishing: early methods on the northwest coast*. University of Washington Press, Seattle.

Streuver, S. 1968. Flotation techniques for the recovery of small-scale archaeological remains. *American Antiquity* 33 (3): 353–62.

Stuart, A. J. 1982. *Pleistocene vertebrates in the British Isles*. Longmans, London.

Summerfelt, R. C. and Hall, G. E. 1987. *Age and growth of fish*. Iowa State University Press, Ames.

Szidat, L. 1944. Über die Erhaltungsfähigkeit von Helmintheneiern in Vor- und Frügeschichtlichen Moorleichen. *Zeitschrift für Parasitenkunde* 13: 265–74.

Tauber, H. 1986. Innovative trends in prehistoric anthropology. In Herrmann, B. (ed.), *Mitteilungen der Berliner Gesellschaft für Anthropologie, Ethnologie und Urgeschichte*, Band 7, pp. 31–8. (Contributions to an international symposium in West Berlin, 26 February–1 March 1986.)

Taubert, B. D. and Coble, D. W. 1977. Daily rings in otoliths of three species of *Lepomis* and *Tilapia mossambica*. *Journal of the Fishery Research Board of Canada* 34: 332–40.

Templeman, W. and Squires, H. J. 1956. Relationship of otolith lengths and weights in the haddock, *Melanogrammus aeglefinus* (L.), to the rate of growth of the fish. *Journal of the Fishery Research Board of Canada* 13: 467–87.

Thompson, W. F. and Freeman, N. L. 1930. History of the Pacific halibut fishery. *Report of the International Fisheries Commission*, No. 5, pp. 1–61.

Topp, R. W. and Cole, C. F. 1968. An osteological study of the sciaenid genus *Sciaenops* Gill (Teleostei, Sciaenidae). *Bulletin of Marine Science* 18: 902–45.

Tortonese, E. 1975. *Osteichthyes – pesci ossei II. Fauna d'Italia*, vol. XI. Bologna.

Trolle-Lassen, T. 1984. A preliminary report on the archaeological and zoological evidence of fish exploitation from a submerged site in Mesolithic Denmark, in Desse-Berset, N. (ed.), 2nd fish osteoarchaeology meeting, CNRS. Centre de recherches archéologiques, *Notes et Monographes Techniques* 16: 133–43.

Uerpmann, H.-P. 1973. Animal bone finds and economic archaeology: a critical study of the 'osteo-archaeological' method. *World Archaeology* 4 (3): 307–22.

Van Neer, W. 1986. Some notes on the fish remains from Wadi Kubbaniya (Upper Egypt; Late Palaeolithic), in Brinkhuizen, D. C. and Clason, A. T. (eds.), *Fish and archaeology*, pp. 103–13. British Archaeological Reports International Series, No. 294, Oxford.

Walker, B. 1982. Scottish methods of preserving white fish, in Gailey, A. and Ó hÓgáin, D. (eds.), *Gold under the furze: studies in folk tradition*, pp. 138–49. Glendale Press, Dublin.

Ward, D. J. 1984. Collecting isolated microvertebrate fossils. *Zoological Journal of the Linnean Society* 82: 245–59.

Watson, H. 1978. Coastal otters (*Lutra lutra* L.) in Shetland. Unpublished M.Sc. thesis, University of Aberdeen.

Weatherley, A. H. and Gill, H. S. 1987. *The biology of fish growth*. Academic Press, London.

Weiler, W. 1968. Otolithi Piscium (Neubaerbeitung). *Fossilium Catalogus I. Animalia* 117: 1–196.

Wheeler, A. 1969. *The fishes of the British Isles and north west Europe*. Macmillan, London.

1977. Fish bone, in Clarke, H. and Carter, A. (eds.), Excavations in King's Lynn 1963–1970, pp. 403–8. *Society for Medieval Archaeology Monograph Ser.*, 7.

1978a. Problems of identification and interpretation of archaeological fish remains, in Brothwell, D. R., Thomas, K. D., and Clutton-Brock, J. (eds.), *Research problems in zooarchaeology*, pp. 69–75. Occasional Papers of the Institute of Archaeology, London, No. 3.

1978b. Why were there no fish remains at Star Carr? *Journal of Archaeological Science* 5: 85–9.

1979a. The fish bones, in Renfrew, C. Investigations in Orkney, pp. 144–9. *Reports of the Research Committee of the Society of Antiquaries of London*, 38.

1979b. *The tidal Thames: the history of a river and its fishes*. Routledge & Kegan Paul, London.

Wheeler, A. and Jones, A. K. G. 1976. Fish remains, in Rogerson, A. Excavations on Fuller's Hill, Great Yarmouth, pp. 208–24. *East Anglian Archaeology* 2: 131–245.

Wheeler, A. and Locker, A. 1985. The estimation of size in sardines (*Sardina pilchardus*) from amphorae in a wreck at Randello, Sicily. *Journal of Archaeological Science* 12: 97–100.

(in press) Randello wreck: the fish remains, in Parker, T. A Roman shipwreck at Randello (Ragusa, Sicily). *International Journal of Nautical Archaeology*.

White, T. E. 1953. A method of calculating the dietary percentage of various food animals utilized by aboriginal peoples. *American Antiquity* 18: 396–8.

Wigforss, J., Lepiksaar, J., Olsson, O. I. and Påsse, T. 1983. Bua Västergård – en 8000 år gammal kustboplats. *Arkeologi i Västsverige* 1. Göteborgs Arkeologiska Museum.

Wilkinson, M. 1979. The fish remains, in Maltby, M. Faunal studies on urban sites, the animal bones from Exeter, 1971–1975, pp. 74–81. *Exeter Archaeological Reports*, 2.

1981. The study of fish remains from British archaeological sites. Unpublished Ph.D. thesis, University of Sheffield, England.

Williams, D. 1973. Flotation at Sīrāf. *Antiquity* 47: 198–202.

Williams, T. and Bedford, B. C. 1974. The use of otoliths for age determination, in Bagenal, T. (ed.), *The ageing of fish*, pp. 114–23. Unwin Brothers Ltd, Old Woking.

Williamson, H. C. 1902. A comparison between the cod (*Gadus callarias* Linn.), the saithe (*Gadus virens* Linn.) and the lythe (*Gadus pollachius* Linn.), in respect to certain external and osteological characters. *Annual Report of the Fisheries Board for Scotland* 20 (3): 228–87.

Wing, E. S. and Reitz, E. J. 1982. Prehistoric fishing economies of the Caribbean. *Journal of New World Archaeology* 5 (2): 13–32.

Zeuner, F. E. 1963. *A history of domesticated animals*. Hutchinson, London.

INDEX

Page references to text figures are set in italic.

abundance, 4, 27, 32, 136, 151, 153
Acanthopterygians, 181
Acanthuridae, 24, *25*, 59, 120
Acipenser, 1, 9, 117, *119*
Acipenseridae, *15*, 17, 110
Acipenseriformes, 17
Africa, 20, 23, 24, 26, 30, 33, 62
  eastern, 18
  Kenya, 173
  Lagos, 155
  Makapansgat, 62
  northern, 33, 69, 113
  South, 20, 22, 171
  West, 20
age, estimation of, 9, 114, 118, 137, 146–7, 155
age pyramid, 32
Agnatha, 14, 79
Agonidae, 120
Akazawa, T., 142
Alosa, 5
Aluteridae, 58
Amiidae, *15*, 17, 110
Amiiformes, *15*, 17
Anabantoidei, 33
anadromous fishes, 5, 136, 160
anatomy
  Agnathans and cartilaginous fishes, 79–86
  bony fishes, 87–125
anchovies, 30
Anderson Smith, W., 68, 69
Anguilla, 75, 138, 164
Anguillidae, 18, *19*, 35
Anguilliformes, 18, *19*, 91, 98, 110
animal contributions to fish bone assemblages,
  76–8
Antarctic, 34, 35
Antigua, Mill Reef, 175
Antilles, 171
Arctic, 22, 34, 108
Argyrosomus, 129
Ariidae, *19*, 20, 33, 36
artifacts, fish bones as, 2, 85, 86, 129
Asia, 18, 20, 22, 26, 33, 172

northern, 166
south-east, 18, 20, 30
western, 51
assemblages
  assessment of, 126, 152–3, 162–7
  hand-collected, 128–9
  publication of, 127–8
  recording, 130–5
  sieved, 130
Atherinidae, 35
Atlantic Ocean, 18, 22, 24, 26, 175
  eastern, 35
  North, 22, 23, 35, 36, 37, 86
  sub-tropical, 22
  western, 35
Australia, 16, 23, 33, 34, 35, 64
  Darling Basin, NSW, 10
  eastern, 18
  New South Wales, 174
  southern, 20, 86
Avery, G., 171

Badham, C. D., 69
Bagenal, T. B., 147
Bagridae, *19*, 20, 33
Balistes, *119*
Balistidae, *25*, 26, 58, 111, 113, 120
Balme, J., 10, 174
Baltic, 4, 169
Bănărescu, P., 11
Bangtson, D. A., 154
Banks, Sir Joseph, 30
baramundi, 33
Barbus, 183
Bardach, J. E., 147
Barker, G., 38
Barkman, R. C., 154
barracuda, 35
basses, 23, 33
  black, 23
  sea, 23
Bateman, N., 28, 60
Batey, C. E., 9

201